HEIDEGGER
AND DERRIDA
ON PHILOSOPHY
AND METAPHOR

PHILOSOPHY AND LITERARY THEORY

Series Editor: Hugh J. Silverman

This series provides full-scale, in-depth assessments of important issues in the context of philosophy and literary theory, as they inscribe themselves in the developing archive of textual studies. It highlights studies that take a philosophical or theoretical position with respect to literature, literary study, and the practice of criticism. The individual volumes focus on semiotics hermeneutics, post-phenomenology, deconstruction, postmodernism, feminism, cultural criticism, and other new developments in the philosophico-literary debate.

Stephen Barker	*Autoesthetics: Strategies of the Self After Nietzsche*
Robert Bernasconi	*Heidegger in Question: The Art of Existing*★
Véronique M. Fóti	*Heidegger and the Poets: Poiēsis/Sophical/Technē*★
Sabine I. Gölz	*The Split Scene of Reading: Nietzsche/Derrida/Kafka/Bachmann*
Richard Kearney	*Poetics of Modernity: Toward a Hermeneutic Imagination*
Jean-François Lyotard	*Toward the Postmodern*★
Jean-François Lyotard and Eberhard Gruber	*The Hyphen: Between Judaism and Christianity*
Louis Marin	*Cross-Readings*
Michael Naas	*Turning: From Persuasion to Philosophy: A Reading of Homer's* Iliad
Jean-Luc Nancy	*The Gravity of Thought*
Giuseppe Stellardi	*Heidegger and Derrida on Philosophy and Metaphor: Imperfect Thought*★
Wilhelm S. Wurzer	*Filming and Judgment: Between Heidegger and Adorno*★

★*Available in Paperback*

PHILOSOPHY
AND
LITERARY
THEORY

HEIDEGGER AND DERRIDA ON PHILOSOPHY AND METAPHOR

IMPERFECT THOUGHT

GIUSEPPE STELLARDI

an imprint of Prometheus Books
59 John Glenn Drive, Amherst, New York 14228-2197

Published 2000 by Humanity Books, an imprint of Prometheus Books

Inquiries should be addressed to
Humanity Books
59 John Glenn Drive
Amherst, New York 14228–2197
VOICE: 716–691–0133, ext. 207
FAX: 716–564–2711

04 03 02 01 00   5 4 3 2 1

Library of Congress Cataloging-in-Publication Data

Heidegger and Derrida on philosophy and metaphor : imperfect thought /
  Giuseppe Stellardi.
       p. cm. — (Philosophy and literary theory)
  Includes bibliographical references and index.
  ISBN 1–57392–824–0 (pbk. : alk. paper)
  1. Semantics (Philosophy). 2. Metaphor. 3. Heidegger, Martin, 1889–1976. 4.
Derrida, Jacques. I. Title. II. Series.

B840.S815 2000
121'.68'0922—dc21   00–026788
                                                                          CIP

Printed in the United States of America on acid-free paper

To Margherita

CONTENTS

ACKNOWLEDGMENTS   13

INTRODUCTION   15

Philosophy and Metaphor: The Dimensions of a Problem   *15*

Field   *19*

   Philosophical Theories of Metaphor   23

   Usage of Metaphors in Philosophy   28

Relationship between Metaphor and Philosophy ... 31

Motives ... *32*

Philosophy before Metaphor ... 33

Metaphor As Philosophy's Problem ... 34

Directions ... *37*

Theory of Metaphor ... 38

Theory of Philosophical Discourse ... 38

Heidegger, Derrida: Imperfect Thoughts ... 38

Notes ... *40*

1. OF METAPHOR ... 43

Preliminary Questions ... *43*

Beyond the Traditional Model ... *47*

Labels and Metaphors ... 47

Toward a Description of Metaphor ... 49

The Mechanism of Metaphor ... *51*

Definitions ... 51

The Trait ... 56

Text, Context, Reader   57

The "Other" of Metaphor   59

Notes   **65**

2. DERRIDA: THE CATASTROPHE OF METAPHOR   **67**

The Ricoeur–Derrida Debate   **70**

Philosophy within Metaphor?   70

The Living Metaphor   78

The Retreat and the Catastrophe   91

Some Questions   99

Metaphors and Indecidables   **105**

Cumbersome Metaphors   105

Derrida's Operation   108

Impossible Foundations   111

Conclusion?   **114**

Notes   **117**

3. HEIDEGGER: METAPHORS THAT HURT   127

Position of the Problem and Initial Questions   *128*

Delimiting the Field   *134*

    Operative Notion of Metaphor   134

    Sample of Texts   135

Metaphor in **Unterwegs zur Sprache**   *136*

    Heidegger and Metaphor   140

    Grayness   141

    Suffering   143

    Control   145

The Structure and Function of Heidegger's Metaphor   *148*

    The Structure of "Die Sprache"   153
      Textual Articulations   *154*
      Logico-rhetorical Resources   *155*
      Metaphors   *156*
      The Poem   *156*

    Metaphor and Suffering: The Threshold   159

    Silence and the Word   162

The Thought of Difference   **165**

   Difference and Analogy: The Trait   165

   Poetry and Thought   170

   Heidegger's Operation   174

   Grayness or Bliss?   177

Notes   **182**

4. OF PHILOSOPHY   **193**

Philosophy among the Modes of Discourse   **194**

   Modes of Discourse   194

   Analysis of Variables   198

   Modes of Discourse and Metaphor   203

   Modes of Discourse and Ethics   205

   Modes of Discourse and Truth   206

Philosophical Discourse   **208**

   Philosophical Truth and Ethics   210

   Forthcoming Thought   215

   Nonrepresentational Thought   218

   Thought As Productive Fiction   222

Heidegger's Reader   225

Etymology, Quotation Marks, Rhetorical Question   229

Philosophy and Metaphor   232

Strategies of Deconstruction,
or the Endless Death of Theory   **235**

Two Metaphors   235

Structuralism and Deconstruction   237

Force and Form   243

Metaphor, Theory, and Supertheory   246

Fidelity and Transgression   249

Life and Death   253

Notes   *255*

IN PLACE OF A CONCLUSION   261

Notes   *265*

BIBLIOGRAPHY   267

INDEX   273

ACKNOWLEDGMENTS

The original French version of this work was presented as a doctoral dissertation to the University of Paris I–Panthéon-Sorbonne.

I am deeply grateful to Peter Hainsworth for his help with the translation in English. All errors, of course, are mine.

INTRODUCTION

PHILOSOPHY AND METAPHOR: THE DIMENSIONS OF A PROBLEM

Not "Metaphor *in* Philosophy," nor "Theory of Philosophical Metaphor," not even "Metaphors in Heidegger and Derrida," but—simply—"Philosophy *and* Metaphor": What moves the present work is the fateful *conjunction* of two unlikely partners (unlikely, that is, as soon as one closely examines them and their relationship). Two "objects" difficult enough to define separately, and whose relationship seems even more difficult to elucidate and legitimate; certainly touching each other, however, somewhere, communicating or mating in a way that one suspects is essential. This contact, this obscure copulation, which constitutes the primary stake and wager of this study, is not approachable in a direct manner, through a straight determination reflecting itself—if such a determination were possible—in its very title, and directing, by means of a rational method, the journey inaugurated by it. Hence the extreme (conjunctive and suspensive) generality of the title under which this work announces itself, which is meant to signal, more than the inordinate ambition of its author, the amplitude and implications of a question which, such as I attempt to shelter and face here, only preserves its sense at the cost of resisting any reduction and fragmentation, and also of renouncing any too strong preliminary methodic decision. The price to be paid for this fidelity to the question, however, will include a large measure of incompleteness, approximation, and imprecision: imperfect thoughts, these of mine will be.

The present work is more the temporary coagulum of a meditation in progress, than the product of an effort of historico-theoretical systematization. I would like to think that what it lacks in terms of encyclopedic completeness and systematic solidity is compensated by the freedom of movement in the tortuous pursuit of the paths of thought that I have deemed necessary to follow. Inevitably, before I directly approach Martin Heidegger and Jacques Derrida, I shall have to discuss the relationship between philosophy and metaphor in its generality. However, my initial task will not be to cover, analytically or synthetically, the immense field of all textual production bearing the trace, explicit or hidden, of the complex and changing relations that metaphor has entertained, and entertains, with philosophy (and vice versa). Rather, it is to deploy, on several levels, attentively but without too many reservations and preconceived, self-imposed limits, the problematic field opened by the two terms of the inquiry; with, once more, an additional specification, which is particularly important for the understanding of the wider implications of this work: It so happens that the elaboration of this particular problematic field is inevitably and deeply linked to a general, or even radical, disquiet concerning philosophical practice today.

This could generate suspicions concerning the initial impartiality of my point of view and transparency of my objectives: Do my questions really concern metaphor *and* philosophy, or rather philosophy alone, via the detour of metaphor? The doubt is not gratuitous, focusing as it does on the way of posing the problem, which in advance decides the treatment and perhaps the outcome. From a certain point of view that I have no qualms in adopting, metaphor can at times seem a key, or a simple pretext, to linger on the borders of philosophy, where the question of its being becomes particularly pressing. We shall see, however, that from a different, slightly shifted but not less valuable point of view, the landscape changes radically, opening up the possibility of an entirely different relationship (and hierarchy) between the two terms of the question: the possibility, that is (and a disquieting one it is), that philosophy itself turn out to be nothing more than metaphor's margin; or the pretext for one among its many tricks. Nothing that I know—but, of course, I might well be the very last one to know about some of the movements of my own text—has been here once and for all decided, concerning metaphor *and* philosophy. I should actually add that although there is here a "philosophical *parti-pris*" in the way I question the link between metaphor and philosophy, no decision has been made in advance that philosophy "must be saved."

This investigation tries to take up position with respect to the trajectories of a series of oscillations, without, however, immobilizing them: "Metaphor" and "philosophy" represent the poles of the most central among these oscillations, but the determination of their respective position and status ought to be left, as much as possible, in suspension. The task, indeed, is not to find the "solution," the "answer," or the "formula"; but rather to negotiate, with very intractable adversaries, provisional formulations whose aim it is, in the first instance, to allow the questioning to survive and to advance. The character, generally "oscillatory" and plurivocal, of the present text's progression, can perhaps find here its justification, in the name of a rigor that is not rigidity. There will be, however, moments of rest, of abandonment to the apparent clarity of definitions and deductions; these will not signal the point of arrival of this research, but rather its point of departure for a new phase of its development. Such moments will be necessary to the extent that they correspond to an instance of "control," or "gathering" of the effort of thought, whose rightful claims are here fully accepted; which, however, does not lend them the status of "ultimate aims," "final results," or "hard cores" of this research. They rather represent its safety notches or its imaginary landmarks: They only deserve a limited degree of trust.

In this introduction I shall endeavor to present the reader with an idea of what this work does *not* do (and indeed *cannot* do, if the radicality of the question is to be preserved, at the cost of renouncing the advantages and comforts of the "already thought"), while actually not rejecting (and even to some extent implying and presupposing) the methodic and systematic approach to the problem in its historical and theoretical dimensions. I shall offer, first of all, a preliminary outline of the problem in its generality; then I shall attempt to specify, insofar as possible, the motivations, points of departure, cores of interest, and aims of this work.

FIELD

An analysis of the theme "philosophy and metaphor," that deemed itself "methodologically exhaustive," should develop along (at least) three levels, which I shall summarily entitle as follows:

(a) historico-critical presentation of *theories of metaphor*, explicit or implicit, produced, or at any rate visible, within different philosophical discourses, as well as discourses that are not strictly philosophical;

(b) study of the *effective usage of metaphor* in philosophical texts; and

(c) theoretic examination of the rapport between "metaphor" and "philosophy" and determination of a *general model* of this rapport.

This tripartition, however, cannot be assumed to be the point of departure of a work that could then safely and comfortably distribute itself in each of the three registers mentioned. Even placing in parentheses the problem of justifying the selection in the first place, it is evident that each of them contributes to a play of presuppositions and interaction, at times evident, at other times less visible, that it is worth mentioning right on the threshold of the present work. The intention is to signal the complexity of this play, certainly not to resolve or overcome it, even less to find in it the pretext for an ecstasy of impotence, but to acknowledge it as inescapably constitutive of the problem and then carry on without ever forgetting it.

For a start, it is difficult to imagine how a "theoretical examination" of the relationship between metaphor and philosophy could legitimately precede, or avoid, an analysis of the effective usage of metaphors in philosophical language, without vowing itself to sterility and emptiness. However, that usage partially depends on a theory or implicit notion of metaphor and its role in philosophical discourse: Such notions also function, consciously or otherwise,[1] by activating mechanisms of admission and exclusion and of distribution of metaphorical effects in a text. Furthermore, a philosophical theory of metaphor cannot separate itself from a point of view on the whole of the relationship between metaphor and philosophy, and can even derive from it: it is, for instance, Heidegger's case precisely, as we shall see.

I will not insist further: The identification of the three levels of analysis mentioned above, though perfectly reasonable and practicable, does not permit a sufficiently radical treatment of the proposed topic if it presupposes the possibility of exhausting its complexity by technically handing it over to three essentially separated projects to be pursued independently. The singularization of each one of the levels remains nevertheless legitimate, but only provisionally and under certain conditions. It is important to signal that this situation will reverberate on the continuation of this work, contributing to the determination of its oscillatory aspect. I will come back to this.

Further difficulties announce themselves. An extension of the discourse in the direction of *that which is not, or ought not to be, metaphorical* seems inevitable. It is impossible, dealing with metaphor from a philosophical point of view, or rather, in a perspective that directly concerns philosophy, not to question the notions of concept, truth, meaning, system: all of which, as we shall see, the philosopher tends to *oppose* to metaphor. One can easily see, at that point, the "whole" (or "the essential") of philosophy comes into play.

Also, the topic "metaphor and philosophy" hardly permits a treatment entirely internal to the philosophical discipline: On the contrary, a certain degree of extraneousness to this field is required if one is to perceive the more radical implications of the problem. Furthermore, once the inevitable questions concerning the specificity of the usage of metaphors in philosophy are uttered, others relating to neighboring discourses impose themselves: the intersections of metaphor and literature, metaphor and science, and metaphor and natural (ordinary) language automatically take place in the problematic field illusorily delimited by the binomial metaphor and philosophy. The "outside" of philosophy is hence pulled into the discourse, and rightly so.

It is in this complex space that the most immediate difficulty must be tackled: the definition of objects and instruments. The old methodological paradox fully applies here: We are indeed called upon to clarify what metaphor and philosophy are *before* we start. But this is precisely the core of the question and can certainly not be given a priori. Nevertheless, if we must enter the circle somewhere, we might as well jump in it by providing provisional, operative notions of metaphor and philosophy as starting points of an investigation that, subsequently, could very well (and without too many qualms) turn against its own foundations.

As regards the first of the two concepts we need, one of the main difficulties is that two different notions of metaphor are pertinent, depending on the context: a *narrow* one, corresponding to a linguistic occurrence, recognizable in a catalogue of rhetorical figures; and a *wide* one, corresponding to the phenomenon of transfer, of referral (*Verweisung*, in Heidegger's sense), or to the structure of the signification in general as described, for instance, by Charles S. Peirce.[2] These two notions constitute the extreme poles on a continuum, where the minimum is represented by the "substitutive" theory of metaphor, focusing on the noun, and the maximum by those theories that end by identifying the metaphoric effect with the production of meaning itself, that is, with the very life of language or thought in general. In between, there would would be room for the theories ("impertinence," "tension," "double reference," and so forth) that, in one way or another, widen the horizon of the analysis of metaphor well beyond the limit of the noun, and of a strict, violently reductive distinction between proper and improper meaning. We shall come back to this at a later stage.

To tackle the problem in the least restrictive way, we need therefore at least two provisional notions of metaphor: one to identify the metaphoric occurrences in the philosophical text; the other to recognize, even in the absence of metaphoric occurrences in a strict sense, the larger or more subtle phenomenon of the displacement of meaning, and to put it in relation to a philosophical project in its entirety, perhaps even in its unity of intent. The first notion is more relevant in an examination focused on the second level mentioned above (study of metaphors used in philosophical texts); the second, in a study concentrating on the third level (theoretic examination of the relationship between metaphor and philosophy). Here, however, both notions will be used, with the intent of opening up a field and keeping it open and active, rather than of closing it by way of conceptual definition.

As we shall see soon enough, the narrow notion of metaphor, which regularly appears here, is (broadly, and reinterpreted in a personal manner) the one first formulated by the Anglo-Saxon line of philosophical, critico-literary, and linguistic research (Ivor A. Richards, Monroe C. Beardsley, Max Black, and so forth).[3] The wide one owes much to Derrida's work, which itself represents the issue of a philosophico-literary tradition of "exaltation" (I shall have to explain myself on this point) of metaphor.

As regards philosophy, it would be pretentious and naive on my part to improvise replies to the question "What is it?" and superfluous to insist on the difficulty of exactly situating the discourse and the field of philosophy today. I shall therefore provisionally accept a pragmatic and wide notion of philosophy, so as to enable me, simply, to identify and assign to the corpus of this discipline the texts and discourses that are perceived as pertinent in the philosophical debate. I will thus avoid the immediate difficulty of having to "justify" the philosophical credentials of Heidegger or Derrida, for instance, while knowing very well that they are not unchallenged. At the conclusion of this study, however, I will take a more decided stance on this matter.

Armed with patience, let us now start from the beginning again (though it no longer is the same beginning), with the strategic distinction of three possible directions of inquiry, whose general coordinates I will now draw. I repeat, once more, that I do not aim to cover exhaustively a field, but rather to indicate paths, exemplify directions of approach, and writing genres through which the question ceaselessly elaborates itself.

Philosophical Theories of Metaphor

The history of metaphor, as the name itself says, begins in Greek. Aristotle's formulation has been for a very long time the only theoretical basis for all subsequent attempts to conceptualize the operation of metaphor. It is also the only theory of metaphor in a strict sense that, generated inside the philosophical field, has resisted and produced sizable effects. According to Aristotle, metaphor is "the transport [*epiphora*] of a foreign name," under four possible scenarios: transport from gender to species, from species to gender, from species to another species, and "by analogy."[4] In this formulation, all the essentials of what metaphor, for centuries to come, will be deemed to be, are already present: the founding dichotomies (thing/name, proper/improper); the privilege accorded to the noun [*onoma*]; the idea of "transport," of "substitution," and of the analogic "ground." All the developments of a "semantic" type (according to the distinction proposed, among others, by Paul Ricoeur, as we shall see) come from there. If one looks closely, there is also, already, with the weight attributed to the faculty of "perceiving resemblances," the core of a possible conjunction between poetics and ontology, which, if carried forth to its logical consequences, would place metaphor right at the heart of the processes of knowledge acquisition. However, the full ontological implications of Aristotle's theory have been, more often than not, suppressed or neglected by interpreters and followers alike. The theory itself, on the other hand, or at least its "substitutive" core, has opened a path that has been followed for centuries, with little hesitation; but not by philosophers, however, or at least not explicitly.

After Aristotle, and as if in posthumous execution of Plato's condemnation, rhetoric and poetics become progressively separated from the whole of philosophical interests,[5] dragging with them the object "metaphor." In this way the destiny of metaphor is determined. Two aspects of this destiny (strictly linked to each other) are particularly interesting: metaphor's reduction to a rhetorical or literary ornament, and the loss of interest in it on the part of philosophy.

From the moment philosophy declares the exteriority and insignificance of rhetoric and poetics (domains of discursive and literary forms and effects, in opposition to the domain of essences and of truth), and thus of metaphor, assigned by the Aristotelian encyclopedia to these two departments of knowledge, the normal attitude of the philosopher with regard to metaphor oscillates between two positions: indifference and violent rejection.

Metaphor has generally been seen as a more or less useless supplement, or a germ of dangerous illnesses for philosophy's own body, for its rational essence. This negative (or denegative) attitude, which perhaps has manifested itself with the greatest virulence in British empiricism (e.g., John Locke, David Hume) and in logical positivism, has not quite disappeared in contemporary philosophy, where it survives at least in the form of a moderate reminding of the need for rigor, and therefore for a levelheaded rejection of rhetoric and figurative language.

If the attitude described above has generally prevailed in the history of Western philosophy, divergent positions have nevertheless been recorded. Suffice to mention here the names of Giambattista Vico[6] and Jean-Jacques Rousseau,[7] to signal the existence of a philosophical current of "supporters" of metaphor, maintaining that it, far from being a trifle with no consequence, is the very source of meaning in language. It cannot be said, however, that this current has produced a new, full-blown theory of metaphor, even though the position reserved to metaphor by the historico-linguistic theories of Vico and Rousseau, as well as by the German Romantics, no doubt implies a notion of metaphor very different from the "ornamental" one proposed by classical rhetoric.

We could make more or less the same remark concerning G. W. F. Hegel, whose notion of metaphor[8] (a shortened comparison, in which the primary role is played by "signification," rather than by "form") is derived directly from the traditional one. Hegel also shares with the tradition an attitude of detached sobriety concerning metaphor's usage: It is an embellishment, not to be confused with the necessary part of the philosophical investigation. A few interesting observations on metaphor's motivations, its "contextual" nature, and the metaphoric origin of certain abstract expressions are not enough to modify the essentially classical arrangement of the question. Hegel's novelty, instead, consists in the insertion of metaphor in the dialectic system, which absorbs it (as indeed any other object) and assigns to it a position in the Spirit's development.

This clearly prevents a simple rejection of metaphor and its fix-
ation in the exteriority of the inessential. At the same time, however, it neutralizes all its specific potentialities to create destabiliza-
tion of meaning. Such valorization-neutralization of metaphor is
perhaps the most refined and efficient way of philosophical contain-
ment of the "metaphoric danger."

A significant (albeit little-known) moment in the philosophical
reflection on metaphor is represented by Benedetto Croce, with his
brief text titled "Noterella sulla metafora" (1939).[9] In it, the Italian
philosopher distinguishes a "strong" usage of metaphor (in poetry,
where the phenomenon should be described in terms of "manifes-
tation of a whole," rather than simply translation of meaning) from
a "weak" usage (for instance in philosophy, where metaphor is used
as an explanatory—and not strictly necessary—tool). Croce also distinguishes *from* metaphor, analogy in the Aristotelian or scholastic
sense, described as an instrument of rational knowledge, rather than
a mere rhetorical figure.[10]

Croce's position on metaphor seems to occupy, curiously, the
intersection of the two philosophical currents mentioned above. On
the one hand, he acknowledges the primordial and creative function
of metaphor (at least, of the particular type of metaphor that
Ricoeur defines as "living"); on the other, he strives, in a rather traditional manner, to safeguard philosophy's (that is, rationality's) own
field of action—a maneuver, by the way, quite similar to that orches-
trated much later by Ricoeur.[11]

Within the philosophical tradition there are at least two other
important moments, each one bearing significant consequences as
regards the appreciation of metaphor's role. I am referring, of
course, to Friedrich Nietzsche and Heidegger.

Nietzsche's position concerning truth and metaphor is well
known:[12] Truth, concepts, are in fact only metaphors whose

metaphoric quality has been forgotten, but not removed. He thus criticizes the idea of truth and submits it to a genealogical analysis, showing how so-called truth is the petrified result of lies and metaphors, forgotten as such, for moral purposes; that is, with the aim of imposing *one* particular type of morality, that of the weak.

However powerful this theory may be, there is in it a difficulty that the commentators have not failed to perceive: Jean Greisch formulates very well an argument that is shared by Derrida, and that brings us back to the fundamental problem of the present inquiry:

> To compare the history of metaphysical thought with the wear of a coin, as Nietzsche, for instance, does, is ambiguous, because the notion of wear is already part and parcel of a strictly "metaphysical" representation of the dichotomy proper/figurative. In other words, it presupposes a theory of metaphor that we no doubt ought to put in question in the first place.[13]

There is, however, also a more general objection that one could move against Nietzsche. In establishing at the same time a genealogy and a critique of truth, he seems to be maintaining, in practice, both the notion and, above all, the pathos of truth: What else is his work, in fact, but the revelation of a truth that has been forgotten underneath layer upon layer of lies? His particular truth is that of the will to power, and of the metaphoric essence of truth itself. In what, essentially and structurally (that is, in its functioning within a discourse), does this truth of Nietzsche's distinguish itself from that of other philosophical systems?

We could perhaps try to sketch a provisional reply along the following lines: Nietzsche's truth does not strive to demonstrate itself as abstractly true, but, rather, openly to *impose* itself as will and style supported by individual values, not as an appeal to a presumed universal consensus of reason based essentially on resignation and weakness. This displacement, from the (rationalistic) point of view of justification and truth to that (vitalistic) of self-asserting existence and force, may be the really revolutionary novelty of Nietzsche's interpretation of the rapport between metaphor, truth, and ethics. The philosopher's active role, therefore, will be not only to unveil and criticize the metaphoric origin of concepts, but also *to accept and impose his own metaphors as such*: Their *force*, not their abstract correspondence to a reality presumed to be absolutely true, is their inner and real truth.[14]

As concerns Heidegger,[15] just as well known is his terse statement that "the metaphorical exists only within metaphysics,"[16] and his explanation (reductive, and criticized by many) of the metaphoric process as transfer from the "sensible" to the "intelligible" level. But I shall come back at length to his positions, as well as to the more recent phases of the philosophical debate on metaphor.

Usage of Metaphors in Philosophy

As we have seen, in general philosophers have not said much about metaphor. Even Aristotle, after all, gave it but a few (albeit rather decisive) lines. One fact is, however, difficult to challenge: Philosophers *do* use metaphors; or rather, there are, at first sight, metaphors in philosophical texts. It remains to be seen who uses what.

The study of metaphors (and generally of images, tropes, and rhetorical figures) in philosophical texts may well feature centrally in works consecrated to the style and language of philosophers; and these are wholly respectable studies that nevertheless only marginally seem to have right of citizenship in philosophy. Certainly the admiration for the beautiful images in the Platonic dialogues, or for the literary qualities of Henri Bergson's texts, is commonplace in philosophy manuals. But the imagination of philosophers and their individual repertoires of metaphors have seldom been seriously studied in their own rights.[17] By the same token, the formal aspects of their works have seldom been perceived as essential for the assessment of their thought.

Of course, for as long as metaphor is defined as ornament or secondary supplement, philosophers' metaphors are destined to silence, or to marginal consideration, as more generally the form of their language (in opposition to the "contents" of their thought). However, recent and numerous contributions on the topic of metaphor no longer support such a definition and, though very different from each other, they all share a tendency to reevaluate and enhance its position and weight. This in turn helps to reinvigorate a line of "exaltation" of metaphor (or of "image") that in philosophy, as we have seen, as well as elsewhere (for instance in the literature and literary theory of the baroque, romanticism, symbolism, surrealism, and so forth) had never died.

On the other hand, the ever more frequent intersections between philosophy and linguistics, literature, and psychoanalysis; the renewed interest in philosophers such as Nietzsche and Heidegger; as well as, in general, the vast influence of works classified, more or less correctly, under the labels of structuralism and poststructuralism, no longer justify the neglect of the problems of the signifier and of form.

The topic of the philosophers' metaphors presents itself today, therefore, in a new light: no longer a mere problem of style (in a reductive sense), unless, of course, philosophy itself were one such massive problem.[18] In this case, however, traditional stylistics would no longer provide analytical tools adequate to the task. The perspective has therefore radically changed: When the question concerning the usage of metaphors and images in philosophical texts is asked today, it is not with a view to investigating their literary worth, but rather to tackling the deep sense and the effects of their presence in those texts.[19] This should require: (a) a detailed analysis of metaphoric occurrences and their quantitative weight and distribution in the different parts of a text (preface, introduction, notes, conclusion, and so forth); (b) a study of the metaphoric fields[20] to which the various metaphors belong (fields that, of course, largely overflow the alleged unities of text and author) and of the system of relations they entertain among themselves in the text; and (c) a proper interrogation of the conscious reasons, the unconscious mechanisms, and the textual needs that all contribute to activate the use of metaphors; in other words, all that—beyond their charm and ornamental value—invokes them and more or less obscurely guides their apparition.

From the point of view I am trying to maintain in this investigation, however, the limits of the particular approach I have been describing above are clear: It operates exclusively on openly metaphoric occurrences, adopting—generally speaking—a notion of metaphor (or image) that is relatively narrow, limited to textual events immediately recognizable, on the basis of a consciously or unconsciously accepted definition, as metaphoric. Such analyses usually disregard more ample or less evident facts, such as "dead metaphors" within philosophical terminology, or the "metaphoric value" of an entire system of thought. Faced with questions of this kind, traditional perception of the metaphoric occurrence is, clearly, still inadequate. Instruments are required, capable of perceiving on one hand the genesis and life of metaphor, and on the other the events of a metaphoric order that escape immediate perception, often because they exceed the span of both the word and the proposition.

Relationship between Metaphor and Philosophy

Explicit theories and actual usage of metaphors are, on the best hypothesis, two ways leading to the problem that is here central: Is there a structural relationship between metaphor and philosophy? Of what kind? And, if so, what are the consequences of this for metaphor and for philosophy? Problems of this sort have been raised in relatively recent times by the revival, in different fields, of the interest in metaphor.

As I have already signaled, in philosophy the polemic against metaphor never died out; or, more precisely, the animosity against a type of discourse that, despite calling itself philosophical, shows a suspiciously liberal usage of "figures" and an obstinate intersection with literature and poetry. However, with the "rebirth" of metaphor, with the widening of its relevance to fields that a hasty but resistant judgement had declared unaffected by it (science, for instance), the topic of metaphor has begun to surface even in philosophy, and to elicit occasionally answers such that the role and status of philosophy itself seem to be called into question.

Important work has been accomplished by several authors separately, aimed at identifying the presence in philosophical texts of metaphors, or figurative cores, whose role cannot be described as purely ornamental or explanatory, and which on the contrary seem to exercise a truly essential function in a particular discursive economy. These are the so called root-metaphors that, according to Stephen C. Pepper,[21] lie very close to foundations of metaphysical constructions; or the "absolute metaphors" of Hans Blumenberg,[22] elements of meaning irreducible to a rational equivalent that are somehow in direct relation with the great questions that philosophy can neither finally answer, nor discard.

Such inquiries, albeit absolutely necessary, are nevertheless still preliminary,[23] and above all still not radical enough to tackle the real core of the question."metaphor and philosophy." The proximity of this core signals itself by a sort of "catastrophe,"[24] in which *all* the elements of the problem—metaphor, philosophy, and more—are truly put in question. The thread of the debate between Ricoeur and Derrida will enable me, in due course, to wander further along this path of reflection.

MOTIVES

The present investigation receives part of its impetus from two sources: on one hand, the relatively recent revival of the interest in rhetoric and, specifically, in metaphor, within as well as outside the field of philosophy; and on the other, more deeply, the uncertain or even critical situation in which philosophy seems to find itself nowadays (and perhaps cyclically), when it comes to achieving consensus regarding its own right to exist and its demand to be listened to.

The ultimate (and certainly remote) aim of this study is therefore, without doubt, the clarification of the status, structure, and legitimacy of philosophical discourse, and its delimitation in relation to neighboring ones. From this point of view, at least in a preliminary phase, metaphor will function as a point of departure and a touchstone: Its presence—and possibly its specific difference from other types of metaphor—within the philosophical text, and more specifically in some texts of Heidegger and Derrida, might tell us something relevant concerning philosophy itself.

It is also possible, however, that this aim will turn out to be unattainable, precisely because of the special bond between metaphor and philosophy, inducing the "catastrophic" effects that we shall see. At any rate, such an aim does not direct the inquiry as an imperative—but at the most, as a hope.

On the contrary, what imperatively moves the investigation at every stage, and even beyond the horizon and the interest of philosophy as discourse and as institution, is a moral duty to search for "the truth." The duty is itself unjustifiable and, I believe, purely philosophical, though free from any disciplinary affiliation (including to philosophy).

Philosophy before Metaphor

It is time to reopen the question of metaphor's double meaning. Within the discourse of philosophy in particular (albeit not exclusively), reference to metaphor can have two meanings:

(a) a narrow one, whereby metaphor is envisaged as a rhetorical or strategic instrument, and its functioning in the philosophical text is analyzed in terms of position, effects, and so on;

(b) a wider one, whereby metaphoricity is perceived as a category constitutive of philosophical discourse and the analysis is effected with a view to clarifying the load-bearing structures of this same discourse.

The very existence of such double meaning signals a revolution in the philosophical approach to the problem of metaphor. Several aspects of this revolution warrant closer attention.

Both the philosopher's theoretical position and practical behavior with regard to metaphor evidently depend to a large extent on the perception he has of metaphor itself; this perception has been changing quite significantly in recent years.

For a very long time the object "metaphor" has appeared almost exclusively in nonphilosophical contexts; for instance, in rhetoric, aesthetics, linguistics, poetics, and literary criticism. Its massive arrival in the philosophical domain is far from self-explanatory: In fact, it signals a change in status of its object, or a modification of the field of objects and instruments pertaining to philosophy, or both.

The status of the object has actually changed: Metaphor is no longer generally seen as "the substitution, for explanatory or ornamental purposes, of a thing's proper name with an improper one." The object ceases thus to be insignificant to the eyes of the philosopher (who only deals with "important things," or rather with "the most important things," leaving to others the marginal, secondary, and inessential ones). On the other hand, even the field and the repertoire of philosophy's instruments have effectively changed; the philosophical investigation has been contaminated with objects and notions of extraphilosophical origin (literature, psychoanalysis, linguistics, and so forth), which, in turn, certainly has something to do with the deterioration of philosophy's own field and methods. More specifically, the massive intrusion, not only in the wider field of discourse but also in the narrower field of philosophy, of the question of language (and of the text, the discourse, and so forth) prepares the ground for a more attentive examination of the object "metaphor," precisely as a linguistic/discursive/textual occurrence.

On the one hand, therefore, in general, philosophy's attention opens up on previously neglected areas; on the other, in particular, metaphor achieves the distinction of a possible (or even obligatory) object of philosophical inquiry. But there is more: It becomes, in effect, less and less appropriate to approach metaphor as, simply, an "object" for philosophy.

Metaphor As Philosophy's Problem

The topic of metaphor, when it appears nowadays in the philosophical field, often evokes a number of problems that far and away overstep the boundaries not only of an analysis of a linguistic or stylistic phenomenon, but also of an analysis of a determined or *determinable* problem in general: The object "metaphor" seems to possess an enormous centrifugal, even explosive, energy. The relationship between metaphor and philosophy, then, is not only the terrain on which the question of metaphor's definition is asked, but also one of the theoretical sites where, more and more urgently, philosophy is asked questions concerning its own status. Such an overdetermination does not come about by pure chance: Both within and outside philosophy, the conditions conducive to a renewed interest in metaphor have materialized. I shall briefly mention them.

Within philosophy: The "epoch of suspicion," and of the "end of the systems," invites a reexamination and a reevaluation of all that is marginal with respect to the traditional core of philosophical activity. Metaphor is very well placed to represent "the marginal," "the secondary," and "the repressed" in philosophy. At the same time, a portion of the philosophical field puts into motion a "defense of philosophy" that, in effect, reopens the old case "rationality versus its enemies" in which, once again, metaphor features centrally. Furthermore, philosophy is (and perhaps has always been, but today more intensely than ever before) particularly sensitive to a radical interrogation of its own status, and the question of metaphor lends itself to catalyze a large number of "problems of philosophy," in both meanings: objects that philosophy problematizes, and problems that threaten philosophy's existence and well-being.

Outside philosophy: The multiplication and growth of new fields of knowledge revolving around the *human*, the *linguistic*, and the *textual* induces a reconsideration of objects deemed secondary by previously ruling disciplines (such as philosophy), among them metaphor. The need for these new disciplines to impose and consolidate themselves (very often in competition with, and at the expense of, philosophy) manifests itself also through the valorization of the objects of their analysis. The result, partly fortuitous, partly necessary, is that metaphor not only relinquishes its secondary and subordinate position, but also claims a very central one within the research strategies of several among the emerging disciplines or discourses, in relationship to which philosophy is forced to locate and justify itself.

Many questions are triggered by a truly modern perception of the problem of metaphor, and they have hovered over the present inquiry from its start.

If the task consists in determining whether metaphor is a rhetorical and artificial tool or, on the contrary, the living force that creates meaning within language and thought, *how* exactly does one come to a decision in this matter? What would the consequences be of such a "decision," or of its impossibility, on the perception of the relationship between metaphor and philosophy? In what way does one begin to deal with such an intractable relationship? How does one begin in such a way as not to prejudge the outcome, for instance in favor of the interests of the philosopher and his caste?[25]

Once again the question of the beginnings surfaces, and this is hardly surprising, since it is impossible simply to ignore it or to solve it once and for all. It will therefore function here as an oscillator, ensuring the instability of a discourse that, in the impossibility of being radical in the sense of achieving the stability of some ultimate ground, nevertheless believes itself to be radical inasmuch as it manages to maintain itself in constant contact with the original *manque* from which it (painfully) rises: that is, to maintain itself constantly mobile and open. The reader will thus hardly be surprised by the lack of a proper answer to the question of the beginning, since the function of such question is precisely as a reminder of the necessity, the impossibility and the arbitrariness of any beginning.

DIRECTIONS

The present inquiry follows in its development three directions that can be separately identified, though they remain strictly interconnected:

(a) theory of metaphor;
(b) theory of philosophical discourse; and
(c) close analysis, with respect to (a) and (b) above, of two types of philosophical writing (texts by Heidegger and Derrida).

As already mentioned, these directions do not warrant or allow entirely separate treatments, and this is reflected in the contents of the various chapters of this work. They are simultaneously present as the three magnetic poles of an inquiry in a constant state of oscillation, affecting and attracting each other at all times. It is according to these forces and their various intersections that the investigation makes its curves, ellipses, and returns. There is no point, therefore, in looking here for the kind of systematization that consists in dealing with something only after having dealt with "that which comes (logically, methodologically, or historically) before"; and this for the very simple reason that it is impossible to tell, concerning metaphor, philosophy, or writing, what comes before and what comes after.[26]

What follows is thus, unfortunately, not the actual plan of research of this study, but rather its virtual frame of reference, which I shall have to disavow consistently, together with its guarantees and promises, in order not to repudiate the most pressing reasons for the inquiry itself.

Theory of Metaphor

Ideally, the task would be (a) to follow in detail and in depth the history of the concept of metaphor, starting from its Greek origins and ending with its recent revival in different domains, such as rhetoric, semiotics, linguistics, poetics, literary criticism, psychoanalysis, and philosophy; and (b) to compare current theories of metaphor and, finally, to select, extrapolate, or build an operational one for the purposes of this inquiry.

Theory of Philosophical Discourse

Even more ideally, this would entail (a) following the evolution of the ideas that philosophy has formed of itself; (b) listing and studying the main metaphors that appear in the canonical texts to describe the site, method, action, and destination of philosophy; (c) analyzing the differences among the various types of discourse that have been practiced under the title of philosophy; and (d) proposing a general theory of the philosophical discourse, founded on its relative difference from neighboring discourses, which enunciate themselves under other titles. The presence, quantity, and quality of "metaphoric" occurrences in all these discourses, including philosophy, would no doubt play a significant role in establishing similarities and differences.

Heidegger, Derrida: Imperfect Thoughts

Authors such as (for instance, but not by chance) Heidegger and Derrida are, each in his own way, relevant in the perspective of the present work, for several reasons:

(a) Because they represent types (or models/antimodels) of philosophical discourse that are at the same time powerful and controversial. Being borderline, they attract questions that inevitably concern the meaning of philosophy itself.

(b) Because they make fundamental points concerning metaphor and its relationship to philosophy (Heidegger: "The metaphoric only exists within metaphysics"; Derrida: "Neither philosophical discourse, nor natural language can escape the movement of metaphor").

(c) Because of the particular quality of their language, their proximity to poetic discourse, and, above all, their intensive recourse to occurrences that we are tempted to recognize as "metaphoric."

(d) Because their paths of thought, albeit different, seem to share an essential quality that I shall provisionally call incompleteness; and this quality seems to have a lot to do with the special (and at times uneasy) relationship they entertain with metaphor.

Imperfect thoughts: Is there a sense in which philosophy can only, ultimately, be "imperfect"?

Clearly, and even putting aside the essential caveats mentioned above and aimed at avoiding an excessive methodological delimitation of the horizon of inquiry, even if I actually wanted to follow the plan so outlined, it would be impossible to complete within the limits of the present work the whole of such an immense program.

Inasmuch as this ideal plan also represents the necessary contextual framework of my discourse, I shall offer my reader the opportunity to reconstitute it, in part, by way of references, when possible, to existing studies, especially as concerns the history and theory of metaphor.

Otherwise, the lacunae of this work will remain open, particularly when this is appropriate in order not to lose track of the question, or not to close its most decisive and less decidable perspectives. One of the aims of this introduction was precisely to signal the breadth of the question and of the field within which it demands to be elaborated, so that what follows will be perceived in its correct proportions, in the light of the intentions I have just declared.

NOTES

1. The relationship between metaphor and unconscious (and in particular Marxist and psychoanalytical contributions to the study of the unconscious dimension of metaphoric activity) is the central topic of Claudine Normand's book, *Métaphore et concept* (Paris: Complexe, 1976), in which further bibliographic references on this subject can be found.

2. See in this respect Jean Greisch, *La parole heureuse. Martin Heidegger entre la parole et les mots* (Paris: Beauchesne, 1987; henceforward PH), p. 194.

3. Ivor A. Richards, *The Philosophy of Rhetoric* (Oxford: Oxford University Press, 1936); Monroe C. Beardsley, *Aesthetics* (New York: Harcourt, Brace and World, 1958); Max Black, *Models and Metaphors* (Ithaca: Cornell University Press, 1962).

4. Aristotle, *Poétique*, trans. J. Hardy (Paris: Editions des Belles Lettres, 1969), 1457 b 6–9. For the commentary to this truly fundamental text, see Paul Ricoeur, *The Rule of Metaphor* (Toronto: University of Toronto Press, 1977), chap. 1; and Jacques Derrida, "White Mythology," in *Margins of Philosophy* (Chicago: University of Chicago Press, 1982).

5. This is the process that Gérard Genette describes in "La rhétorique restreinte," in *Figures III* (Paris: Editions du Seuil, 1972), pp. 21–40: the reduction of rhetoric to a theory of elocution, then to a theory of tropes, and its subsequent losing contact with philosophy.

6. Giambattista Vico, *Principi di scienza nuova* (1744), book 2: "Della sapienza poetica," in *Opere filosofiche* (Firenze: Sansoni, 1971).

7. Jean-Jacques Rousseau, *Discours sur l'origine et les fondements de l'inégalité* (1754), in *Oeuvres Complètes*, vol. 3 (Paris: Gallimard, Bibliothèque de la Pléiade, 1964). On Rousseau and metaphor, the reader can usefully consult Paul de Man's article "Theory of Metaphor in Rousseau's 'Second Discourse,' " *Studies in Romanticism* 12 (1973): 475–98.

8. G. W. F. Hegel, *Aesthetics: Lectures on Fine Arts* (Oxford: Clarendon Press, 1974–75), chap. 3.

9. Benedetto Croce, *Problemi di estetica* (Bari: Laterza, 1966), pp. 159–63.

10. In this respect, see "The Living Metaphor" in chap. 2.

11. See chap. 2.

12. See Friedrich Nietzsche, "Erkenntnistheoretische Einleitung über Wahreit und Lüge im aussermoralishen Sinne" ["Introduction théorétique sur vérité et mensonge en un sens extra-moral"] (1873), in *Das Philosophenbuch / Le livre du philosophe* (Paris: Flammarion, 1969).

13. PH, p. 9: "Comparer l'histoire de la pensée métaphysique avec l'usure d'une monnaie, comme le fait par example Nietzsche, est ambigu, car la notion d'usure est déjà solidaire d'une représentation toute «métaphysique» du propre et du figuré, autrement dit, elle suppose une théorie de la métaphore, qu'il s'agit sans doute de mettre en question." Unless otherwise stated, translations in English are my own.

14. See, in this respect, Sarah Kofman, *Nietzsche et la métaphore* (Paris: Payot, 1972); and Luisa Bonesio, ed., *Nietzsche: la critica della verità* (Bologna: Zanichelli, 1977).

15. See in particular Martin Heidegger, *Der Satz vom Grund* (Pfullingen: Neske, 1957), *The Principle of Reason* (Bloomington: Indiana University Press, 1991); and "Das Wesen der Sprache," in *Unterwegs zur Sprache* (Pfullingen: Neske, 1959), "The Nature of Language," in *On the Way to Language* (New York: Harper & Row, 1971).

16. Heidegger, *Der Satz vom Grund*, p. 89; *The Principle of Reason*, p. 48.

17. This is also the opinion expressed by Michèle Le Doeuff in *The Philosophical Imaginary* (London: Athlone Press, 1989).

18. See in this respect, for instance, Jacques Derrida, *Eperons. Les styles de Nietzsche* (Paris: Flammarion, 1978).

19. As an early example of this kind of analysis, one could cite David W. Tarbet, "The Fabric of Metaphors in Kant's Critique of Pure Reason," *Journal of the History of Philosophy* (1968): 257–70.

20. The notion of "metaphoric field" has been introduced by Harald Weinrich in "Münze und Wort. Untersuchungen an einem Bildfeld," in *Festschrift für Gerhard Rohlfs*, eds. Heinrich Lausberg and Harald Weinrich (Halle: Niemeyer, 1968), pp. 508–21.

21. Stephen C. Pepper, "Philosophy and Metaphor," *Journal of Philosophy* 25 (1928): 130–32; "The Root Metaphor Theory of Metaphysics," *Journal of Philosophy* 14 (1935): 365–74; *World Hypotheses. A Study in Evidence* (Berkeley: University of California Press, 1942).

22. Hans Blumenberg, *Paradigmi per una metaforologia*, trans. M. V. S. Hansberg (Bologna: Il Mulino, 1969).

23. Blumenberg himself indicates that the object of "metaphorology" (which as a discipline depends on philosophy) is of an eminently historical interest. Ibid., p. 22.

24. On this notion of "catastrophe," see in chap. 2 the discussion of "Le retrait de la métaphore," by Jacques Derrida.

25. I implicitly refer here to the sociological critique—from Theodor Adorno, *The Jargon of Authenticity* (London: Routledge and Kegan Paul, 1973), to Pierre Bourdieu, *The Political Ontology of Martin Heidegger* (Cambridge: Polity, 1991), and to the more recent debate on Heidegger's Nazism—that attempts to link "intellectual positions" to a "position of the intellectual" (Heidegger in this case) in a given social structure, or in a given cultural and ideologico-political field.

26. For the same reason, the reader will not be overly shocked, I hope, to find that the order of chronological succession of the authors with whom I deal is not respected in the present work.

1

OF METAPHOR

I shall not repeat here the task (so necessary, and fortunately several times accomplished) of presentation of the historical development of the concept of metaphor. I will proceed, instead, with the direct object of the present chapter, that is, an approach to a viable (within the context outlined) notion of metaphor.

PRELIMINARY QUESTIONS

A preliminary question, already mentioned at the start of this work, immediately surfaces: Is it possible to speak theoretically (that is, to produce the theory) of metaphor without speaking the language of philosophy? The question is obviously fundamental to determining the relationship between metaphor and philosophy.

First of all, one ought to ask: What does "to speak the language of philosophy" mean? Two types of answer seem possible:

(a) Philosophy is a discipline, that is, a *specific* field of intellectual elaboration, endowed with specific vocabulary and syntax, among other fields that differentiate themselves by their specific vocabularies and syntaxes; in this case, nothing prevents any theoretical discipline, other than philosophy, from taking charge of the theory of metaphor in a language different from that of philosophy. It is through a similar reasoning that various human sciences can aspire to replacing philosophy in the analysis of certain objects (Pierre Bourdieu and Jacques Lacan, among many others, are good examples of this).

(b) Philosophy is *not a specific* field of intellectual elaboration; it certainly has its own tradition, lexicon, and habits, but fundamentally it reflects the structures of the language called "natural" or, more precisely as far as we are concerned, the syntax of Indo-European languages. There is, therefore, no theoretical treatment of any object whatsoever that is truly external to philosophy. And, consequently, underneath the veneer of the different disciplines, there is no nonphilosophical theory of metaphor. This is the reasoning *à la Derrida* through which we learn that metaphysics rules the whole universe of the sayable (even beyond the limits of language) within which we make sense of our world, and philosophy—both as articulation and as deconstruction of metaphysics—firmly maintains its indirect but powerful control over any discourse (as long as it—however loosely—makes sense).

It is in this sense that Jean Greisch writes the following:

> [A] metaphysical "device" only deserves its name if it deploys its effects also outside the proper boundaries of philosophy. Otherwise it would simply be a theoretical construction attributable to an author or to a school of thought.[1]

However, if the largest and most powerful "metaphysical device" is language itself, we could legitimately say that there simply is no (sensible) linguistic production occurring outside metaphysics; and, if philosophy is the discourse where metaphysics presents itself as theory, then there is no theory outside philosophy. In other terms: Philosophy, in this scenario, would not be _a_ discipline, _a_ type of discourse, but rather _the_ metadiscursive domain in which the analysis of the articulations of language (concepts) takes place, and since any metadiscourse (any theory) is concerned with this and thus belongs to that domain, there would be no theoretical site external to philosophy.

If language is not a determined field or object, if there is no site truly external to language, if therefore there is never total control of language, neither is there absolute theoretical definition of the linguistic materials we "use." Bottomlessness, or utter lack of foundation, would be the essential dimension of language. Language would then be more the eternally imperfect articulation of our relationship to an irreducible alterity than the utilization of a means of communication and control; which, in turn, would not be without serious consequences at the level of philosophical discourse.

Paradoxically, the same totalizing approach that excludes the possibility of speaking nonphilosophically of metaphor brings us rather directly to a symmetrical radical impasse; that is, the impossibility of speaking philosophically of metaphor (in a strong sense:

"telling the truth" on metaphor). Indeed, if an essential (and fundamentally unavoidable) connection is established between natural language and metaphysics, or even between metaphysics and metaphor (which happens, for instance, with Heidegger, as well as with Nietzsche); if, therefore, metaphor is introduced to the very heart of what we may call the "theoretical device," one ends up by depriving oneself, in principle, of any possibility of absolute theoretical control of metaphor.

But there is more: The recognition of a fundamental complicity between metaphor and philosophy translates directly into the undecidibility of priorities and hierarchies, and perhaps even into the impossibility of *founding* philosophy as an autonomous discourse. Does this signify the end of philosophical discourse, or simply its condemnation to essential imperfection?

Perhaps it is impossible both to speak philosophically of metaphor and to speak of it (theoretically) in any other way. However, if the fundamental concepts of philosophy are metaphors, would it be possible (or even inevitable) to speak *metaphorically* of metaphor, of philosophy, of truth? What would the meaning be of such a project (or condition) from a philosophical point of view? To what extent can philosophy—without terminally damaging itself—*accept* metaphor?

I jump momentarily over the impasse and I set out on the path leading to a provisional descriptive theory of metaphor. My text's oscillations will soon enough bring me back, irresistibly, to the realm of paradoxes.

BEYOND THE TRADITIONAL MODEL

Labels and Metaphors

Within the traditional perception of the phenomenon, metaphor can be defined as the transposition of a foreign name to something which, as a consequence, does not obtain its proper denomination, but another one, and through this improper but analogically justifiable denomination receives some sort of additional illumination, or is perceived from a different angle. This notion of metaphor has proven exceptionally hardy; it has been, in effect, the most common one since Aristotle.

One of the foundations of the traditional notion of metaphor is, therefore, the perception of language as a repertoire of labels. Everything is assigned a label that can be exchanged, lost, replaced, and so on; metaphor corresponds to one of these possibilities, namely, the exchange of labels. This model has its advantages even though, used in isolation, it does not go very far. Furthermore, and more to the point, the idea of label in itself can become misleading when considering the function of metaphor. However, rather than reject the "labels model," I prefer to use it for what it can offer in terms of usefulness and economy by inserting it in a wider frame.

The attribution of labels seems a perfectly legitimate procedure and a correct description of some aspects of our relationship to language; the problem is that it only concerns one aspect of this relationship. The attribution of labels is but one of the possible, and numerous, linguistic games, one of the mechanisms at work in the production of meaning. Among the other admissible linguistic games, some cannot be accomplished without the intervention of other mechanisms: to communicate, to express, even to "perform" (in the sense of the linguistic performative), all require much more than the attribution and utilization of labels.

Without going too deeply into the detail of linguistic theory, I shall simply say, for the time being, that the constitution of language requires at least two poles, one rigid and one mobile, in order to acquire both the stability and the flexibility that are needed for its full functioning. I shall place labels near the rigid pole, and metaphors near the mobile pole of language.

Contrary to the traditional point of view, I am therefore opposing (though not absolutely) labels and metaphors not because metaphor is devoid of all label-like traces, but because metaphor plays in language a role that is dialectically opposed to the one played by labels. It plays a role of mobilization in discourse: Through analogy, it establishes connections between not only different objects, but also different semantic fields and linguistic games. This is entirely neglected in the classical theory of metaphor, but it has been often stressed by more recent theoreticians of metaphor.

Another important element has been perceived and has come to enrich the modern notion of metaphor, contributing simultaneously to casting doubts on the idea of metaphors as labels. Metaphor has been interpreted as producing a shock in the order of discourse; this shock would be perceived, normally, as "impertinence," and immediately followed by processes aimed at reducing the impertinence. The happy outcome of the process triggers not so much a redistribution of labels, but rather a new effect of sense, which I shall describe in more detail.

Toward a Description of Metaphor

On the basis of what has been said so far, and as a first approximation to the object, I now propose the following provisional description: *Metaphor* is the presence, in a given context or with reference
to a given referent, of a signifier that, on the basis of the codes
applicable in the specific circumstance (a), is not pertinent in relation to the immediate context or referent (b), but can nevertheless
be connected (c) to such context or referent on the basis of an extraordinary code (d), whose acceptability depends on the activation of
a "register of metaphoric pertinence" (e). Dead (or lexicalized)
metaphors (f) are not perceived as impertinent because the repeated
usage has made them elements in a code.

A few points concerning the preceding formulation:

(a) The codes relevant in the specific circumstances can include
the genre and its norms; the practical conditions of the
enunciation, the public, the language, symbolic systems, ide-
ologies, traditions, and so forth. Circumstances select the
relevant codes, making the others instantly inactive.

(b) "Nonpertinent," in this case, is a signifier that the relevant
codes cannot admit as possible (in other terms, an unexpected one).

(c) "To connect" means finding a way to make at least partially
pertinent the unexpected signifier; (partially) deactivating
the metaphoric tension, therefore, without which the occurrence, rather than a metaphor, would be and remain a gratuitous or absurd image.

(d), (e) The presence of a metaphor, recognized as such by effect of
an amount of tension (and consequent distension), activates
a supplementary and extraordinary code, on the basis of

which the limits of pertinence of the signifier are widened, allowing it to "connect" with the context or with the referent. The metaphoric register is the situation generated by the presence of metaphor and the necessary condition for the activation of an extraordinary code of pertinence.

(f) A "dead" metaphor no longer engenders tension (or very little) and does not demand the application of an extraordinary code, because it has already found a place and a role (and is therefore expected) within the ordinary codes. In extreme cases, it is no longer seen as a metaphor at all. In fact, we could say that both "dead metaphor" and "living metaphor" represent two extreme positions: In between there is room for the majority of metaphors, all more or less lexicalized, more or less expected.

The preceding outline of a theory of metaphor extracts and underlines a specific phenomenon (and particularly some aspects of it) for the purposes of this analysis, without actually opposing the thesis of the metaphoricity of language in general. On the contrary, nothing prevents us, in this perspective, from considering the whole of language as a fabric consisting of metaphors, "used" (or dead) within the diverse codes for the greater part, and with a constant activity of creation of new metaphors or regeneration of old ones.

The more rigid the active code (for instance, in scientific discourses), the more structured in the form of a network of relatively fixed expectations is the specific pertinence in a specific context; the more explosive is the impertinence. Or, more exactly: Strict and formalized scientific discourses (excluding, therefore, divulgative ones) rely on the total presupposition of all terms they use. They abolish surprise and only admit tension when it is impossible to do without it; although it no doubt remains to be seen whether precisely those moments, perhaps, do not constitute their most important theoretical articulations.

With poetic discourse, on the contrary, we are often in a situation of permanent expectation of "metaphoric surprise." The metaphoric register is there always at home, and extraordinary codes are always potentially active.

I shall carry forth the analysis of metaphor with reference to the modes of discourse in chapter 4. It is now time, on the basis of the results seen so far, to proceed more decidedly toward a useful theory of metaphor, which in the course of the present work I shall no longer actively attempt to modify. I hope, nevertheless, that what precedes, and especially the path and the way by which we reach this formulation (despite its peremptory and definitive appearance), show well enough its dynamic status; that is, its provisional character, or its limited validity in the wider context of the question of metaphor and philosophy. This is indeed one of the moments of rest and recollection that I announced in the introduction: Necessary though it may be for the time being, it does not represent a point of arrival or a "result" of the investigation.

THE MECHANISM OF METAPHOR

Definitions

Metaphor is a meaning–effect generated by way of interaction between two contexts with reference to a text. A *meaning-effect* is a commotion of the order of discourse, produced by a successful effort of reabsorption of an irregularity, measured on the basis of previous expectations. The *text* is the literal sequence of signs in which the metaphoric occurrence is included (the "zero level of writing," or its "material residue");[2] in itself, without a context, text is always illegible.

The two contexts are: (1) the ordinary context of a particular text; and (2) a secondary context. The *ordinary context* is constituted by the whole of the presuppositions, data, circumstances, norms, codes, and so on enabling and governing the reading of a given text. The *secondary context* is activated only when a portion, or the whole, of the text is not interpretable by reference to the ordinary context exclusively.

Let us take, for instance, the French expression *jeune loup* (young wolf).[3] According to its ordinary context, the occurrence *jeune loup* can be interpreted as metaphorical, or not. Let us assume that the ordinary context is comprised of the following circumstantial determination: classified ads, "lost animals" section. In this case the ordinary context is sufficient to the production of meaning and the occurrence does not require interpretation as metaphorical:

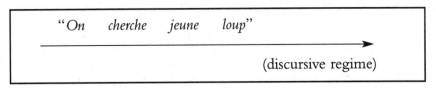

If, however, the ordinary context is determined by the inclusion of the statement in the "help wanted" section of the classified ads, then there certainly is an interruption of sense that requires mending through the intervention of a supplementary context; namely, one including some special connotations of the expression *jeune loup* with reference to the requirements of the job market in our society; the occurrence is therefore going to be interpreted as metaphorical, and a meaning-effect is generated:

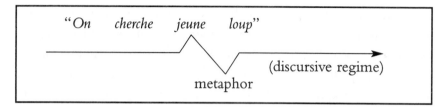

The meaning-effect consists here of the superposition of the expression _jeune loup_, charged with a context that, given the ordinary context, can only be exceptional to another expression (_x_) that is absent and actually does not need to be made explicit or even imagined existent, and which would not have provoked any disruption, had it been employed:

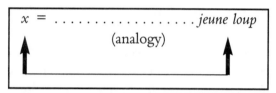

However, the core of this process is not at all the mysterious _x_, but the new context imported into the discourse in order to make further sense.

Contexts are external to the text. A text can therefore never provide the integral key to its own sense, that is, all the contexts sufficient and necessary to its own reading, for two reasons: First, any text is historical, which means it is surrounded by a constantly changing universe of contexts; second, any individual reader is the unstable holder of contexts that are not only different from reader to reader, but also themselves constantly changing. So from both sides, the possible infinity of contexts breaks the well-defined limits established by the literality (or materiality) of the text.

When the codes activated by the ordinary context are insufficient or in any way unsatisfactory, in the process of construing an acceptable meaning based on the text, extraordinary contexts may be (and in most cases indeed automatically are) brought in, until a secondary context is located that allows a pertinent reading of the text, where *pertinent* means "making sense," or rather the particular type of sense required by the particular linguistic game being played; assuming, of course, that the game demands that meaning be generated, which is most often—but not always—the case. Evidently the contexts are relative to the reader and therefore subjective, which here means "dependent on the reader as actualizer of contexts," rather than "created by the reader." And this explains why metaphors, together with all other meaning-effects, can be interpreted in different ways, particularly when they are "new."

The search for extraordinary contexts stops if the hypothesis (always available) of *incorrectness* (grammatical, logical, orthographic, and so on) of the text seems plausible. In any event, the activation of a secondary context does not extinguish the efficacy of the ordinary one; this distinguishes, for instance, metaphor from cryptogram, and the interpretation of metaphors from cryptography. Indeed, if the secondary context is activated and makes sense alone, with complete (though perhaps temporary) obliteration of the ordinary one, the effect is not truly metaphoric. There is metaphor only when ordinary and special context interact, that is, when the meaning produced depends on the two contexts simultaneously.

The secondary context can itself be constituted by an indeterminate number of elements, linguistic as well as extralinguistic. When a metaphoric process is active, the secondary context becomes predominant and the ordinary context serves as frame, or as reference. Without the secondary context we would not know that there is metaphor (and, in fact, there would not be one); without the ordinary context (or at least the awareness of its existence) we would not know how to interpret a metaphor, or even the text itself.

If a secondary context is not immediately available, the reading of the metaphoric text causes an interruption of sense that opens up a further search. If, on the other hand, the reading based on the active ordinary context does not generate any interruption (justifying in turn the acquisition of a secondary sense), the metaphoric effect is void. In lexicalized metaphors, the metaphoric (lexicalized) sense has replaced the "proper" sense and has become part and parcel of the ordinary context. The "proper" sense can then be reactualized by means of a secondary context (for instance, etymological information). Is the effect, in this case, a metaphoric one? Probably not in a strict sense, since the ordinary context (or at least one among its qualifying elements, the lexicalized metaphoric meaning) is no longer required once the secondary context has been introduced. There certainly is, however, a special effect of mobilization of the sense, and this is often used, for instance, by both Hegel and Heidegger.[4]

The metaphoric occurrence and the activation of a secondary context cannot be entirely arbitrary; there must be a relation between the occurrence requiring an extraordinary context and the meaning generated by the activation of the extraordinary context. I shall call this relation, this link justifying and explaining the metaphoric occurrence, "analogy." Either the analogy has previously been instituted (deposited in language), or it has not; in the latter case, the metaphoric occurrence (if successful) institutes the analogy. Such institution, however, is not creation: The _possibility_ of the analogy must in all cases preexist, albeit not always explicitly, as a differential space in language, or rather in the general text of the inscribing of all traces, of all forms. A _trait_ capable of sustaining the analogy must exist in advance somewhere.

The Trait

The analogy-bearing trait is the effect of a structure: It is instituted by a structural network (the general network of the inscription, also known as "culture," or "the world") constituted by relations. No trait is, in itself, identifiable as analogical; nor is it reproducible, or even perceptible, unless it is activated by an analogy.

The trait cannot, in effect, be isolated or said; it is neither a signifier nor a signified, nor a meaning; it does not subsist in isolation, but only in association with two representations, without which it simply is unthinkable. The analogical trait is not representable; without the analogical trait, however, there is no metaphor, since metaphoric representations would make no sense. The analogical trait is neither a *primum* nor a source; it is never natural (original), always derived not from representation, which it always precedes, but from the previous "disposition" of the world as we perceive and interpret it. This disposition regularly eludes any possibility of exhaustive analysis; it includes the trace of all signifying events having taken place and having been recorded, and in particular (in the perspective of this work), the metaphors deposited in the treasure of language.

The world in question is, of course, not the "natural" world, but rather a structure of relations and differences that the reader, as bearer of codes, schemes, norms, forms, and so forth, does not create but activate. No perception in the reader is isolated or pure; only relations, or objects in relation to each other, can be perceived. Analogy, as one possibility of relation, is therefore already at the heart of perception, and is not preceded by the terms that constitute it.

The reader perceives neither the world as a complete whole nor its isolated elements; he perceives always and only a certain state of a certain region of the world. Furthermore, the reader's operation (reading) is never a simple perception but always also an act of modification of the existing state of the world. The modification introduced by the reader may consist of the addition of something to the structure of relations constituting the state of the examined region of the world. At any rate, to truly read a text means making of it something it had never been before.

To sum it up, the trait is the basis of representation, and of perception; only a "trait in relation" is perceptible; a "trait in relation" requires a difference. Analogy is the perception of the same trait (or of traits perceived as identical) in two or more different positions of a relatively homogeneous structure, or of a structure that as a result of the analogy becomes relatively homogeneous. A trait is only perceptible within a system of differences, as we learn from Ferdinand de Saussure. The system is given, in the sense that it precedes any act of perception-reproduction; it is open, in the sense that it is determined by an indeterminate number of factors; it is variable, in the sense that it is historically and geographically relative.

We have seen that "the world" presents itself as a system of differential traits, and that analogy is the identification of a trait perceived as identical within two or more subsystems. Metaphor is, then, the place where such identification produces or reproduces itself. But the metaphoric effect is not limited to the simple identification of an analogical trait. It rather consists of the interference generated between the two contexts of the trait, which are different from one another.

Text, Context, Reader

There is no "zero level of meaning," a proper sense perceptible out of any context. The text is illegible: It is the context that activates the system of differences, which in turn makes the text readable. If *metaphoric meaning* is understood in dichotomic opposition to *proper meaning*, all meaning is metaphoric and proper meaning simply does not exist. However, in relation to a given ordinary context, an "effect of immediate pertinence" is generated, on the basis of the previous habits registered in the agent who actualizes the sense. Metaphoric meaning is not metaphoric in itself, but only in relation to the ordinary context applied by the agent mentioned above, "the reader."

In relationship to the reader the ordinary context, as well as the secondary one, can be divided into external and internal context. This, however, is only useful in first approximation, because the internal and external contexts are only active insofar as a reader actualizes them. One could therefore say that the context is entirely internal (because all must go through the reader), or that it is entirely external (because the reader does not represent a free and creative instance, but a perceptive-reproductive one; in other words, an interference and not a source). At any rate, the designation of the reader as the place of separation between internal and external is not really useful at this moment; the reader should rather be seen as the sole context-actuating device, whatever the context may be. Without a reader (precisely as without text or context) there is no meaning. However—and this is the most important—the reader does not generate meaning; he rather perceives it at the intersection of a context (possibly multiple, as in the case of metaphor) and a text.

The reader is a reader only inasmuch as he carries (at least) a context. The wider context is the world, and the context actualized in the reader is a portion of the world. The reader cannot fully assess the portion of the world constituting his own ordinary context, at least not integrally, because he cannot have of it a complete and instantaneous[5] perception, but only a partial (that is, relative, dynamic, and open) one. The reader is neither necessarily nor entirely conscious of the ordinary context that makes him one; and he is not necessarily conscious of the secondary context. However, whether the reader is or is not aware of the active contexts is of very little significance from the present point of view: The reader could very well be a machine, an automaton.

TEXT	CONTEXT	READER

The three ingredients separately, or even in groups of two in the absence of the third one, are totally inactive. Only the combination of the three of them produces effects; these effects can in turn make sense, but not necessarily. In some cases the effect achieved is one of nonmeaning; for instance, in the case of a text that remains illegible in relation to all applied contexts.

The "Other" of Metaphor

In this conclusive section I shall discuss that which, on the basis of the preceding analysis, is not metaphor, and yet maintains a link with metaphor, be it of similarity or difference. I will thus mention other "tropes" or "figures," but not treat them in the fashion of a manual of rhetoric, that is, systematically and exhaustively. I will only pause at topics that can be of interest in the perspective of the present work, and I shall only discuss the aspects that relate to the problem of "metaphor and philosophy."

On the basis of what I have said above, the word or expression is metaphoric which (a) in a different context would *not* be metaphoric, since it would be interpretable without leaving or having to add to the immediate context; (b) has *not* been redefined and co-opted by the ordinary context in a network (or through an act of definition) that fully determines its position and meaning within it; and (c) makes sense (is interpretable).

Conversely, the word or expression is *not* metaphoric which either (a) is fully interpretable within the ordinary context; (b) despite being foreign to the immediate context, is immediately captured in a network of relations, obeying precise rules, which determine its exact position and meaning; or (c) does not make sense (is not interpretable).

The metaphoricity of the sense depends on the linguistic game being played (which determines to a large extent the ordinary context). If, in a conversation, I speak of a "wave of sympathy," the word "wave" is most probably a metaphor. If, however, I read the expression "electromagnetic wave" in a text of physics, the word "wave" is no longer a metaphor in the same degree (it is a metaphor from a genetic point of view, but not in its present functioning: The original metaphor is partly inactive, and inasmuch as a metaphoric meaning remains active—the connotations of the word "wave" taken out of its normal context—it is entirely constrained within a system of definitions, graphs, formulas, and so on).

In general, what we call "proper," "usual," or "strict" meaning ought always be seen in a nonabsolute dimension; that is, in relation to a given discursive situation. Any occurrence at all can be used in a proper or metaphoric sense, and that does not depend on its objectual referent, but on the ordinary context in which it appears. For instance, the word "animal" applied to a dog will generate an effect of proper sense in most contexts; however, if I shout, addressing my dog in a state of rage after it has just broken a precious vase, "You animal!" then the new context makes the occurrence a metaphoric one, even though the referent actually is a dog, and therefore an animal.

I see, from this point of view, only subtle differences between "proper," "usual," and "strict": *Proper meaning* can be defined here as the result of an interpretative process that does not call upon an extraordinary context; the *usual meaning* is the one we expect in a given context, and therefore does not generate any meaning-effect (a perturbation of the relationship between text and reader requiring, to be settled, the intervention of an unusual context); with reference to an expression that, in the same context, can have also a metaphoric meaning, we speak of *strict sense* when it does not have it, that is, when it does not demand a supplementary context.

Comparison ("she is as beautiful as an angel") generates little tension and demands no resolution, since it is introduced and conducted according to codified forms that "present" and explicitly declare the analogy. There certainly is intervention of a special register and of an extraordinary code, but the reach, the limits, and the application of the analogy are well defined.

Image, according to Hermann Pongs,[6] is a creative and purely subjective phenomenon, in contrast to metaphor, which is a logical and objective one. Gaston Bachelard[7] goes in the same direction, when he opposes image (prereflexive, variational) to concept (reflexive, constitutional). I should say that image (when, of course, this word is not employed as a synonym of metaphor) is a violent disruption of discursive sense that does not demand or allow a resolution of the tension it generates. On the contrary, its purpose is precisely to engender and maintain as long as possible a high level of tension. Partial pertinence (based on an analogical ground) is possible, albeit not necessary. The register activated is not the same one as for metaphor, since it does not trigger an extraordinary code and does not rely upon it to establish a sensible relationship as the foundation for the intended meaning. Thus image, with its irreconcilable charge of disruption, and not metaphor is the preferred instrument of surrealists, futurists, and other avant-gardes. On the other hand, it is entirely useless in philosophical discourse, for the reasons we shall soon discuss.

Catachresis, traditionally, "consists in a sign, already connected to a first idea, being also connected to a new one that itself never had or no longer has a proper sign in language."[8] Cicero defines it as *metaphora inopiae causa*, and indeed the distinction between metaphor and catachresis is sometimes a source of ambiguity, particularly if it helps to consolidate the notion that language is in essence the application of labels to things or ideas: in which case, catachresis would be the improper use of a label for a thing or an idea that, before such attribution, has none. I prefer to speak of catachresis in relation to occurrences that could not be replaced by a nonmetaphoric designation. The phenomenon has special relevance in philosophy, where often the task consists precisely in producing conceptual sense where none is available.

Metonymy and *synecdoche* can be considered special cases of metaphor; their particularity resides in the fact that they do not really demand the search for and intervention of an extraordinary context, but rather the extension of the ordinary one to another element of the semantic field to which the occurrence is linked. If, for instance, I say: "I drank two bottles," there is no need to look for a new context for "bottles" in order to understand what I am saying; perceiving "wine" and "bottle" as belonging to the same semantic field, and extracting from it the element that pacifies the tension, is normally enough.

Allegory is a series of chained metaphors whose effects compose a complex symbolic meaning. The result of the allegory, when, of course, it is correctly interpreted, is a precise message that explains it point by point.

The notion of *concept* would require here, for obvious reasons, a far more detailed analysis. In the perspective opened up by the provisional theory of metaphor that I have just presented, concept can be defined as the result of a process of recontextualization of a metaphor within the discourse that houses it. For instance, in philosophical discourse the word "substance" certainly has a metaphoric origin. However, within a context that fixes its sense and includes it in a wider network, it ceases to function in the metaphoric register and starts to function in the conceptual one: It becomes a concept, endowed with a well-defined meaning that almost entirely replaces the previous one. It is in a somewhat similar manner, I believe, that Ricoeur (indeed continuing a long tradition) sees it.[9]

I have no serious objection to this way of looking at the idea of concept, except on one point that I deem capital in understanding what philosophy is. It is, actually, a "simple" matter of stress. We can stress either (1) the concept, that is, the "end product," ready to use; or (2) the production of concepts, that is, the process that at the same time exploits and controls metaphor. The stress is important: I believe, in effect, that philosophy, essentially, has more to do with the process of transformation of metaphors into concepts than with the management and utilization of concepts, for two reasons:

(a) Because what is specific to the philosophical discourse is the elaboration of pockets and layers of meaning that escape other modes of discourse; that is, the presentation, in the space of the sayable and according to rational forms, of that which is not scientifically verifiable. The general field of discourses constantly creates and modifies this sort of raw material (which, by the way, ensures the continued existence of philosophy).

(b) Because philosophical work is by its nature to a great extent transitory and volatile. Scientific discourses control the procedures that rigorously select acceptable statements and data and, as a result, ensure a relatively long duration to their own theoretical productions. The role of philosophy is entirely different and has very little to do with the accumulation of

knowledge in time. Thus the frequent succession of con-
trasting philosophical theories, far from being a defect, is
precisely philosophy's strength.

Evidently, the transformation of metaphors into concepts
requires their inclusion in a network. Therefore a certain degree of
"construction of theoretical buildings," requiring in turn the utilization of concepts, is indispensable. The purpose, however, is not the
accumulation of knowledge or the accomplishment of any particular project. The aim is always the opening up and the control of
spaces of meaning that other modes of discourse can (and indeed
will) create and modify, but cannot cover using only their own
means. These spaces cannot be listed once and for all, and that control can be neither total nor permanent. From this point of view
deconstruction (both as a notion and as a motion) seems to represent very well the central core of the operation of philosophy: Its
very name (a rare word reintroduced in the vocabulary of philosophy through a semantic reactualization that is always suspended,
since there is no "conceptual definition" of deconstruction) con-
centrates the complex graph of the relationship of dependence and
mastery that philosophy entertains with the spaces of sense in which
it is active.

In the following chapter and later on, I shall say more concerning deconstruction and philosophical discourse; I conclude at
this point this outline of a portrait of metaphor and the partial enu-
meration of the "others" of metaphor, at least of those that touch
most directly upon philosophical discourse.

NOTES

1. Jean Greisch, *La parole heureuse. Martin Heidegger entre la parole et les mots* (Paris: Beauchesne, 1987; henceforward PH), p. 190: "un «dispositif» métaphysique ne mérite son nom que s'il déploie ses effets également hors du domaine de la philosophie proprement dite. Sinon il serait une simple construction théorique attribuable à un auteur ou à une école de pensée."

2. I use here, for the time being, the words *text, reading*, and *reader* in a very large sense, one that includes the production and interpretation of nearly any kind of signifying traces.

3. I am assured this example is untranslatable in English. *Jeune loup* means, metaphorically, a very determined, aggressive, ruthless young person, the kind deemed to be very desirable to modern employers.

4. See in this respect "Etymology, Quotation Marks, Rhetorical Questions" in chap. 4.

5. Which instead, according to Jacques Derrida, represents the fundamental presupposition of any structuralism: see "Force and Signification," in *Writing and Difference* (Chicago: University of Chicago Press, 1978), and "Strategies of Deconstruction, or the Endless Death of Theory," in chap. 4 of the present work.

6. Hermann Pongs, *Das Bild in der Dichtung,* Book 1: "Versuch einer Morphologie der Metaphorischen Formen" (1927; reprint: N.G. Elwert, 1960).

7. Gaston Bachelard, *The Poetics of Space* (Boston: Beacon Paperback, 1976).

8. Pierre Fontanier, *Les figures du discours* (Paris: Flammarion, 1977), p. 213.

9. See in this respect chap. 2.

2

DERRIDA

THE CATASTROPHE
OF METAPHOR

The debate between Derrida and Ricoeur on metaphor and philosophy still best represents and synthesizes a cluster of problems that contemporary theory has definitely not yet been able to dispose of. In spite of its relative distance from the frantically fugitive time of the present moment (in spite, therefore, of its relative "datedness"), Derrida's contribution still represents the unsurpassed edge of what our epoch has been able to produce as truly radical reflection on the enormously intricate problem that goes under the working title "metaphor and philosophy," or "metaphor and concept." His contribution thus remains not only "interesting," but also strictly speaking unavoidable, at least until a complete remodeling of the philosophical field in which it was generated becomes possible.

I should add immediately that perhaps what makes Derrida's contribution so interesting for us may reside today precisely in the fact that it renders inevitable a complete remodeling of the field and of the way of questioning it. In other words, that hurting itself, at the extreme limits of its own lucidity, to the point of its own impotence, it makes the end of deconstructive radicality unavoidable, at least inasmuch as deconstruction is, and cannot totally avoid being, a philosophical position and the proposition of a reproducible paradigm of thought.

In this chapter I will present Derrida's contribution to the question of metaphor. It will appear evident how much I judge it relevant, and even necessary, within the framework of an elaboration of the question of metaphor and philosophy. In order to better describe his theses, I will set against Derrida a powerful adversary, in the person of Ricoeur. By the same token I will offer an outline of Ricoeur's own fundamental contribution to metaphor studies.

Before I begin the discussion of the theoretical positions of Derrida and Ricoeur, and by way of introduction, I wish to raise the question of "style." The difference between two theoretical positions can indeed be faced at the level of the concrete reality of the language of the authors concerned, and of the patent functioning of their respective "thinking/writing machines."

At first glance, a considerable difference is visible between the two discourses of Derrida and Ricoeur, which nevertheless both no doubt elect to appertain to the philosophical genre. Let us read, for example, a few lines of Derrida's "Le retrait de la métaphore":

Qu'est-ce qui se passe, aujourd'hui, avec la métaphore? Et de la métaphore qu'est-ce qui se passe?

C'est un très vieux sujet. Il occupe l'Occident, il l'habite ou se laisse habiter. . . .[1]

This passage is representative of the usual style of Derrida. The immediate impression is that this author partly plays with his own text, partly lets himself be played by it (*"je dérive"*; *"je dérape et je dérive irrésistiblement"*[2]): He follows the hazards of language, stresses them, carefully chooses and distributes cores of meaning, lets them proliferate and cross-fecundate; but also (up to a point, but which point exactly?) he abandons himself to his own writing.

This is, by the way, precisely the reproach that most commonly is leveled against Derrida (and frequently also against Heidegger): a lack of rigor and control over language, or, worse, a hypocritical and interested exploitation of obscurity and a vagueness created on purpose, namely with the purpose of snaring the reader.

On close examination of Derrida's text, it emerges that the "beams" of his discourse are not concepts, but significant elements that, quite correctly, have been named "indecidables." In general, it does not seem illegitimate to affirm that the structure of this discourse overtly avoids definition and systematicity, and that its progress does not follow a precise and authorized logic. From my point of view it is essential to note that Derrida's discourse is often and at all levels openly metaphorical ("under tension," one might say, in the sense of the modern notion of metaphor, in the sense in which Ricoeur himself speaks of "tensional truth" [*vérité tensionnelle*]).

In Ricoeur's discourse the movement is different, the flux of sense is strictly checked through a principle of univocity of meaning, the drift controlled, the concepts defined. This cannot be proved by quoting a few lines of text: It is by following the text's movement at length that one perceives its internal rigor. Ricoeur's discourse is never openly metaphorical; even if it originated in a metaphorical source, in its effects the metaphorical tension, though by no means absent, is never overtly exploited beyond certain narrow limits. In Ricoeur's text, in perfect agreement with his theories, metaphor seems indeed to fall under the control of the "power of distantiation that opens up the space of speculative thought,"[3] to quote his own statement (on which I will soon have the occasion to comment).

What can we learn from these rather impressionistic observations? That Ricoeur's language is closer to an ideal "philosophical norm" of conceptual precision, whereas Derrida's dangerously approaches the literary threshold? But where is this threshold located? And what exactly does it separate?

It is beyond the purpose of these notes on "philosophical styles," and furthermore beyond the scope of my work, to determine which of the two is the true philosophical language, style, and approach. Let us, for the time being, as a starting point and not as a conclusion, simply notice the difference: The play of meaning is larger in Derrida; the conceptual precision is stricter in Ricoeur. There is in Derrida a surplus of metaphor, not only in quantitative terms, that is absent in Ricoeur. It will be interesting to set this in relation with the theoretical positions of the two authors.

THE RICOEUR-DERRIDA DEBATE

This exchange is in three main stages and takes shape in three texts, each representing a central moment of the contemporary elaboration of the question concerning the relationship between metaphor and philosophy.

Philosophy within Metaphor?

"La métaphore dans le texte philosophique" ("Metaphor in the Text of Philosophy") is the subtitle of "White Mythology,"[4] by Jacques

Derrida, and its argument. Following its implicit hints, an innocent reader would probably expect an investigation in the classic style, whose program and implications would be, broadly speaking, the following: there is a philosophical text, that is, (a) the sum of written works traditionally assigned to the discipline named "philosophy," and, by abstraction, (b) a *type* of text, a literary genre or a methodic procedure which, by its fulfilling certain requirements and corresponding to a certain form, is recognizable as "philosophical." There is, then, and in the first place *outside* the philosophical text (outside its proper form, its main structure, its specific requirements), metaphor.

Metaphor, that is, a rhetorical instrument, a stylistic element that has no essential connection with philosophy, but that can be found in its text, either as embellishment, ornament, or explanatory image adopted by a discourse that does not concern it thematically, but uses it; or as an object of research, classification, and systematization within a discourse that concerns and contains it, that establishes its place and its right without being itself affected by it.

The program, then, would be more or less the following: to see how philosophers have used, subdued, and employed metaphor to the advantage of philosophy, how they have inscribed it in the world of philosophy's objects; and to extract then from all this the global structure, or the law, of the relationship between philosophy and metaphor.

This imaginary description of the system of expectations, on the threshold of "White Mythology," of an imaginary, "innocent" reader, represents fairly accurately the state of affairs concerning "metaphor and philosophy" that has long prevailed, and still prevails in everyday practice, in Western philosophy and theory. Derrida's text distances itself from this typical approach, though at the same time following its trace faithfully from the first lines of the essay. It is to the entire work of Derrida[5] that we must turn in order to understand the reasons for an attitude that can generate perplexity, and that consists in assuming a double posture concerning the philosophical tradition, or rather, in Derridean terms, the general text of the logocentric epoch (which is much larger than the philosophical text in a strict sense).

In fact, the deconstruction that Derrida proposes as the engine and the aim of his work is not at all a movement of absolute refusal and destruction. It aims at a structure of which we are part ourselves, including the improbable "subject" of deconstruction. This structure is the logocentric epoch, whose form is that of a text that contains all sorts of inscriptions: graphic, artistic, economic, institutional, and so forth. The efficacy of philosophy within this structure is not limited to the specific field of the discipline called "philosophy," since the logocentric conceptual devices that philosophy puts into discourse command (more or less overtly) the totality of all processes that constitute the epoch. But at the same time (and precisely for the same reason), this same epoch is not to be seen as a monolithic structure to be destroyed from its outside. At the heart of the epoch, finitude, perishableness, the outside, and the beyond are already present, already at work, and it is possible to bring them to the fore.

This is, therefore, the uncertain place and the difficult task of deconstruction, as I read it in Derrida's texts: Placed inevitably within the epoch, the deconstructor endeavors to promote the recognition and proliferation of the signs of alterity. He discovers in the text of philosophy, of literature, of art (but not only), on the one hand the powerful (albeit often unperceived) machinery of dominant conceptual structures; and on the other, the subtle but inevitable apparition of all sorts of disruptive traces of the outside, of the other. The deconstructor does not play here the part of the classical subject (the center of knowledge and activity), but at most that (far less glamorous) of a decentered and displaced subject, the territory of movements that overcome or carry it, and that in any case it does not master.

But let us go back to Derrida's text and try to follow its movement. Derrida faces there the problem of the so-called dead metaphors. Among the metaphors used in any philosophical text, there are some (for example "theory," "logos," "*eidos,*" and many others) that, because of their being constantly used, obliterate their own metaphorical value and become integrated into the proper field and vocabulary of philosophy. They cease, therefore, to be aids to representation or explanation, and are elevated to the rank of concepts. These dead metaphors in their whole constitute metaphysics as a sort of white mythology, that is, a conceptual edifice whose difference from common mythology is its discolored presentation, which hides its shameful origin. It is, in fact, Nietzsche's argument.[6] Derrida, without subscribing to it, takes it over in a much subtler way, dismembers it and makes it play on all possible registers: In short, he deconstructs it, and I will not relate here all that is accomplished in Derrida's text in terms of reelaboration and reinscription.

The result of the "reverse metaphorization" of concepts (reactivation of their metaphorical surge and essence) and of the Derridean deconstruction of white mythology is that the serene primary evidence of the relationship between metaphor and philosophy begins to become irreparably ambiguous. This evidence rested on the watertight distinction, even at the point of greatest proximity, between the "proper substance" of philosophy and the metaphorical tool. This exterior tool is now to be discovered (albeit in disguise) at the very heart of philosophy, as an essential part of its mechanism. The consequences thereof, should they escape the philosopher's control, could be serious: Philosophy's striving to affirm itself as rational thought, in opposition to mythic thought, would be annulled or severely impaired at its very root. In fact, an essential opposition is not so easy to prove if a difference in nature (and not only in appearance) cannot be shown between analogy-figure-allegory-myth on the one side, and concept-idea-system on the other. If an essential difference cannot be shown in the relationship between, on the one hand, the mythical-analogical thought, and on the other, rational thought and truth, reality, and being.

Analogy's domain (to which metaphor belongs) does not stop at the point where the world of rational ideas begins: It invades the field of truth, of the "proper." From this moment onward, throughout Derrida's text, metaphorical power keeps winning further terrain: Rapidly the whole of philosophical discourse, the whole of language itself, is swallowed by metaphoricity; that is, by analogy, by impropriety. In this vortex of dissemination any privileged relationship between words and meaning, effect and origin (that is, philosophy's privilege), is forever lost, and philosophy becomes little more then one of metaphor's drifts.

Metaphor's mutiny against philosophy has a curious side effect on metaphor's identity itself. What about the theoretical relationship by which philosophy grasps, identifies, and dominates metaphor? What about philosophy's claim to be entitled to give metaphor its place, to describe its mechanism conceptually, to tell its truth? What, then, is metaphor? What can still meaningfully and rationally be said of metaphor, if all is metaphor? (The same questions, of course, apply to linguistics, rhetoric, and any other discipline attempting to provide a theory of metaphor).

In examining the history of the philosophical discourse, Derrida sheds light on a double movement. On one side, philosophy takes possession of metaphor, assimilates it, interiorizes it, makes it into a concept. On the other, philosophy ends in being submerged by metaphor's uncontrollable tow. This movement, according to Derrida, is, however, not exceptional in the least: Something similar happens with any of philosophy's points of foundation. The point of foundation is philosophy's blind spot, where its domination is suspended and visibility is impaired through excessive proximity, and from where a massive return of what was supposed to be under control remains a constant possibility; in fact, happens all the time.

The existence and functioning of metaphor, such as they are perceived—for instance—in the Aristotelian model, are theoretically visible only *within* metaphysics (this is also Heidegger's much discussed opinion). Metaphor installs itself in the space that has been opened by philosophy's fundamental oppositions: proper/improper, sensible/unintelligible, same/other, true/false, and so on. Producing a metaphorology absolutely independent from the philosophical field would therefore appear unthinkable. But at same time it is metaphor that "lifts" philosophy, that generates it through its own "poetic" power, that gives it instruments and energy, and that therefore finds itself protected from philosophy's eye. It is a circle without origin, because if there is a "proper" of metaphor, it is precisely its difference from the proper, its distance from origin. This difference and this distance are insurmountable, after the generalization of metaphor, which extends its power right to the heart—no longer intact—of language, of thought, of being. What to do with metaphor in the philosophical text? And furthermore, what about the philosophical text itself? What is left of the "philosophical text" after the invasion of metaphor?

According to Derrida, two possibilities offer themselves when facing the relationship between metaphor and philosophy. First of all, the classic stance: trying to reduce the metaphorical power, conceived as negative; to contain, to overcome metaphor, also in the sense of Hegel's *Aufhebung*. The concept must overcome metaphor, and this must always be possible because the very existence of metaphor points to the existence of that which metaphor hides and indicates: truth. This stance involves, from Derrida's point of view, an oversight and a form of blindness. Metaphor itself is responsible for this blindness, inasmuch as it structurally covers and hides, through its own visible splendor, the original gap from which it emerges.

There is a second possibility. Instigating the generalization of metaphorical power, allowing its proliferation, accepting the effects thereof: the loss of the proper, the intensification of syntactic energy to the detriment of the semantic privilege, and finally, the emptying of the fundamental oppositions of metaphysics and of all oppositions (including syntactic/semantic) that form a system with them. Dissemination of meaning (in Derrida's sense, beyond the limits of polysemy, which remains a well-ordained, finite, and therefore masterable plurality). This second option is, needless to say, deconstruction's stance.

But it is essential to keep in mind at all times something that I have already stressed. Deconstruction is not the free and autonomous operation of a subject pursuing a particular aim: It is first of all a movement that is *already* happening within the epoch, a movement of transformation with no subject and no aim. The deconstructionist's role consists in recognizing this movement, in following its trace, perhaps in facilitating it.

Metaphor has its place precisely in the wake of this movement, or rather *is* perhaps this movement itself. This movement is not one of negation or pure destruction. It superimposes itself on the legal, reproductive movement of a given structure, but at same time, through an often very subtle difference, it upsets it. This is precisely what we have seen with regard to metaphor, whose functioning strictly reproduces and implements the system of metaphysical oppositions, but at the same time nullifies its pertinence, neutralizes its power, and thus makes room for something that still is unthinkable for the time being: the "beyond" of those oppositions, of philosophy, of the epoch.

The trajectory of metaphor is exemplary within Derrida's theoretic field. It gives us the opportunity to witness a "labor of the negative" that repudiates any Hegelian paternity,[7] in that it refuses idealist overcoming, the reabsorption and redemption into the positive, into the absolute. Death is at hand, with no resurrection in sight: the death of an epoch whose end is not yet visible, but which nevertheless obscurely announces, by sometimes unrecognizable signs, the possibility of its own disappearance. This possibility is very close, intimate, nonexorcizable; but constantly exorcized, for instance by philosophy.

From this perspective, it obviously becomes necessary to rethink the problem of the nature of the "philosophical text," of the form of philosophy, of the border between *within* and *without* philosophy. It is difficult, from Derrida's point of view, to safeguard the relevance and meaning of these notions. One can always rely on tradition in order to be able to identify the canonical corpus of the discipline as the collection of the texts transmitted and classified under the title "philosophy." But the identification of the philosophical genre for the present and for the future (i.e., the question of its distinction, status, and legitimacy), is a different matter altogether.

The difficulty is, clearly, not exclusively internal to Derrida's discourse. It also comes from the more general circumstance that philosophy seems prone today to a double movement of broadening and lessening: broadening in that it exceeds the limits of its "proper" and of its text, invading neighboring genres and even, in principle, the entire *texte général*, that is, the world; lessening in that philosophy witnesses, with some degree of impotence, a progressive reduction in its own privilege, function, and direct link with being and truth, and must content itself with a position that tends to become mar-

ginal, accessory, or even useless in the modern economics of power
and know-how.

What, then, about philosophy today? I will leave this question
unanswered for the time being, and move to the second moment of
the debate.

The Living Metaphor

I will deal here specifically with the eighth chapter of Paul Ricoeur's
excellent work, *The Rule of Metaphor,* a chapter dedicated to
"metaphor and philosophical discourse."

Ricoeur immediately declares his aims. The question that, at the
end of *The Rule of Metaphor,* requires an answer is: Which philosophy is implied in the way of treating metaphor that has been pro-
pounded all through the book? We are thus confronted with a
second-degree reflection that aims to unfold the idea of philosophy
that is implicitly at work in the interpretation of metaphor that
Ricoeur presents in the first seven studies of his book. But it soon
becomes clear that what is at stake goes beyond the mere possibility
of a choice between one or other form of philosophy, and concerns
nothing less than the *possibility* and the *autonomy* of philosophy itself.
The danger comes precisely from metaphor, analogy, and the poetic
discourse that relies on them. The question is: Is there an essential
difference between philosophical discourse and poetic discourse?

This is the driving motivation and the ultimate reason behind
Ricoeur's effort "to recognize in principle, the *discontinuity* that
assures the autonomy of speculative discourse."[8] This does not
exclude—quite the contrary—the possibility of an "interanimation
of philosophical and poetic discourse."[9] One can easily measure the
distance that separates this position from Derrida's; we will soon see
in greater detail the terms of the opposition.

In two words, the operation in which Ricoeur engages in the first seven chapters consists in displacing the point of insistency of the metaphor from the *noun* to the *phrase*, and then from the phrase to the *discourse*. The canonical theory of metaphor, established by Aristotle and essentially accepted by different forms of classical rhetoric, is founded on a semiotic concentration on the noun as the minimal meaningful unit in language. Metaphor exerts its power on the noun, and indeed it can be described as the attribution to something of a noun that is not its own. It follows that the metaphorical movement consists of transfer, substitution, and deviant denomination resulting in a displacement or widening of meaning.

The first act of Ricoeur's strategy consists in transporting the entire framework of the analysis from the level of the noun to the level of the phrase. Now the supporting linguistic theory is of a semantic orientation (for example, Emile Benveniste's). The minimal complete meaningful unit is borne by the phrase, not by the noun. Metaphor works not on the vertical coordinate of denomination, but on the horizontal axis of predication, and its operation belongs to the order of "predicative impertinence," rather than to the order of "denominative deviance" (which implies much larger ontological presuppositions).

Finally, Ricoeur's path brings the reader to the last step: the jump from the level of the phrase to the level of the discourse. By the same token, the semantic theoretic milieu is abandoned to make room for a hermeneutic point of view. Metaphor is now founded on a double reference: a first-degree reference to reality, and a second-degree reference of a poetic nature. The metaphorical power plays in the space between those two limits, and must be understood not in the form of a rhetorical figure centered on the word, or as a semantic impertinence internal to the linguistic code, but rather as the redescription of reality within the space of *one* of many possible "modes of discourse": the poetic discourse. This type of discourse requires its own structure and activates its own specific kind of truth: a tensional truth, a "metaphorical truth" implemented in the copula, the *is* which means at the same time *is not* and *is as*.

Through these three steps, which are not to be seen as a uniform progression from falsity to truth, since each point of view is supported by a different and legitimate theoretic approach, Ricoeur questions certain philosophical notions, such as those of reality and truth, and introduces the idea of a plurality of autonomous and specific modes of discourse, and also of the possibility of interactions among them. The ground is thus prepared for the question that occupies the eighth study: the status of philosophical discourse, its links with metaphorical power, and its relationship with poetic discourse.

Ricoeur opens the discussion with the refutation of a counterexample that one could oppose to the initial hypothesis of the difference between philosophical and poetic discourse: It is the theme of the analogy (or equivocalness) of being, as it is found, for instance, in Aristotle. "Being is defined in many ways," says Aristotle in the *Metaphysics*: Is this equivocalness the same as the poetic one? Does analogy generate in a similar way metaphorical utterance, predication in general, and speculative predication in particular?

Ricoeur's answer is short and negative. There is nothing in common between the orderly equivocalness of being and poetic metaphor. The multiple significations of being are disposed according to a line of filiation that is not yet the one of the dialectic order and of the division by *genus* and *species*, but represents nevertheless a centered and well-regulated polysemy that is capable of founding and managing the predicative function as such. It is already an order of categories. Nothing to do with metaphor, with poetic analogy, with Platonic participation between ideas and "other things," that is, with the sort of "participation" that, according to

Aristotle, is precisely no more than a metaphor devoid of any speculative meaning.[10]

An initial distance is thus imposed between philosophical and poetic discourse, between innocent polysemy and deadly (for philosophy) dissemination. Henceforth, "philosophical discourse sets itself up as the vigilant watchman overseeing the ordered extensions of meaning; against this background, the unfettered extensions of meaning in poetic discourse spring free."[11]

These, at least, are the explicit intentions. But what about the real functioning of Aristotle's text? Here things become more complex. Following the positioning of the initial disparity, we witness a progressive weakening of that criterion, and finally a crossing between a derived concept of analogy and the categories theory. But we should notice that "by entering the sphere of the problem of being, analogy at once retains its own conceptual structure and receives a transcendental aspect from the field to which it is applied."[12]

This same "problem of being," furthermore, designates the locus of an interminable investigation: ontology remains forever the "sought-after science" (*science recherchée*), rather than the found one. The deep motivation of this uninterrupted search resides perhaps in the necessity, once recognized and never repudiated, of maintaining the difference between the analogy of being and poetic metaphor.

To sum up: Transcendental analogy takes place only on the basis of a difference with regard to poetic resemblance. This difference is the very gesture that founds speculative discourse, after which it remains necessary to accomplish a further leap toward a concept of the unity of Being totally independent of analogy itself. The defeat suffered in trying to complete this program does not make void (according to Ricoeur) the decisive importance for philosophy of having been able to elude somewhat the power of poetic discourse, while retaining the latter's polysemic or "equivocal" demand. It is precisely to the fruitful crossing with two different discourses (poetry on one side, theology on the other) that Aristotle's philosophy, as an autonomous discourse, owes its impetus toward an endless quest.

A second counterexample that one could oppose to the thesis of the discontinuity between speculative and poetic discourse is represented by ontotheology, and particularly by the Thomist doctrine of analogy.[13]

The issue there consists in the extension of the problem of analogy generated by the equivocalness of the notion of "being" to the question of "divine names." The encounter and union between ontology and theology presents serious difficulties. How can we talk of God without ruining divine transcendence? By what right can a truthful discourse on God be founded? Are we then condemned to total incommunicability between the two levels, that of the creator and that of creatures?

The notion of analogy helps in overcoming these difficulties. It remains to be seen whether the price to pay for this intervention is not too high. The explicit aim of Thomist doctrine is "to establish theological discourse at the level of science and thereby to free it completely from the poetical forms of religious discourse."[14] It will therefore be necessary to find a concept of analogy independent of poetic metaphor and capable of preserving the disparity, dissimilarity, and incommensurability between the two terms of the analogy (God and the world); and this knowledge will be a science, not a mystic intuition.

The Thomist solution, the product of an enormous theoretical effort, relies on the notion of a *creating causality*: The act of creation establishes between beings and God a bond of participation that makes the analogical relationship ontologically possible. The *communication of an act*, and not an unseemly *similarity*, justifies the analogy in the first place. Two orders of priority are possible in the "attribution of names," one on the basis of "the thing itself" and one on the basis of signification. The former relies on what is first (God), the latter on what is for us best known (created things). Only the former is able to found pure analogy, the latter can only generate metaphors. Analogy relies on the predication of transcendental terms, metaphor on the predication of meanings that carry with them their material content.[15]

The problem is that analogy and participation, in the shape in which Thomas conceives them, form a circle that invalidates the entire ontotheologic edifice, as many critics have pointed out. But this should not prevent us (Ricoeur recommends) from admiring the titanic effort in order to stress the difference between analogy and metaphor and the refusal of all compromise with poetic discourse: "I would call such concern" says Ricoeur, "the distinctive feature of the semantic aim of speculative discourse."[16] And he concludes: "Such is the magnificent exercise of thought that preserved the difference between speculative discourse and poetic discourse at the very point of their greatest proximity."[17]

After the discussion of the two counterexamples Ricoeur deals with a very central problem. He examines the possibility of an implication of a totally different kind "between philosophy and metaphor, . . . which links them at the level of their hidden presuppositions rather than at the level of their stated intentions."[18] It is now time to summon Heidegger and Derrida.

Heidegger's explicit utterances concerning metaphor are certainly not numerous. According to the most famous one, which I have quoted already, "the metaphoric exists only within metaphysics." Taking into account Heidegger's thought in general, this declaration is probably to be interpreted as the unearthing of an essential, hidden link between metaphor and metaphysics, both made the object of one act of transgression. The secret link between metaphor and metaphysics becomes visible when considering a double transfer, which must be recognized as being one and the same: transfer from the proper to the figurative in the metaphor, transfer from the sensible to the intelligible in metaphysics. Metaphor thus belongs essentially to metaphysics, to representational and instrumental thought, and reproduces its central movement.

In the course of a detailed analysis, Ricoeur does his best to destabilize Heidegger's position. On the one hand, the identification of the distinction between sensible and intelligible as the fundamental trait of metaphysics, and of metaphysics itself (so described) as the central mechanism of Western thinking, is an unacceptable act of violence: "Only a reading forced beyond any justification can make Western philosophy lie on this Procrustean bed."[19] On the other, the identification of the distinction between proper and figurative (applied to isolated words) as metaphor's main axis is an equally illegitimate way of "proving" the existence of an essential link between metaphor and philosophy, as a step in the overall strategy aimed at throwing metaphysics into discredit.

Furthermore, an attentive examination of the context of Heidegger's statements (Ricoeur refers here more specifically to *Der Satz vom Grund*, the text from which the aforementioned declaration is quoted) reveals that the attack against metaphor concerns one specific type of metaphoric expression only: the so-called *dead metaphors*, and even more specifically the metaphors generated by philosophical discourse itself. However, Heidegger's appreciation of "true poetry" (the poetry that "awakens the largest vision," that "makes the world appear") is universally known. But, asks Ricoeur, "is this not what *living* metaphor does?"[20] Ricoeur's opinion is that Heidegger's attack on metaphor on the one hand is ineffective, and on the other aims at the wrong target. "The constant use Heidegger makes of metaphor is finally more important than what he says in passing against metaphor."[21]

Ricoeur's discussion of Derrida's position comes all too naturally after that of Heidegger. Ricoeur believes that a deep bond establishes a direct communication between Heidegger's "limited critique" and Derrida's "unlimited deconstruction." Indeed, does not Derrida go further in the direction of the so-called hermeneutics of suspicion (that is, Heidegger's deconstruction, Nietzsche's genealogy, and the Marxist critique of ideology) by buttressing "the universal suspicion of Western metaphysics with a more heightened suspicion directed at what in metaphor itself is left unsaid? Now the unstated in metaphor is used, worn-out metaphor."[22]

We have already summarized Derrida's argument. According to Ricoeur, it is possible to distinguish in it two central statements: The first concerns the efficacy of usual metaphor in philosophical discourse, and the second concerns the deep unity of metaphoric and analogical transfer from visible being to intelligible being.[23] Both are (in Ricoeur's opinion) unsustainable. The hypothesis of a specific fecundity of usual metaphor goes against the grain of Ricoeur's work, which regularly puts the stress on *living* metaphor and finds that "dead metaphors are no longer metaphors, but instead are associated with literal meaning, extending its polysemy."[24] It is clear that the adjective "literal" here does not mean "original" or "proper," but rather "usual" or "customary."

It is only within the frame of semiotic theories imposing the primacy of denomination (and thus envisaging metaphor as simple substitution of meaning) that the efficacy of usual metaphor can be exaggerated. But the true problems of metaphoricity concern the play of semantic pertinence and impertinence. From this point of view, when a metaphor is usual—or dead—it loses its metaphoric power together with its predicative impertinence. In philosophy as well, it is necessary to distinguish between dead and living metaphors: The former are no longer metaphors, and when they become concepts it does not happen exclusively because of use and wear. "That there are philosophical terms is due to the fact that a concept can be active as thought in a metaphor which is itself dead."[25] A worn metaphor is not enough to make a concept. A further dialectic operation of overcoming (*relève*) is required to create "a proper sense in the spiritual order out of an improper sense coming from the sensible order."[26]

Concept lives in metaphor's death, and not in its "white" disguise. In fact, only this independence of the content (spiritual meaning) from its carrier (in this case, worn metaphor) makes philosophical discourse (including deconstruction) possible at all. "The act of positing the concept proceeds dialectically from metaphor itself":[27] there is therefore no circularity in the concept of metaphor. This concept is not the idealization of its own metaphor (as Derrida—according to Ricoeur—claims), but (exactly as any other concept) a new spiritual production (autonomous and perfectly legitimate, of an order totally different from the metaphoric one) that installs itself in the metaphoric production.

We have already stated Ricoeur's opposition concerning "the theoretical core common to Heidegger and Derrida, namely, the supposed collusion between the metaphorical pair of the proper and figurative and the metaphysical pair of the visible and invisible,"[28] the alleged unity of *meta*-phoric and *meta*-physic gesture. If the theory of metaphor as substitution presents some affinity to the dialectic overcoming of the sensible in the intelligible, the tensional theory of metaphor (centered on the play of semantic impertinence) has nothing to do with it. In conclusion, "it is not, then, metaphor that carries the structure of Platonic metaphysics; metaphysics instead seizes the metaphorical process in order to make it work to the benefit of metaphysics."[29]

Ricoeur's essay ends with a clarification concerning the two questions (strictly linked to each other) of the *content* of the ontology that is implicit in the proposed interpretation of metaphor, and of the *mode* of implication between the poetic and philosophical discourses. First of all, it is necessary to abandon two theses: (1) the naive idea that the metaphoric process contains a ready-made, immediate ontology, and that philosophy has only to disentangle it; and (2) the argument (suggested by Ludwig Wittgenstein in *Philosophical Investigations*) that different language games are radically heterogeneous. On the contrary, a general theory of the interferences between different modes of discourse is now urgently required.

Specifically concerning philosophy, Ricoeur declares that "on the one hand, speculative discourse has its condition of *possibility* in the semantic dynamism of metaphorical utterance, and that, on the other hand, speculative discourse has its *necessity* in itself."[30] And he states once again the irreducible difference between poetry and philosophy, between the metaphoric implicit and the conceptual explicit, even if the former can always be reengaged in the latter. The tension that is generated by the semantic shock of metaphor is a *demand of concept*, not yet a *knowledge through concept*; the passage to explicit ontology entails a passage to a concept.

All enunciation is characterized by a "dynamism of signification" due to the instability of signification itself. In metaphor this dynamism is pushed to its maximum as a result of the tension generated by the double reference, as we have seen. However, "that speculative discourse finds something like the sketch of a conceptual determination in the dynamism described above does not bar it from beginning in itself and from finding the principle of its articulation within itself. . . . The *necessity* of this discourse is not the extension of its possibility. . . . Its necessity proceeds instead from the very structures of the mind, which is the task of transcendental philosophy to articulate. . . . [S]peculative discourse is the discourse that establishes the primary notions, the principles, that articulate primordially the space of the concept. . . . [T]he speculative is the condition of the possibility of the conceptual."[31]

Ricoeur quotes Edmund Husserl, who says that the speculative is what allows us to say that "understanding a [logical] expression" is something other than "finding images."[32] *Imaginatio* and *intellectio* belong to two different levels of discourse. Metaphor appertains to *imaginatio*; on the contrary, the conceptual order, because of its own ability to form a system, is capable of freeing itself from the play of double signification, and therefore from metaphoric tension.

The discontinuity between the metaphoric and conceptual orders does not prevent exchange and communication. It is possible to imagine a mixed discourse, where interpretation would satisfy simultaneously the needs proper to concept (conceptual clarity) and the tension inherent to metaphor (dynamism of signification). According to Ricoeur, the universe of discourse, in spite of being divided according to the different modes of discourse (each centered on a particular semantic intention), is mobilized by a constant play of attractions and repulsions, which generates all sorts of interactions and intersections.

Speculative discourse relies on language's ability to produce a distance from itself, and to consider itself as a totality related to the totality of being: It is *the knowledge of its own relation to being*. The fact that there is no linguistic space outside language, and that all utterances *on* language are by necessity included *in* language, should not justify any intellectual paralysis. The philosophy of language, and philosophy *tout court*, find their rightful space and task in the *capacity of distantiation* that is inherent to language.

From this point of view, reality is "the final category upon which the whole of language can be thought, although not known, as the being-said of reality."[33] This notion of reality must be duly enlarged beyond its positivist meaning (which is inevitably linked to a verificationist notion of truth) in order to become acceptable in this perspective; for example, "feeling is no less ontological than representation."[34] This obviously shatters the accepted boundaries of objectual representation and shakes the very distinction between "outside" and "inside," as well as the distinction between discovering and creating, finding and imagining. "We must thus dismantle the reign of objects in order to let be, and to allow to be uttered, our primordial belonging to a world that we inhabit, that is to say, which at once precedes us and receives the imprint of our works."[35]

But a very serious problem presents itself: "When the reference to objects set over against a *judging* subject is suspended, is not the very structure of utterance shaken? . . . [D]oes not the notion of speculative discourse itself evaporate, and with this notion the dialectic of speculative and poetic?"[36] There is no space here to deal with this complex question. I will only say that, to solve the problem, Ricoeur appeals to Aristotle, who says that "to bring before the eyes" is "to signify things in action."[37] Beyond representational thought, beyond any technical or artistic artifice, the task is "to seek after the place where appearance signifies 'generating what grows' "[38]: This is precisely what poetic discourse expects speculative discourse to be able to think.

Here we must again cross Heidegger's path. This path represents for Ricoeur, at the same time, a necessary endeavor and an inevitable temptation: the attempt (which remains valid and fruitful) to build speculative thought on the basis of the investigation (started by Aristotle) into the multiple senses of the notion of being; and the temptation (to be rejected) to efface the difference between speculative and poetic.

At the heart of Heidegger's reflection in his later years is the reciprocal belonging of *Erörterung* (the quest for the "place" and at the same time the "commentary" on this quest) and *Ereignis* (the "thing itself" that ought to be thought). This reciprocal belonging delimits speculative thought in its "constitutive gesture." It also hints at the double war that will have to be waged, against the seduction of the unspeakable on the one hand, and against the subtle power of "ordinary speech" on the other. Even if one designates *Erörterung* and *Ereignis* as metaphors, they remain philosophical (as opposed to poetic) metaphors: Heidegger's thought, according to Ricoeur, in its most illuminating movements, and precisely at the point where it seems to melt into poetry, clearly preserves the distinction. When Heidegger presses upon poetic texts, the effort of thought that he accomplishes remains separate from them; his path and intention are different. And the metaphors that he employs come to the help of thought by giving him the possibility of semantic innovation, but they are not poetic metaphors: There is indeed an insuperable disparity between the *same* that remains to be thought (philosophy) and metaphoric resemblance (poetry).

Ricoeur's interpretation does obviously not respect in the least Heidegger's wish to break (prudently but decidedly) away from metaphysics. This is precisely the point of contention: Ricoeur strongly disputes Heidegger's pretension to shut the entire history of Western thought in the enclosure that he calls "metaphysics," and even more his pretension to secure for himself the exclusive benefit of breaking it open. The most interesting part of Heidegger's thought is precisely what links it to the tradition of speculative philosophy: its contribution to the incessant elaboration of the primordial problem of the relation between thinking and being. "The invincible ambiguity" of Heidegger's last works come from an internal crack between the logic of continuity with speculative thought and the logic of rupture from metaphysics. But this second logic precipitates thinking toward hermeticism[39] and "a kind of despair of language."[40] On the contrary, thought can only live and prosper—according to Ricoeur—as the critical instance of *distantiation*, contemporary with the experience of *belonging* that poetic discourse opens, or reconquers.

The Retreat and the Catastrophe

In the lecture titled "Le retrait de la métaphore," delivered in 1978 and published the same year, Derrida deals with Ricoeur's criticisms and reopens the discussion on Heidegger.

Derrida's position concerning Ricoeur's criticisms cannot be reduced to a simple disagreement: On the contrary, very often Derrida's answer consists in showing that the objections that Ricoeur makes to him are already clearly legible in his own text. This is explained as the result of a certain blindness that affects Ricoeur when he faces Derrida's text. It remains to be seen what mechanism is responsible for this selective blindness—in other words, what is the real motivation for the disagreement— beyond the reasons presented by Ricoeur, which are insufficient in Derrida's opinion.

We have seen that Ricoeur charges Derrida with a consistent radicalization and extension of Heidegger's movement, based on a common theoretic core, that is the alleged connivance between the metaphoric couple of proper and figurative and the metaphysical couple of visible and invisible. Derrida replies, on the one hand, that in "White Mythology" he constantly questions the current, philosophical interpretation of metaphor as transfer from sensible to intelligible, as well as the privilege bestowed on noun and word in those semiotic theories that center on the primacy of denomination, and explicitly opposes to it a consistent attention to the syntactic motif. On the other, that he rejects the assimilation[41] of Heidegger's program to his own, stating furthermore that "here, for essential reasons, there is no core and especially no theoretical core."[42]

Another point on which Ricoeur is responsible for having unduly simplified Derrida's thought (according to the latter) concerns the efficacy of worn metaphor (*métaphore usée*): the simplification consists in reducing the "play of wear" (*usure*) to only one of its many meanings (erosion, impoverishment, extenuation), and in reducing Derrida's position precisely to the statement that the latter questions, "namely, that the relation of metaphor to concept, and the process of metaphoricity in general would be understood under the concept or the scheme of *usure* [wear and tear] as a becoming-worn or becoming-worn-out."[43] But the "scheme of *usure*" in Derrida's text, functions also in different ways and meanings: For instance, "as the production of surplus value [*plus-value*] according to laws other than those of a continuous and linearly accumulative capitalization."[44] Furthermore, Derrida never had the intention of accrediting "the schema of the *us* but to deconstruct a philosophical concept, a philosophical construction erected on this schema of worn-out metaphor or privileging, for significant reasons, the trope named metaphor."[45]

One last point, of capital importance, attracts Derrida's attention in his rapid reply to Ricoeur. As we have seen, Ricoeur charges Heidegger, and implicitly Derrida, of (unduly) regarding metaphysics as the homogeneous unity of a whole, in order to secure (but illusorily, says Ricoeur) the possibility of jumping out of it. Derrida's answer to that is clear: "I have never believed in the existence or in the consistency of something like metaphysics *itself*."[46] An expression such as "the closure of metaphysics" (*la clôture de la métaphysique*)—Derrida often stresses this point, also in "White Mythology"—does not indicate "the circular limit bordering a homogeneous field but a more twisted structure . . . :

'invaginated.' "[47] Obviously, there is a sort of epochal coherence, signaled, for instance, by the persistence of certain thought structures;
but "representation of a linear and circular closure surrounding a
homogeneous space is, precisely, . . . an autorepresentation of philosophy in its ontoencyclopedic logic."[48] As we have seen already,
deconstruction presupposes that the epoch (as well as metaphysics
and philosophy) is already internally troubled by its outside; and it
does not seek (at least not immediately, not unreservedly) to jump
out of the metaphysical _clôture_.

As he carries on with his reflection on metaphor, Derrida once
again encounters Heidegger. Heidegger, who only seldom and very
allusively deals with metaphor as such, nevertheless makes abundant
use, in his own text, of metaphoric power. Or such, at least, is
Ricoeur's thesis: The metaphoric power of Heidegger's text is richer
and more significant than Heidegger's explicit theses on metaphor.

Derrida, on this matter, asks two questions: Is there an essential
relationship between Heidegger's reserve in openly speaking of
metaphor and what is written in Heidegger's text—metaphorically
or metonymically—on metaphor? What are

> the meaning and necessity which link this apparently univocal,
> simplifying, and reductive denunciation of the "metaphysical"
> concept of metaphor on the one hand, and, on the other, the
> apparently metaphoric power of a text whose author no longer
> wishes that what happens in that text and what claims to get along
> without metaphor there be understood precisely as "metaphoric,"
> nor even under any concept of metalinguistics or rhetoric?[49]

In order to follow in Heidegger's text in the most _economic_ way,
the most significant leads among many possible itineraries; in order
to give order to the readings and the rewritings that he proposes,

Derrida choses one title and one theme: *le retrait*. Why *retrait*, and why *retrait* of metaphor?

First, the word *retrait* is endowed with a rich polysemy that makes it apt "to capture the greatest quantity of energy and information in the Heideggerian text,"[50] within the limits of the problem and the context at hand. And secondly, it corresponds quite precisely to certain central themes in Heidegger's thought. For instance the *épochè* of being, that is, its suspensive retreat, its veiling and concealing itself (*Verborgenheit, Verhüllung*); and this is the distinctive trait of metaphysics according to Heidegger: "This whole of this aforesaid history of Western metaphysics would be a vast structural process where the *épochè* of Being withholding itself, holding itself in withdrawal, would take or rather *would present* an (interlaced) series of guises, of turns, of modes, that is to say, of figures or of tropical aspects [*allures*] which we could be tempted to describe with the aid of rhetorical conceptuality."[51] Which means that, inasmuch as the being can only be named in a metaphoric/metonymic swerve, metaphysics not only deals with and construes the concept of metaphor; "it would itself be in a tropical position with respect to Being or the thought of Being."[52]

So nothing happens without metaphor, everything (the whole of what is) is in a metaphoric position. But at the same time, being cannot be said or named *more metaphorico* (at least if we follow the dominant metaphysical usage of the word "metaphor"), and even less literally or properly. "We will speak of being only *quasi-metaphorically*,"[53] with a metaphor doubled with a *re-trait*, a supplementary fold. If metaphysical discourse, which produces and contains the concept of metaphor, is itself quasi-metaphoric, the narrow concept of metaphor can only have a strictly metaphoric meaning. On the other hand, metaphysical discourse can only be outflanked through a *retreat* of metaphor (as a metaphysical concept). But since

this *retreat* does not generate a discourse of the proper and the literal, it will have the meaning of a return and a fold, therefore not
of a disappearance of metaphor, but of an "abyssal generalization of
the metaphoric."[54]

We must note that the word *retrait* does not function here literally or metaphorically. We cannot rely on the *retrait* (as if it were
something we know well) to think metaphorically *being* and
metaphor, neither can we speak of the *retrait* literally. Here we have
an example of the "metaphoric fold" that produces a sort of reversal,
a catastrophe[55]:"*Withdrawal-of-Being-or-of-metaphor* would be by way
less of leading us to think Being or metaphor than the Being or the
metaphor *of withdrawal*, by way of leading us to think about the way
and the vehicle, or their fraying."[56] The metaphoric trajectory is
reversed "at the moment when, having become excessive,
metaphoricity no longer allows itself to be contained in its so-called
metaphysical concept."[57] What is the effect of this "generalizing catastrophe" (*catastrophe généralisante*)? A breaking down of discourse, or
simply a conversion of meaning, "repeating in its depth the circulation of the hermeneutic circle"?[58] For Derrida a text (any text) necessarily includes both motifs.

The very same generalizing catastrophe is at work in one of the
best known among Heidegger's "apparent metaphors": "language is
the house of Being."[59] At first sight, the meaning is clear: In order to
understand what "language" is, we should leave it and proceed
toward the notion "house":

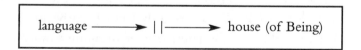

The trouble is that we will never get there; the voyage is interrupted before we reach the destination, and the meaning is set free

again. The representation "home" points to a nonrepresentable, invisible reality.

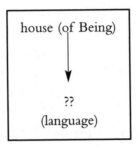

Is that a catachresis? An icon? Not exactly. The home should make language's being nearer for us, but, following the inversion and generalization of this image, it becomes something nonevident, it is put "on hold"[60]: waiting for a destination. In the end, what is left if not the circle of references and the emptiness of meaning?

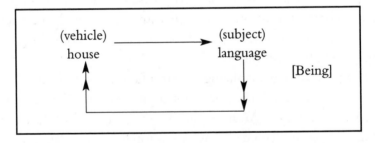

Not exactly emptiness. In the loss of representational meaning, room is made for a beginning of sense, for a future meaning. Meaning is "catastrophied" (reversed, but not linearly, and generalized). Or rather, the infinite deferment of meaning toward its own absence is generalized.[61]

Being cannot be named, neither properly, nor literally, nor metaphorically, nor "catachretically." In fact, Being is not some thing or another, it is nothing. (And could not the same be said of all purely discursive entities, devoid of any objectual referent?) "Now what happens here _with_ the quasi-metaphor of the house of Being, and what does _without_ metaphor in its cursive direction," says Derrida, "is that it is Being which, from the very moment of its withdrawal, would let or promise to let the house and the habitat be thought."[62]

We should note that it is not a simple inversion, whereby—against the common belief—Being becomes the better known (the nearer) and the home the less known. The movement here is no longer simply metaphoric, it is neither metaphoric nor literal: "Stating nonliterally the condition of metaphoricity, it frees both its unlimited extension and its withdrawal."[63] Thus no more metalanguage, no more metaphysics; but "always another metaphor when metaphor withdraws in expanding [_évasant_] its limits."[64]

Another example of catastrophic metaphor: Heidegger says of dialect that it is not only "the language of the mother," but also and primarily "the mother of language."[65] In this metaphor we end up by no longer knowing which is the "vehicle" and which is the "tenor," which is the direction of meaning: "A mother tongue would not be a metaphor in order to determine the meaning of language [_le sens de la langue_], but the essential turn in order to understand what 'mother' means."[66]

One last example of generalizing metaphor is particularly interesting, since it concerns the relationship between thinking and poetry (_Denken_ and _Dichten_, in "Das Wesen der Sprache"[67]). This relationship is determined as _vicinity_. But "to call metaphor, as if we knew what it was, any value of neighborliness between poetry and thought, to act as if one were first of all assured of the proximity of proximity and of the neighborliness of neighborhood [_voisinage du voisinage_], is to close oneself to the necessity of the other movement";[68] that is, the upsetting, catastrophic movement, whereby proximity is no longer close, propriety is no longer proper, and so on. The point is not to discover vicinity, since we sojourn and move in it. But we must "return where we are already": this is the quasi-metaphoric operation of Heidegger's text, which should not be confused with a simple "figurative way of speaking" (*Bildlicher Redeweise*), for the reasons that I have tried to explain.[69]

The proximity of *Denken* and *Dichten* gives us access to vicinity along a path—neither metaphoric nor literal—that reopens the question of metaphor. What is this trait, this "value of proximity" that reconciles *Denken* and *Dichten*, that divides them and that they share, that attracts them while signifying their irreducible difference?

It is the *trait* itself (*Riß*): the limit, the margin, the mark. This dividing trait refers *Denken* and *Dichten* to one another, but does not belong to either. "This is why it is not a common trait or a general concept, nor a metaphor anymore."[70] If such a trait were something, it would be something older than both, their common origin, while remaining singular and different. But it is not original, nor is it derived; it opens a differential drift, it opens the very possibility of naming in language, and therefore is not "itself namable as separation, neither literally, properly, nor metaphorically."[71] *Denken* and *Dichten* are two parallels crossing each other to infinity, signing "in some way the one in the body of the other, the one in the place of the other, the contract without contract of their neighborliness."[72] The trait, the cut (*Riß, Aufriß*) opens up *Denken* and *Dichten* in the getting closer of the one to the other. "This approximating does not draw them into proximity again from another place where they would already be themselves."[73]

This getting close is the *Ereignis*. It is not an autonomous agency, original in respect to the two that are separated and allied by it; it is nothing, it does not appear itself, it is structurally in retreat. "Its inscription . . . succeeds only in being effaced."[74] It is not derived or secondary, either. The oppositions organizing the discourse called metaphysical (before/after, matter/form, substance/accident) are not pertinent here. "If metaphysics had a unity, it would be the regime of these oppositions which appears and is determined only *by way of* [*à partir de*] the withdrawal of the trait, of the withdrawal of the withdrawal, and so on. The *by way of* is engulfed in it [*s'y abîme*]."[75]

The trait is retreat. The trait is therefore nothing. "When trait or *retrait* is said in a context where truth is in question, 'trait' is no longer a metaphor of what we usually believe we recognize by this word."[76]

What happens, then, between retreat and metaphor? This is Derrida's answer, and the close of his text: "Nothing, no response, if not that withdrawal of/from metaphor happens and with(out) itself."[77]

Some Questions

The difference between Ricoeur and Derrida is not clear-cut: It seems sometimes insignificant, and sometimes enormous. One could legitimately wonder, after all, whether it really exists; that is, whether it concerns, beyond some superficial peculiarities, beyond even explicit refusals and denials, the deep unity of the "act of thought" of each one of the two philosophers. This "act," this deep reason, could be more or less the same: a questioning, a radical self-interrogation of philosophy in the quest for its own statute, for its own place (to be found or maintained), with one final aim: the confirmation of its own privilege.

This task seems today more necessary than ever, from philosophy's point of view, at a time when its position is challenged on various fronts: for instance, by scientific and technocratic ideology; by the requirements of the market, which tend to invade all sectors and to install everywhere the rule and the procedures of technical and economic power; by human sciences, which in their quest for more room and more recognition tend to take possession of what used to be the proper domain of philosophy, and to submit it to so-called scientific criteria of investigation; by the demands of politics, and of social agencies in general; and also by the pressure of literary and poetic discourse, which invades philosophy—taking advantage of its current identity crisis—and replaces the traditional procedures of its discourse with its own more analogical, metaphoric, and allusive ways.

Hence, for philosophy, there is a double urgency: on the one hand, to enliven its discourse, to fecundate it through some sort of conjunction with neighboring discourses; but even more important, on the other hand—lest philosophy should lose its specificity and surrender to the pretenders to its throne—to resite and refound itself more subtly, so as to be able to respond to the ever increasing complexity of interactions between the diverse modes of discourse without losing its right to a dominant position.

It is particularly important to note that philosophy so envisaged—once again we can call it radical, in the absence of better qualification—can hardly content itself with a position of equality with other discourses and disciplines. Either it can maintain its specific (and higher) position—"the point of view over the totality," "the control over the region of principles," and so on—and thus authorize itself as metadiscourse, metalanguage, master discourse in the theoretical space; or it stands to lose everything, and to disappear.

Such could be (but let's not forget it is an hypothesis) philosophy's pretension, and the deep source of energy that two thinkers (and two theoretic fields) as different as Derrida (deconstruction) and Ricoeur (hermeneutics) might have in common. Let us go back to the texts and try to shed some light on this intricate question.

Concerning the relation between metaphor and philosophy, Ricoeur's and Derrida's conclusions—but are we entitled to speak of conclusions for the latter?—do not appear to be very divergent. Apart from Ricoeur's efforts to provide a more adequate concept of metaphor (efforts and results that Derrida never questions and rather tends to praise), if Derrida's protestation that most of Ricoeur's criticisms against him are due not to a real disagreement, but to a defective and therefore unsustainable reading of his texts, we are left with two apparently similar points of view on the relationship between metaphor and philosophy.

For Ricoeur the so-called philosophical metaphors are no longer true metaphors: They are dead metaphors, lexicalized and then subjected to a process of conceptual reforging that transforms them into philosophical tools; and they are radically different from poetic metaphor, even when they look very like them, as in Heidegger's later texts.

For Derrida, too, philosophical metaphors are not common metaphors. He, too, uses Heidegger to show how certain quasi-metaphors (vicinity, home, *Ereignis*, *Riß*, and so forth) are actually *reverse* metaphors, where the distinction between proper (literal) and figurative (metaphoric) is finally lost. It is here, in this step beyond metaphor, that an access to the unthinkable is opened up. Similarly, for Ricoeur, it is only through the conceptual overcoming of metaphor that the speculative power is set free.

For both, the thin line separating poetry from philosophy is to be preserved. But the apparent proximity suddenly becomes an insuperable distance when Derrida explains that the step beyond metaphor can only be a total generalization of metaphor itself which, by freeing metaphor from its metaphysical definition (proper/figurative), drags it away from the grip of speculation, and even unveils metaphor's hold on metaphysics (on language, on the

whole of Being) and opens the path for a thought that, in spite of
its being chained to metaphysics because of the necessity of articu-
lating itself in the present, nevertheless is on its way toward something (or somewhere) else, which for the time being cannot yet be
determined.

This is, I believe, the point where a radical difference between
the two philosophers becomes clear. Ricoeur rejects the idea that
metaphysics is in a metaphoric position vis-à-vis Being, the idea that
philosophical metaphors are in fact metaphors raised to an infinite
power, and first and foremost the idea of "overcoming metaphysics."
Ricoeur, as well as Derrida, comes near the point where all metaphysical distinctions (inside/outside, discovery/creation, and so on)
vacillate and where the necessity is clearly felt for a new approach to
the *Ereignis*. But even there he affirms the power of distantiation
proper to speculative discourse, its critical specificity. He rejects all
hermeticisms and despair of language and denies the possibility, the
necessity and the opportunity of a rupture with the tradition of
speculative philosophy. For him the task of any true philosopher
remains always the same:

> What philosopher worthy of the name prior to Heidegger has not
> meditated on the metaphor of the way and considered himself to
> be the first to embark on a path that is language itself addressing
> him? Who among them has not sought the "ground" and the
> "foundation," the "dwelling" and the "clearing"? Who has not
> believed that truth was "near" and yet difficult to perceive and
> even more difficult to say, that it was hidden and yet manifest,
> open and yet veiled? . . .[78]

Ricoeur's dialectics of belonging and distantiation, in which
speculative thought (sometimes using—but without renouncing its

own specificity—metaphoric energy) installs itself, does not correspond to Derrida's interlacing of belonging and overcoming. To be very concise, only the latter puts thought (even if only by supposition) in danger of losing itself, puts it in a position of relative difference, that is, of partial exteriority to the traditional, speculative line of thought. But this is precisely the position and the difference that Ricoeur rejects outright.

Ricoeur's philosophy is constantly "in quest," open to all manner of interactions with other modes of discourse, and it looks for different ways and forms. But it never risks its own point of foundation, because "speculative discourse has its *necessity* in itself, in putting the resources of conceptual articulation to work. These are resources that doubtless belong to the mind itself, that are the mind itself reflecting upon itself."[79] Must we, then, to escape despair and impotence, have resort to *l'esprit lui-même*? Ricoeur does not seem to hesitate in this regard.

Once we have found the crux of the difference, other questions must follow, for instance: What is the precise sense and extent of the "risk" that deconstruction is prepared to accept? Is not this risk, by some chance, the last trick of a philosophy hard to kill, still trying to have the last word, to cry out the last truth, be it a self-destructive or self-paralyzing one? Why deconstruction? What is the specific value of the discourse that calls itself by this name?[80] These questions will not find a definitive answer here.

At the end of this short voyage with Ricoeur and Derrida, what is the state of the question concerning the relationship between metaphor and philosophy? Simplifying once again, I should say that from Ricoeur's side almost nothing has changed with reference to the traditional philosophical point of view on this matter. It is certainly true that the strict metaphysical theory of metaphor is refuted and a very interesting and rich reworking is carried through in order to produce a more adequate and comprehensive theory of metaphor. It is also true that the value and fecundity, for philosophical discourse, of the energy carried by the semantic dynamism that characterizes metaphor are duly recognized, and that a dialectic line of communication is opened between the experience of belonging (proper to poetic discourse) and the power of distantiation on which speculative thought relies. But, in the end, the metaphoric power remains totally external to philosophy, and is accepted only inasmuch as philosophy is able to master it and to put it to work to its own benefit. The only alternative, for philosophy, is to be drowned by metaphor, to lose its identity in it. We recognize here the usual scheme, the typical idealistic dialectics of reabsorption and reelaboration of the negative. It remains to be seen, admittedly, whether this "usual scheme" is not in fact the most economic and effective way of approaching and dealing with the intractable relationship between metaphor and philosophy. Is there a better one?

In Derrida this reassuring dynamic is upset. It is metaphor, the metaphoric necessity, that puts philosophy at work. Philosophy must therefore give up its attempt to produce (and believe in) a non-metaphoric knowledge of metaphor, since this can only result, ironically, in a replication and generalization of metaphor itself. Philosophy's identity has already been lost from its very beginning; its specificity cannot be preserved like a treasure endangered by an inimical power, but at most like a mobile mark constantly displaced over the body of language, with no haven of rest, with no home, always facing its unconquerable others.

There is no respite in this irresistible drifting dragging philosophy from metaphor to metaphor, from difference to difference. But is one drift different from another? Can one chose one's own drift? And if so, why and how should one choose?

METAPHORS AND INDECIDABLES

In the second part of my exploration of deconstruction's territories, I will pursue and deepen the examination of Derrida's "machine," and more particularly of some of its most central mechanisms, whose movement appears to be similar to that of metaphor.

Cumbersome Metaphors

The debate on the question of the relationship between metaphor and philosophy reaches with Derrida, as we have seen, an extreme point, beyond which the disposition of all relevant factors changes radically. This mutation does not have a merely local significance. It is indeed exemplary of a certain twist to which philosophy is subjected everywhere in Derrida's writing.

The example of the discussion on metaphor, however, is not chosen by chance, and it has more importance than other possible examples. It is marked by a privilege deriving from the key position metaphor occupies in Derrida's writing, from a double point of view: (1) its eminent position, as an object for analysis, in the patent economy of Derrida's writings and thought; and (2) its essential function, as an instrument for articulation and argumentation, in the strategy and in the style of Derrida's writing.

The latter statement is not self-explanatory, except for some of Derrida's (as well as Heidegger's) detractors, from whose pens come abundant accusations of etymologism, excessive and dishonest usage of metaphors, and, in general, perversion and lack of restraint in the use of language.[81]

In this regard, however, I would prefer to suspend judgement and not to take for granted what, more or less implicitly, underlies such accusations: a clear-cut opposition between metaphor and con-

cept, sustaining in its turn that between natural language and philosophical language, between philosophy and poetry, and so on. Once
again, for the time being, I will not deliberate concerning the
"philosophical quality" of Derrida's writing. Instead, I will limit
myself to tracing in it a certain insistence (albeit "diverted," as we
shall see) of the metaphorical.

The discovery of an essential presence of metaphor inside philosophy's own body is not something new and cannot be attributed
to deconstruction exclusively. Ernest Renan, Nietzsche, and Anatole France, with very diverse intentions from each other, have all
indicated (or denounced) in metaphysics (and in Nietzsche's case,
also in science) a deposit of forgotten metaphors, of blanched
tropes, of catachreses surreptitiously elevated to concepts—long
before Derrida.[82] From this viewpoint, philosophy's "sin" is not classified under the title "use and abuse of metaphors," as happens in the
antimetaphoric line that runs through the Western tradition from
Aristotle to the empiricists, positivists, and today's "scienticists" of all
kinds. It is rather a sin committed by philosophy against metaphor
and against itself, at least an act of oblivion and denial of its own origins, resulting in the end in a loss of vitality,[83] in a sclerosis of its own
possibilities of innovation and articulation.

In any case, philosophy's metaphors and catachreses may well be
dead today, but they must have been alive yesterday. There has therefore been a moment (or several, if one does not believe in the unity
and homogeneity of "Western philosophy") when a philosophical
discourse in its dawning state would open its own original (albeit not
entirely autonomous, not absolutely different, not "purely conceptual") space of sense by means of metaphors, catachreses, and neologisms. After which, those acts of metaphoric definition left behind
only a sclerotic and systematized slough: metaphysics, a depository
and sanctuary of meaningless and truthless junk, an inventory of nec-

essary (at least for philosophers) fictions. But can we really believe that the metaphorical origin has not left any trace at all, any active presence, in the discourse that, admittedly, has so successfully managed to forget it? One can doubt it, and this would be the starting point, both of a militant critique of metaphysics as a herbarium of dead metaphors, and of a (more or less, depending on individual positions) radical "apology" of living metaphor in philosophy.

The following step, however, that is, the return (or the more or less radical surrender) to metaphor is still a very difficult one for a philosopher to take. The best proof of this is deconstruction itself, that is, the contemporary philosophical discourse which enjoys perhaps the largest degree of freedom from tradition, yet cannot bring itself to openly and unreservedly "accept" metaphor. Understandably, because the recognition of an universal presence of metaphor in every discourse (including philosophy's) does not necessarily imply a demise of all differences, or the complete surrender to metaphor, that is, to a total lack of control, of ground, of reason, of sense. The question of identity (philosophy's identity, the conceptual identity of a particular type of discourse) is therefore certainly not eliminated, but displaced. We ought to ask ourselves whether, when mentioning metaphor after the generalization of the metaphorical, we are always naming the same thing. Isn't there, next to the point of view of "essences" (that is, of an essential—and probably deceptive—distinction between metaphor and concept), also a problem of degrees and forms? Even admitting that everything in language and thinking is metaphor, it remains possible to think that there is metaphor and _metaphor_, and that philosophy is still entrusted with a duty to make the choice between types of metaphors, between ways of dealing with metaphors, between different manners of surrendering to metaphor.

Derrida's Operation

Derrida's writing is a practice of philosophy as linguistic alchemy, much more than as adhesion to a tradition or participation in a linguistic game according to the rules of an instituted grammar; hence, for some, a radical doubt concerning its authenticity and its philosophical legitimacy.

Metaphor is not the only alembic in this experiment. On the contrary, it could be denied (and not without ground, from a certain point of view) that metaphor plays an essential function in it. In Derrida's text we encounter a good many "indecidables,"[84] but none among the key notions is explicitly described as a "metaphor." What is the difference between an indecidable and a metaphor?

First of all, an indecidable (*marge, différance, supplément,* and so on) is negatively defined by its inability to tolerate any definition. It could, however, be described as a nonfinite bundle of "signifieds," disposed within the space of an opposition (within/without, more/less, before/after, or signifier/signified, for instance) that has been *barred.* This space of meaning, which the indecidable ought to (but structurally cannot) cover, is not, in effect, directly approachable. Hence a resemblance (explicitly and firmly denied by Derrida[85]) with the ways of negative theology. I shall not pause over this, as something else provides the focus of the present discussion, that is, a possible similarity between the operation of the indecidable and the operation of metaphor.

Deconstruction chooses indecidability as its own space, in defiance of rationality, but not without reason. Actually, to say that "deconstruction *chooses* indecidability as its own space" is incorrect, at least in part. In fact, deconstruction in a sense *generates* it, taking advantage of clefts in the "text of the epoch," where amounts of "indecidable energy" can be liberated. Indecidable is what makes

classic, binary logic no longer exclusively relevant, resists alignment
with the chronological axis of history and metaphysics, and rejects
the choice between the two terms of the opposition between historical and logical. It is that which allows the _clôture_ (the logical
space governed by metaphysics) to be attacked or disassembled from
within, without leaving it. A notion (_une marque_[86]) is systematically
kept out of the symbolic space that it is supposed to indicate, and
effectively does indicate, but without being allowed to establish itself
by instituting an analogy. On the contrary, such a notion is forced
to activate the deconstruction of the opposition that is meant to
support the analogy: This is, perhaps, what an indecidable is.

I now wish to propose an hypothesis: An indecidable is a
metaphor (or, more precisely, a catachresis) kept "alive"—in
Ricoeur's sense—by means of constant negation. In other terms, a
perpetually unresolved metaphor. One example, significant albeit
slightly particular, is provided by deconstruction's key word, _dif-
férance_.[87] This is an indecidable, the signification (or, at least, the
meaning-effects) of which can be described according to the following scheme:

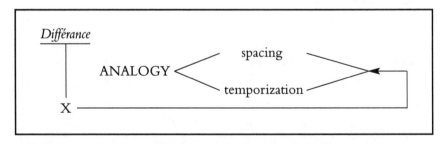

Différance is a metaphor, or rather a catachresis, which replaces an
unthinkable _x_ and offers it to our thought, by way of analogy,
through the notions of "spacing" and "temporization." Those two
notions, however, are already secondary with regard to _différance_,

which generates them. In truth *différance* (what it represents) is nothing. It is not. There is therefore, in this case, no literal meaning, and analogy is deprived of a ground. The *a* of *différance* indicates precisely the original torsion that has barred and made unusable any possible "proper" sense of the word. The analogies which could make the object *x* (replaced by the term *différance*) thinkable, are in their turn systematically barred.

We could consider *différance* as a metaphor for "metaphor," on the basis of the analogy "displacement of sense." But the analogy is immediately barred: There is neither proper nor improper, the sense is in motion, but it has already, and always, been displaced. Does "*différance*" make for us the idea of metaphor more visible, more clear? Does it place it "before our eyes"? Or is it, on the contrary, metaphor that tells us something about *différance*, of which nothing can be said? If *différance is* something, it is perhaps (as we have seen in the first part of this chapter) the *generalizing catastrophe* of metaphor: the site where metaphor, bending back on itself, explodes and overflows its limits.

Différance, with its supplementary *a*, is a neographism. To the good reasons presented by Derrida in order to justify the license he takes with the dictionary, we could add this one: The graphic difference which marks *différance* "energizes" the catachresis, thus increasing the suspension effect that Derrida's discourse creates preventing interpretation from resting on a sense (whether etymological or analogical), if not univocal, at least delimitable. Except for the neographism, the same happens to all other indecidables. To summarize, a "mark," which does not belong to philosophy's dictionary, or has become foreign to it, is applied in a context where it can only be interpreted metaphorically. But the very same context immediately neutralizes the analogical foundation of the application. The meaning, initially drawn in a particular direction, is diverted and kept in a sort of relative and relatively calculated (but up to what point?) freedom. We are therefore in the presence of something more and something less than a metaphor, according to a scheme similar to that (which we have already encountered) of the "generalizing catastrophe," analyzed by Derrida in certain among Heidegger's "metaphors," such as those concerning habitation and the "home of Being," where the metaphorical direction is inverted and generalized, confounding all usual relations between predicate and subject, vehicle and tenor, discourse and referent, with the results that we have seen.

Impossible Foundations

What is the aim of Derrida's "operation"? Is it still a philosophical operation? In this case, what makes it different from poetic creation? First of all, to be attentive to Derrida's indications, we should say that what is happening is not an operation, and that there is no aim. Less brutally: The notions of "operation" and "aim" should be displaced and twisted in order to extract them from the diverse philosophical discourses that monopolize their intelligibility and channel it through the concepts of the subject, history, and so on. The continued utilization of "old names," such as "aim" and "operation," can therefore only have a limited meaning, and one which is strategic and tends toward its self-elimination.

Whether this is philosophy, and in what way exactly this is different from, say, poetry, is in question; this indeed is *the question*. The radicalness of Derrida's questioning, however, does not reside so much in the question itself, but in the absence of a reassuring answer.[88] The possibility of philosophy losing its way never abandons Derrida's horizon of thought: I should say that, to a large extent, that possibility constitutes it. This "disposition" appears everywhere in

Derrida's work. We have isolated it, in its most general form, in connection with the theme of metaphor. The act of assigning to the place of the foundations (that is, to the "blind spot") of philosophy—as well as of any discourse—the structure of a metaphor certainly is nothing more than another metaphor; but doesn't it, at least, suggest something important about metaphor, and about philosophy?

Derrida's writing, in a way, represents the extreme point of presence of metaphor in philosophy, and vice versa. The border of literature is not far, perhaps it has even been (but not inadvertently) crossed. Philosophy, however, is not disavowed, precisely as metaphysics is not simply overcome or erased. Derrida's text has the merit of explicitly inscribing the question of metaphor in its amplest capacity. Precisely for this reason, Derrida brings us up to the point where philosophy's specificity is at risk of losing itself because, as it seems, of an extreme proximity to the "metaphoric sun," which is also the (barred) origin of sense. The catastrophic generalisation of metaphor is therefore nothing less, perhaps, than deconstruction's central gesture.

The reversal of the metaphor/concept dichotomy can even be conceived as the necessary precondition of any possible deconstruction, and its unjustifiable foundation. Concept (from a Derridean viewpoint) is no longer philosophy's element, for this would assume the "stricture" of a system of relations, dominated by a thinking and reflecting subject. To encourage the proliferation of metaphors means not so much reestablishing truth, but redistributing meaning: relax the stricture, allow language to distil and reassemble itself in figures of sense as yet unthought, or forgotten. This philosophical (deconstructive) metaphor will always and in each case be *living*, that is, active, since it will never be allowed to sediment in a concept.

But why speak of indecidables, and not of metaphors? Probably because the object "metaphor" still deeply belongs (in spite of all modern modifications) to a tradition that makes it inadequate to fulfil a deconstructive role. This becomes evident if one considers that the "foundation" of metaphor, according to the tradition that, as we have seen, has dominated Western philosophy, is analogy. What does that mean, if not that the gap of sense is immediately stopped, and the metaphorical energy distributed along the axis of a finite analogy that restores the order disturbed by metaphor itself? All tropic displacements rest on this basis and, thanks to analogical chains, they partake of the solidity of language's native soil. Even more recent theories of metaphor end up by converging toward the idea of a "reduction of the gap," of a "reabsorption of the shock," of a "reestablishment of the order of signification."

The indecidable, on the contrary, resists indefinitely the reestablishment of order. It immediately belies the analogical ghost that it seems to evoke, and it fulfils a role that is opposed to that of metaphor: to keep meaning's gaps open and visible, leaking and seeping. It is, therefore, precisely for this reason, a deconstructive agent.

If indecidables are not metaphors, they are not concepts either, since they escape—and are not able to enforce—totalization and control. They are movements of language, thanks to which the space of sense is opened that the philosophical operation of deconstruction needs. The indecidable is a metaphor denied or, better, a metaphor that denies its second constitutive moment, the moment of the reduction of the gap.

The indecidables keep *différance* active; and *différance* bars the origin. If the thought of *différance* is the radical thought of metaphor, deconstruction is recognizing the insistence of metaphor (as *différance* without origin, as impropriety in the absence of a "proper") in all key points of the discourse of metaphysics. Would it be acceptable to say that deconstruction's "theory" is the theory of a generalized (and catastrophic) metaphor, as the site of philosophy?

If so, it would be a particular type of metaphor, a modified metaphor. But is there a discourse (including that of science) that is not the result of a certain modification of metaphoric energy, that is, of the movement of the production/displacement of sense?

Derrida's philosophy is the place where a "catastrophe" of sense takes place. The sense, however, is not lost completely, rather it changes direction and metaphorically presents thought with its unthinkable origin. "Philosophy" is certainly many things, and very diverse. Hegel's philosophical game is indeed not Derrida's. "Philosophy" for Derrida (if I dare define with such peremptoriness something that so badly tolerates definition) is forcing upon language a certain bend in the free (and arbitrary) play of metaphors in which its dynamism has its source. But this certainly would not suffice to mark philosophy's specificity, even less Derrida's originality. For the philosophical cocktail to function, an ethical component is needed: an intention, a duty of truth, without rule and without external obligation. A voluntary submission to the truth-power (which certainly does not mean "to the prevailing ideological structures") that is inherent in a language, in a tradition, in a state of the field, and that one cannot control, or only marginally.[89]

CONCLUSION?

Let us summarize, before momentarily concluding, the reasons why Derrida represents the point of maximum advance in the questioning about metaphor and philosophy: (a) because he explicitly poses the question and deals with it up to its extreme consequences; (b) because in his writing the "metaphorical capacity" is more apparent than elsewhere; and (c) because in his texts the status and the site of philosophy are constantly under examination, which allows the relationship between metaphor and philosophy to be analyzed beyond the traditional and reassuring scheme.

But the price of this operation is very high: Everything is in question, there is no point of departure or reference, and as a consequence there is a very real risk of going nowhere, or of reaching, after long exertions, only impotence and silence.

Derrida's path of thought brings philosophical discourse as close as possible to its point of support, not in order to found it, but to signal the lack of foundation on which it erects itself, its bottomlessness. It brings it closest to the point where philosophy, together with its last cards, puts its identity on the table and most certainly loses it, at least for those who do not feel the need for such a wager. This wager is indeed not justifiable, and particularly not from deconstruction's viewpoint. Nothing legitimates deconstruction, not a truth criterion or a reality instance, which, however, are not simply annulled, but rather put into question and therefore deprived of their legitimizing function.

Deconstruction, nevertheless, has no need to prove its own right to existence: It exists, it happens, as any other event, in the order of discourse and elsewhere, according to a formula where repetition and difference mix, giving birth to a new combination. What (possibly) makes deconstruction an acceptable (and perhaps reproducible) discourse, if not a "philosophical school," at least a "philosophical position," is not its truth, nor the simple fact of its existence, but an indefinite series of factors interacting in a given (but not entirely controllable) field. This indefinite series can always, for economy's and convenience's sake, be metonymically replaced by such short-cutting notions as "necessity," "relevance," "efficacy," and so on.

However, something should immediately be added. Precisely that which makes deconstruction a position, which gives us the possibility of partially mastering its movement, simultaneously condemns it to the inevitable destiny of all positions: obsolescence, oblivion, death. This perhaps explains, among other things, why deconstruction, albeit unable to renounce any "purposive intention," without which there would be no philosophical discourse, so obstinately resists definition, control, the closing (*clôture*) of its own discourse.

Deconstruction is not the end of philosophy. Even if (theoretically) philosophy has the means to declare its own end, it cannot commit suicide: If the end comes, it will come in a different form. But furthermore, and more to the point, with Derrida, philosophy is not even trying to kill itself. On the contrary, it survives indefinitely by elaborating its own mourning.[90] In effect, if the metaphysical project is fundamentally flawed and impossible, so is the antimetaphysical one. The latter is prone to an even higher degree of blindness if it entails the false belief that metaphysics can be excluded by decision. Catching a glimpse of the impossibility of "closing" a discourse does not mean declaring its end; on the contrary, it opens (almost) infinite avenues for continuation.

Deconstruction knows all this. Between the two impossibilities, philosophy—according at least to Derrida—prospers, in forms that certainly less and less correspond to the great traditional models and therefore elicit all sorts of questions. These questions are not made less valid or redundant by our suspicion that there is no answer for them, at least if the answer must be a definitive solution. There is no philosophy, for us, without them. Let's therefore start again asking ourselves what philosophy is, what difference there is between a displacement of sense and the other, and how does metaphor make philosophy (and all the rest) happen. If Derrida's discourse has the disadvantage of not offering answers (except in the form of demonstrating the impossibility of certain answers), it nevertheless offers the advantage of not liquidating the questions.[91] Of course, it remains to be seen to what extent a discourse that claims to be philosophical can waive the possibility (and the duty?) of providing answers. This is a question to be added to the others.

This conclusion, with all the questions that it generates and leaves unanswered, could mark the point where research into metaphor loses itself in philosophy's "general catastrophe." In fact, in Derrida's perspective—as we have seen—metaphor is precisely one of the ways by which philosophy is brought as near as possible to the point of its perdition. But isn't this "wanting to get to the point where everything can be lost" one of the purest determinations of philosophy's vocation and destiny? It is one of them, but certainly not the only one.

It seems to me that here two possibilities—irreconcilable, but both acceptable—present themselves. The first one: to elect domicile in this region of thought where paradox flourishes and rules. This "choice," which some critics will describe as a glorified cul-de-sac, is nevertheless entirely decent, and (depending on the way it is implemented) does not forfeit the innermost intention of philosophy. The second one, also acceptable, respectful of a different determination of that same intention, and probably even historically imminent, is to forget Derrida. To forget, radically, the radicalness of a knowledge too acute for comfort, too hostile to hope, and the well-being of thought. To start again, therefore, on a different trajectory, chosing a different drift of language, or taking up again, as Ricoeur for instance suggests, the old path: the way that the speculative tradition has opened and entrusted to us.[92]

NOTES

1. Jacques Derrida, "Le retrait de la métaphore," *Po&sie* 7 (1978; henceforth RM): 104. "The *Retrait* of Metaphor," *Enclitic*, 2, no. 2 (1978): 6: "What is happening, today, with metaphor? And without metaphor

what is happening? It is a very old subject. It occupies the West, inhabits it or lets itself be inhabited. . . ."

2. RM, pp. 104–105. "The *retrait* of Metaphor," p. 7: "I drift . . . I skid and I drift irresistibly."

3. Paul Ricoeur, *The Rule of Metaphor* (Toronto: University of Toronto Press, 1977), p. 313. *La métaphore vive* (Paris: Editions du Seuil, 1975; henceforward MV), p. 398: ". . . le pouvoir de distanciation qui ouvre l'espace de la pensée spéculative."

4. Jacques Derrida, "La mythologie blanche," in *Marges de la philosophie* (Paris: Editions de Minuit, 1972); "White Mythology," in *Margins of Philosophy* (Chicago: University of Chicago Press, 1982).

5. And in particular: Jacques Derrida, *De la grammatologie* (Paris: Editions de Minuit, 1967); *L'écriture et la différence* (Paris: Editions du Seuil, 1967); *La dissémination* (Paris: Editions du Seuil, 1972); and *Marges de la philosophie*.

6. See Friedrich Nietzsche, "Erkenntnistheoretische Einleitung über Wahreit und Lüge im aussermoralishen Sinne" ["Introduction théorétique sur vérité et mensonge en un sens extra-moral"] (1873), in *Das Philosophen-Buch / Le livre du philosophe* (Paris: Flammarion, 1969).

7. Reference is made to the theme of the "labor of the negative," as it is developed in G. W. F. Hegel's *Phenomenology of Spirit* (Oxford: Oxford University Press, 1979).

8. Ricoeur, *The Rule of Metaphor*, p. 258. MV, p. 324: "reconnaître, dans son principe, la discontinuité qui assure au discours spéculatif son autonomie."

9. Ibid. MV, p. 325: "vivification mutuelle du discours philosophique et du discours poétique."

10. Aristotle, *La métaphysique*, trans. J. Tricot (Paris: Vrin, 1981), A,9,991 a 19–22.

11. Ricoeur, *The Rule of Metaphor*, p. 261. MV, p. 327: "le discours philosophique s'instaure comme gardien vigilant des extensions de sens réglées sur le fond desquelles se détachent les extensions de sens inédites du discours poétique."

12. Ibid., p. 270. MV, p. 340: "en entrant dans la mouvance de la problématique de l'être, l'analogie à la fois apporte sa conceptualité propre et reçoit la qualification transcendantale du champ auquel elle est appliquée."

13. Concerning the difference between analogy and metaphor in the discourse of speculative theology, see also Janet Martin, "Metaphor amongst Tropes," *Religious Studies* (1981).

14. Ricoeur, *The Rule of Metaphor*, p. 273. MV, p. 344: "d'établir le discours théologique au niveau d'une science et ainsi de le soustraire entièrement aux formes poétiques du discours religieux."

15. Ibid., p. 280. MV, p. 356.

16. Ibid., p. 277. MV, p. 353: "pour ma part je vois dans ce souci le trait distinctif de la visée sémantique du discours spéculatif."

17. Ibid., p. 280. MV, p. 356: "Tel est l'admirable travail de pensée par lequel a été préservée la différence entre le discours spéculatif et le discours poétique au lieu même de leur plus grande proximité."

18. Ibid., p. 280. MV, p. 357: "entre philosophie et métaphore, une implication d'un tout autre genre . . . qui les enchaîne au niveau de leurs présuppositions cachées, plutôt qu'à celui de leurs intentions déclarées."

19. Ibid., p. 282. MV, p. 360: "seul un coup de force, impossible à justifier, couche la philosophie occidentale sur ce lit de Procuste."

20. Ibid., p. 284. MV, p. 361: "Or, n'est-ce pas là ce que fait la métaphore *vive?*"

21. Ibid., p. 280. MV, p. 357: "l'usage constant que Heidegger fait de la métaphore a finalement plus d'importance que ce qu'il dit incidemment contre la métaphore."

22. Ibid., p. 284. MV, p. 362: "[Derrida] étayerait l'universelle suspicion à l'endroit de la métaphysique occidentale par une suspicion plus aiguë adressée au non-dit de la métaphore elle-même. Or le non-dit de la métaphore, c'est la métaphore usée."

23. Ibid., p. 285. MV, p. 362.

24. Ibid., p. 290. MV, p. 368: "Cette anlyse incline à penser que les métaphores mortes ne sont plus des métaphores, mais qu'elles s'adjoignent à la signification littérale pour en étendre la polysémie."

25. Ibid., p. 293. MV, p. 371: "Il y a philosophème parce qu'un concept peut être actif en tant que pensée dans une métaphore elle-même morte."

26. Ibid., p. 292. MV, p. 371: "du non-propre issu du sensible un propre spirituel."

27. Ibid., p. 293. MV, p. 372: "La position du concept procède dialectiquement de la métaphore elle-même."

28. Ibid., p. 294. MV, p. 373: "le noyau théorique commun à Heidegger et Derrida, à savoir la prétendue connivence entre le couple métaphorique du propre et du figuré et le couple métaphysique du visible et de l'invisible."

29. Ibid., pp. 294–95. MV, p. 374: "Ce n'est donc pas la métaphore qui porte l'édifice de la métaphysique platonisante; c'est plutôt celle-ci qui s'empare du procès métaphorique pour le faire travailler à son bénéfice."

30. Ibid., p. 296. MV, p. 375: "d'une part, que le discours spéculatif a sa *possibilité* dans le dynamisme sémantique de l'énonciation métaphorique, d'autre part, que le discours spéculatif a sa *nécessité* en lui-même."

31. Ibid., p. 300. MV, p. 380: "le discours spéculatif commence de soi et trouve en lui-même le principe de son articulation. . . . Sa *nécessité* ne prolonge pas sa possibilité. . . . Elle procède plutôt des structures même de l'esprit que la philosophie transcendantale a pour tâche d'articuler. . . . le discours spéculatif est celui qui met en place les notions premières, les principes, qui articulent à titre primordial l'espace du concept. . . . le spéculatif est la condition de possibilité du conceptuel."

32. Ibid., p. 301. MV, p. 381.

33. Ibid., p. 304. MV, p. 386: "la catégorie ultime à partir de laquelle le tout du langage peut être pensé, quoique non connu, comme l'être-dit de la réalité."

34. Ibid., p. 305. MV, p. 387: "le sentiment n'est pas moins ontologique que la représentation."

35. Ibid., p. 306. MV, p. 387: "Il faut donc ébranler le règne de l'objet, pour laisser être et laisser se dire notre appartenance primordiale à

un monde que nous habitons, c'est-à-dire qui, tout à la fois, nous précède et reçoit l'empreinte de nos oeuvres."

36. Ibid. MV, p. 388: "avec la suspension de la référence à des objets faisant face à un sujet *jugeant*, n'est-ce pas la structure même de l'énonciation qui vacille? . . . n'est-ce pas la notion même de discours spéculatif qui s'évanouit, et avec cette notion la dialectique du spéculatif et du poétique?"

37. Aristotle, *Rhétorique*, trans. M. Dufour and A. Wartelle (Paris: Editions des Belles Lettres), III, 1411 b 24–25.

38. Ricoeur, *The Rule of Metaphor*, p. 308. MV, p. 392: "se mettre en quête du lieu où apparaître signifie génération de ce qui croît."

39. Ibid., p. 313. MV, p. 397.

40. Ibid. MV, p. 398: "quelque désespoir du langage."

41. Derrida, "The *Retrait* of Metaphor," p. 12: "This continuist assimilation or setting into filiation. . . ." RM, p. 109: "l'assimilation continuiste et la mise en filiale. . . ."

42. Ibid., p. 13. RM, p. 109: "il n'y a ici, pour des raisons essentielles, ni noyau ni noyau théorique surtout."

43. Ibid. RM, pp. 109–10: "à savoir que le rapport de la métaphore au concept et en général le procès de la métaphoricité se laisseraient comprendre sous le concept ou le schème de l'usure comme devenir-usagé ou devenir-usé."

44. Ibid. RM, p. 110: "comme production de plus-value selon d'autres lois que celles d'une capitalisation continue et linéairement accumulatrice."

45. Ibid., p. 14. RM, p. 110: "d'accréditer le schème de l'*us* mais bien de déconstruire un concept philosophique, une construction philosophique édifiée sur ce schème de la métaphore usée ou privilégiant pour des raisons signifiantes le trope nommé métaphore."

46. Ibid. RM, p. 110: "Je n'ai jamais cru à l'existence ou à la consistance de quelque chose comme *la* métaphysique."

47. Ibid. RM, p. 110: ". . . la limite circulaire bordant un champ homogène mais une structure plus retorse . . . : *invaginée*."

48. Ibid. RM, pp. 110–11: "la représentation d'une clôture linéaire entourant un espace homogène, c'est justement . . . une auto-représentation de la philosophie dans sa logique onto-encyclopédique."

49. Ibid., p. 20. RM, p. 115: "le sens et la nécessité qui lient entre elles la dénonciation apparemment univoque, simplifiante et réductrice du concept «métaphysique» de métaphore et d'autre part la puissance apparemment métaphorique d'un texte dont l'auteur ne veut plus qu'on comprenne comme «métaphorique», justement, ni même sous aucun concept de la métalinguistique ou de la rhétorique, ce qui s'y passe et prétend s'y passer de la métaphore."

50. Ibid., p. 19. RM, p. 114: ". . . à capter la plus grande quantité d'énergie et d'information dans le texte heideggerien."

51. Ibid., p. 20. RM, p. 116: "Toute ladite histoire de la métaphysique occidentale serait un vaste processus structural où l'*épochè* de l'être se retenant, se tenant en retrait, prendrait ou plutôt présenterait une série (entrelacée) de guises, de tours, de modes, c'est-à-dire de figures ou d'allures tropiques qu'on pourrait être tenté de décrire à l'aide d'une conceptualité rhétoricienne."

52. Ibid., p. 21. RM, p. 116: ". . . elle serait elle-même en situation tropique au regard de l'être, ou de la pensée de l'être."

53. Ibid. RM, p. 116: "On en parlera toujours *quasi* métaphoriquement."

54. Ibid., p. 22. RM, p. 117: "généralisation abyssale du métaphorique."

55. Ibid., p. 25. RM, p. 118.

56. Ibid., p. 23. RM, p. 118: "*Retrait-de-l'être-ou-de-la-métaphore* serait en voie de nous donner à penser moins l'être ou la métaphore que l'être ou la métaphore *du retrait*, en voie de nous donner à penser la voie et le véhicule, ou leur frayage."

57. Ibid. RM, p. 118: "au moment où, devenue débordante, la métaphoricité ne se laisse plus contenir dans son concept dit métaphysique."

58. Ibid. RM, p. 118: "répétant en profondeur la circulation du cercle herméneutique."

59. This metaphor is presented in Martin Heidegger, "Letter on Humanism," in *Basic Writings* (London: Routledge, 1993), p. 237.

60. *En souffrance* is the expression used in French for a letter that cannot be delivered.

61. This deferment seems to have a structure similar to that of a chiasmus, in the general sense of an arrangement where the components are disposed crosswise. The chiastic structure is massively present in Heidegger's writing. In this respect, see Jean-François Mattéi, "Le chiasme heideggerien ou la mise à l'«écart» de la philosophie," in Dominique Janicaud and Jean-François Mattéi, *La métaphysique à la limite. Cinq études sur Heidegger* (Paris: P.U.F., 1983).

62. "The *Retrait* of Metaphor," p. 24. RM, p. 119: "Or, ce qui se passe ici, avec la quasi-métaphore de la maison de l'être, et ce qui se passe de la métaphore en sa direction cursive, c'est que c'est l'être qui donnerait ou promettrait de donner, depuis son retrait même, à penser la maison ou l'habitat."

63. Ibid., p. 25. RM, p. 120: "Enonçant non-littéralement la condition de la métaphoricité, il en libère et l'extension illimitée et le retrait."

64. Ibid. RM, p. 120: "Toujours une métaphore de plus au moment où la métaphore se retire en évasant ses limites."

65. "Die Mundart ist nicht nur die Sprache der Mutter, sondern zugleich und zuvor die Mutter der Sprache" (*Sprache und Heimat*, quoted by Derrida, RM, p. 114; "The *retrait* of Metaphor," p. 18).

66. Ibid. RM, p. 114: "langue maternelle ne serait pas ici une métaphore pour déterminer le sens de la langue mais le tour essentiel pour comprendre ce que «la mère» veut dire."

67. Martin Heidegger, "The Nature of Language," in *On the Way to Language* (New York: Harper & Row, 1971); "Das Wesen der Sprache," in *Unterwegs zur Sprache* (Pfullingen: Neske, 1959).

68. Derrida, "The *Retrait* of Metaphor," p. 26. RM, p. 120: "appeler métaphore, comme si on savait ce que c'était, telle valeur de voisinage entre poésie et pensée, faire comme si on était d'abord assuré de la proximité de la proximité et du voisinage du voisinage, c'est se fermer à la nécessité de l'autre mouvement."

69. In the next chapter I shall resume, from a different angle, the examination of this point.

70. Derrida, "The *Retrait* of Metaphor," p. 28. RM, p. 122: "C'est pourquoi ce n'est pas un trait commun ou un concept général, ni davantage une métaphore."

71. Ibid. RM, p. 122: "... il n'est lui-même nommable, en tant qu'écartement, ni littéralement ni métaphoriquement."

72. Ibid, p. 29. RM, p. 122: "... et signent en quelque sorte l'une dans le corps de l'autre, l'une au lieu de l'autre, le contrat sans contrat de leur voisinage."

73. Ibid. RM, p. 123: "Cet approchement ne les rapproche pas depuis un autre lieu où il seraient déjà eux-mêmes. . . ."

74. Ibid. RM, p. 123: "Son inscription n'arrive qu'à s'effacer."

75. Ibid., p. 30. RM, p. 123: "Si *la* métaphysique avait une unité, ce serait le régime de ces oppositions qui n'apparaît et ne se détermine qu'*à partir* du retrait du trait, du retrait du retrait etc. Le *à partir de* s'y abîme lui-même."

76. Ibid., p. 33. RM, pp. 125–26: "Quand on dit trait ou retrait dans un contexte où il y va de la vérité, *trait* n'est plus une métaphore de ce que nous croyons usuellement reconnaître sous ce mot."

77. Ibid. RM, p. 126: "Rien, pas de réponse, sinon que de la métaphore le retrait se passe et de lui-même."

78. Ricoeur, *The Rule of Metaphor*, p. 311. MV, p. 396: "Quel philosophe digne de ce nom n'a pas, avant lui [Heidegger], médité sur la métaphore du chemin, et ne s'est pas tenu pour le premier à se mettre sur un chemin qui est le langage lui-même s'adressant à lui? Quel n'a pas cherché le «sol» et le «fond», la «demeure» et la «clairière»? Quel n'a pas cru que la vérité était «proche» et pourtant difficile à apercevoir et plus difficile encore à dire, qu'elle était cachée et pourtant manifeste, ouverte et pourtant voilée? . . ."

79. Ibid., p. 296. MV, p. 375: "le discours spéculatif à sa nécessité en lui-même, dans la mise en oeuvre des ressources d'articulation conceptuelle qui sans doute tiennent à l'esprit lui-même, qui sont l'esprit lui-même se réfléchissant."

80. "Difficult to say why the fact of expressing discontent and a desire

(that cannot be motivated by any specific reason) of something else, however usual and respectable this way of behaving might be, should be considered as specifically philosophical" ("Difficile dire en quoi le fait d'exprimer un mécontentement et un désir d'autre chose qui ne peuvent être motivés par aucune raison particulière, aussi habituelle et respectable que soit cette façon de faire, devrait être considérée comme spécifiquement philosophique.") (Jacques Bouveresse, *Le philosophe chez les autophages* [Paris: Editions de Minuit, 1984], p. 181). The same remark could obviously be addressed to Heidegger, and to all "regressive" philosophies of the times of crisis, according to Perelman's distinction (*Rhétorique et philosophie. Pour une théorie de l'argumentation en philosophie* [Paris: P.U.F., 1952], chap. 4). For my part, I find Bouveresse's question perfectly legitimate, but cannot help feeling (and I do not mean it as a criticism) that philosophy, by constitution, is *never* able to justify or even explain its own deepest reasons.

81. As an example: "When he approaches philosophical subjects, Derrida shows himself to be dangerously inclined to metaphorizing, which translates into a phosphorescent halo that, enveloping the page, hampers the perception and precise definition of the conceptual web of the discourse. Speculation, with Derrida, tends to convert itself into metaphor. . . ." Tito Perlini, "Ontologia come violenza," *Nuova corrente* 63 (1973): 24.

82. For the references, see Derrida, *Margins*, pp. 214–18; *Marges*, pp. 254–56.

83. Let's note, incidentally, that the same reproach is sometimes moved, in the name of a sort of poetry which is seen as "living," against a type of poetry qualified as "dead," that is, as artificial, empty, exclusively formal: "No hubo música en su alma; sólo un vano / Herbario de metáforas y argucias / Y la veneración de las astucias / Y el desdén de lo humano y sobrehumano" (Jorge Luis Borges, "Baltasar Gracián," in *Obra póetica* (Buenos Aires: Emecé Editores, 1975), p. 143.

84. A nonexhaustive list of "indecidables" appears, thanks to Lucette Finas, in an appendix to L. Finas et al., *Ecarts. Quatre essais à propos de Jacques Derrida* (Paris: Fayard, Digraphe, 1973).

85. See Derrida, *Marges*, p. 6; *Margins*, p. 6.

86. The word *"marque"* (an indecidable in its own right) is preferred by Derrida thanks to its relative foreignness to the linguistico-metaphysical constellation of the concept of "sign."

87. See Derrida, "La différance," in *Marges*.

88. A good example of "reassuring answer" is offered, in my opinion, at the conclusion of Ricoeur's *The Rule of Metaphor*, where the autonomy of speculative discourse is stated and guaranteed on the basis of the "very structures of the mind" (p. 300; MV, p. 380).

89. This discussion will be continued in chap. 4.

90. On this, see in particular Jacques Derrida, *Glas* (Lincoln and London: University of Nebraska Press, 1986).

91. In this, his gesture is faithful to Heidegger's deepest and most explicit intention: "An answer is no more than the final step of the very asking; and an answer that bids adieu to the inquiry annihilates itself as an answer." (Martin Heidegger, *Nietzsche* [San Francisco: Harper & Row, 1984], vol. 2, p. 192).

92. The reader is referred to chap. 4 for a discussion of the "mode of discourse" called philosophy. A detailed discussion becomes necessary, also in order to understand how two profoundly incompatible discourses (such as Derrida's and Ricoeur's) can nevertheless both legitimately be seen as acceptable expressions—irrespective of the fortune and durability of each—of that mode of discourse.

3

HEIDEGGER
METAPHORS THAT HURT

The preceding discussion on Derrida and Ricoeur gave me the opportunity to mention Heidegger's name. In this chapter, I will take up again the discourse on Heidegger and on his peculiar relationship to metaphor, with the intention of developing it in a more open and personal way. I will propose here some interpretative hypotheses, strictly interwoven with close textual analyses, concerning particularly some texts enclosed in the collection *Unterwegs zur Sprache.*[1]

POSITION OF THE PROBLEM
AND INITIAL QUESTIONS

> *". . . we must, of course, first rid ourselves of the calculative frame of mind."*
>
> —Martin Heidegger[2]

Before approaching Heidegger once again, I will venture some preliminary propositions that, however banal or provocative they may appear, should help in clearing the ground of some misunderstandings that always lurk in the shadows of this kind of endeavor.

(1) The objective here is not to establish whether Heidegger's text speaks the truth or lies (in any one among the possible senses of this dichotomic pair of terms). It is, rather, to see if and how a discursive machine, within the framework of a given context, functions in this text, perhaps even (partially) in a way that is unknown to its author.

(2) "Mastering" Heidegger's text (as any other text, in principle) is impossible. The task would be better described in terms of "journeying over" it. Not surprisingly, the choice of one course excludes another without, however, making the latter forever unusable; which means that the whole textual field, albeit physically limited, cannot be entirely covered in one journey, and not even in several.

(3) Asking Heidegger's text questions is not a "simple" or "initial" act. It is always a secondary act, situated (in consequence of decisions made in advance, though not necessarily by a deliberating subject) somewhere between connivance, or repetition, and violence.

Before Heidegger's text, we ask the question of metaphor: this is the apparently minimal point of departure of this analysis. But how does one place oneself _before_ Heidegger's text? _Before a text_, in general? To a certain extent, the reader finds himself more _in_ than _before_ Heidegger's text. This means, on the one hand, that once the reading starts the reader is no longer external and foreign to the text, in spite of all possible wishes to the contrary; and, on the other, as I have just suggested, that one does not master this text (or any other), that one cannot master an element in which one is immersed: at the most, one can swim in it. To say that we are more _in_ than _before_[3] this text means therefore that we are partly lost, partly impotent, in this relationship.

How then should one approach Heidegger's text? According to Jean Greisch, "[O]ne should first of all learn to bear the intransigence of a thought that, in order to be understood, demands that one follows its own itinerary."[4] I share only in part this point of view which, taken radically, would give space exclusively to a servile repetition of Heidegger's path. I would rather try to find some sort of interactive balance, precariously oscillating between fidelity and violence; that is, between listening or even abandoning oneself to the demands of the text, and criticism. From my point of view, as I have already stated, the problem is not one of truth and falsehood, or of right and wrong. For what concerns the analysis of Heidegger's texts, it would be more (but not exclusively) a question of internal coherence: Does Heidegger do what he sets out to do? Does he do what he needs to do in order not to contradict himself? The stumbling block, of course, is that he doesn't always say clearly what he intends to do, and how, and that the kind of contradiction that would be relevant here is not to be described in strictly logical terms unless we are prepared to lose all contact with Heidegger's enterprise.

In Heidegger's text there is metaphor. This trivial statement, once again (as had been the case with Derrida), does not go without saying. It is, for instance, explicitly belied with much force by Heidegger himself, when he insistently sets out to discredit metaphor, and precisely in circumstances where the presence of metaphor, in his own text or in the poetic text that is being analyzed, seems to be indubitable. "Blue is not an image [*Bild*] to indicate the sense of the holy . . . ,"[5] he writes, commenting on a poem by Georg Trakl.[6] Elsewhere, he says, "It would mean that we stay bogged down in metaphysics if we were to take the name Hölderlin gives here to 'words, like flowers' as being a metaphor."[7]

"Bogged down in metaphysics": If we stick to Heidegger's scarce explicit declarations, the rejection of metaphor is based upon a presupposition of complicity, which, however, is never entirely made explicit or justified, between the latter and metaphysics, as a whole and in its fundamental gesture: "The metaphorical exists only within metaphysics."[8] The same transfer, the same enhanced referral (from sensibility to intelligibility) would appear to be the central mechanism that both metaphysics and metaphor have in common. The management and exploitation of Being appear to be the dimension and framework of both. This, at least, is what the majority of Heidegger's commentators[9] have inferred from his lapidary declarations.

If metaphor then entertains such close links with metaphysics, a thinker bent on overcoming metaphysics will have to condemn metaphor. The examination of Heidegger's rapport with metaphor, however, is not going to be made easier by the fact that metaphor and metaphysics are viewed as conniving and perceived as being one and the same target in a struggle for overcoming the latter. On the contrary, it is well known how fraught with complications the Heideggerian notion of *Überwindung* is. But there seems to be no choice. In order to understand the meaning of the "rejection of metaphor" we will have to go back to the old question: What exactly is the meaning that Heidegger attributes to the "overcoming of metaphysics"? How does one do that? What remains to be done, if that cannot be done (forthwith)? These are all questions that I will put on one side for the present.

Let us try to get a closer look, first of all, at the way in which metaphor, according to Heidegger, depends on and belongs to metaphysics. It must be said immediately, with Ricoeur, that at first sight such a connection can only seem relevant within the framework of a traditional and by now outmoded notion of metaphor. In metaphor, according to the traditional description, we move—by means of an analogy—from something known to something less known, or even unknown. Metaphor is therefore aimed at presenting, analogically, a nonlinguistic reality, or at providing an approximate, immediate, and lively representation of a truth or an idea that cannot be logically or conceptually expressed in the given context. This movement pertaining to metaphor is similar to the transfer from sensible (*aistheton*) to intelligible (*noéton*),[10] which constitutes, according to Heidegger, the central movement of the metaphysical machine; and, if fact, it is the same movement.

Heidegger sees metaphor (disapprovingly in both instances) either as a means for using language in order to overcome it with the intention of reaching the intelligible and the unspeakable that lies beyond language, or as an instrument for the establishment of the total interdependence that permits the exploitation of Being. For him, however, the true and essential relationship between language and Being takes place on a completely different level: *die Sprache spricht*. Language is the path. The inexpressible does not reside elsewhere. The *Ungesprochene* is not a mystico-romantic unspeakable, but the essential reserve of language. Language speaks, and when it speaks according to its own essence it does not speak by way of metaphors, but by way of "nominations," of showing/hiding indications. If, with metaphor, in most among the current senses of the term, we move through analogy from a known to a less known or unknown, in poetry and in true thinking, on the contrary, according to Heidegger, that which is (apparently) known is referred back to that which, in the very act of retiring, shows the essential. Thus the play of known and unknown takes on in Heidegger a different form, and reveals a different connection.

The ordinary movement of metaphor, with its hopping from image to image, is structurally opposed to the coming of that which wants to be thought. Here metaphor discloses itself as an agent and instrument of representation: Heidegger's rejection of "images" is therefore strictly dependent on his suspicion with regard to representational thinking—first and foremost as an instrument of the metaphysical/technical epoch. Heidegger's repression of metaphor does not, therefore, stem from a necessity to safeguard concept, as is traditionally the case. Quite on the contrary, it derives from the perception of and essential *complicity* between metaphor and concept.[11] For sure, a concept is not always metaphorical or representational. It can very well always have a metaphorical origin, and perhaps it does remain always metaphorical in the sense of a residual and unavoidable possibility of nonpropriety, of nonunivocity, of dissemination. But, on the other hand, concept can in certain circumstances function in a nonrepresentational (and therefore, in this sense, nonmetaphorical) way. Let us consider, for instance, in a mathematical discourse, the abstract concepts of "infinity," "whole number," "root." The representational bond, which remains visible in the words themselves with their particular etymological meanings, is nevertheless replaced here by a strong, precise position within a structure. Those concepts can only function as part of a structure that rigorously defines them and makes them operative. But the problem is elsewhere. There is in effect a much deeper (albeit perfectly visible) solidarity between concept and metaphor. Even a nonrepresentational concept cooperates in the technico-metaphysical enslavement of the world, thereby declaring its essential complicity with representation, of which it is more an extreme consequence than the absolute opposite. For Heidegger, it is therefore imperative to abandon both metaphor and concept, representation and abstraction, since both belong to the enslaving movement of *logos*, of *techné*, and both are responsible for blocking the possibility of the "other movement."

How, then, is this clear-cut position compatible with the presence in Heidegger's text of so many metaphors? Of course, it remains to be proved that this is the case. And, of course, it remains possible—and even necessary—to distinguish between metaphor and *metaphor*, and to say with Ricoeur[12] that Heidegger's text is filled with a particular type of metaphor (the "living" metaphor), different from the one Heidegger criticizes.[13] We can, however, already propose a different explanatory hypothesis: Perhaps Heidegger's text is overrun by metaphor. It does not control it: Expelled, metaphor comes back, uninvited, all the time, which would explain the occasional reaction, at times almost violent, of the author and master. We ought then to distinguish between declarations of intent and textual facts, and ask two separate sets of questions: (1) How does Heidegger see metaphor, how does he see his own "usage" of language, and why does he reject metaphor?[14] (2) How does metaphor function in Heidegger's text, and how does language work there, irrespective of all of the author's explicit statements and of his inferable position?

Is it possible to prove that Heidegger's text is filled with metaphors? In order to do so, would it suffice to define metaphor and check whether an object corresponding to such a definition is present in the text, in which form, in which proportion, and with which effects on the text itself? An attempt of this kind (which I shall undertake) could yield some interesting results. However, this sort of analysis remains inevitably insufficient and secondary in the elaboration of a question that does not tolerate too strong a framing for its initial position, even less a definitive limitation of its scope.

DELIMITING THE FIELD

Operative Notion of Metaphor

Once again, I shall draw the essential traits of the provisional definition of metaphor, which I gave in chapter 1.

No text is "legible" in the absence of a net of references, which we shall call "context." We call "metaphor" an occurrence whose interpretation requires the activation of a supplementary context in addition to the "ordinary" context of a discourse. The ordinary context is the minimal context determined by the genre and object of discourse, the situation and quality of the enunciator and the reader, the language used, and so on. All of this is projected onto the level of the reader, who alone can actualize the context, which is therefore always different from one reader to the other. Elements participating in the composition of ordinary context vary in number and type. No discourse is accessible in the absence of ordinary context. But comprehension of a particular occurrence is not always guaranteed by the ordinary context alone, in which case (which is, for instance, the case of metaphor) a supplementary context can be activated.

Metaphor's peculiarity resides in the fact that both contexts (ordinary and supplementary) are simultaneously active. Metaphor thus takes place at the intersection of two different contexts, of which the second is foreign to the isotopy (that is, to the initial interpretable configuration) of the text. If the activation of supplementary contexts does not modify the noncomprehension of the occurrence, then there is no metaphor: The occurrence remains irreducibly foreign to the discourse, which will not necessarily prevent it from possibly producing other types of effects. However, one other condition is required by metaphor: The intersection of the two contexts must not be gratuitous (in this case one would rather speak of "image," in the surrealist sense of the term), but instead motivated by an *analogical trait*. The question whether this trait is anterior to the metaphoric occurrence itself, or instituted by it, is a very important one, in view of the analysis of Heidegger's text, but also, in general, in view of the central problems facing this enquiry.

Sample of Texts

I have chosen, for my attempt at analyzing metaphor's incidence in Heidegger's text, the essays collected under the title *Unterwegs zur Sprache*. The volume includes texts first published or read in public between 1950 and 1959.

This choice is partly based on the following: (1) In the later Heidegger, and more particularly in these texts, the usage of "metaphors" is more apparent, the proximity to poetic discourse is more pronounced, and the necessity of submitting to close scrutiny the titles of philosophical legitimization of such a discourse is more evident than elsewhere in his work; (2) the immediate topics of this collection of texts often coincide with the preoccupations which are at the heart of the present enquiry; and (3) the situation of *Unterwegs zur Sprache* appears to be central in Heidegger's work, and in a current of thinking that stems from it (focusing on the question of language, though in a very different way from the linguistic disciplines).

However, it remains true that the choice is in part arbitrary and accidental, which is both inevitable and justifiable, given the exploratory character of this inquiry.

METAPHOR IN
UNTERWEGS ZUR SPRACHE

The first task is the determination of the ordinary context of this group of texts. Such a determination will necessarily and always remain incomplete and subjective, not only because of lack of information, but also for more essential reasons. In effect, ordinary and extraordinary contexts do not exist a priori, in the void and as absolute entities, but only in the presence of the instance which actualizes them: the reader. It follows from this that the actualizing instance, in the very act of bringing the contexts to life, is also bound to modify them. This means that a text is not immutable; it can never remain the same, since the contexts through which it is read change with each reader.

A few elements can nevertheless be listed as very general points of reference. For instance, the German language, as used in the intellectual exchange in cultivated circles of the time, obviously constitutes the largest part of the ordinary context of these texts. Furthermore, the genre, to which the author's history and position in the field of philosophy assigns them, immediately activates a supplementary specification: that of the "philosophical tradition," with all its distinctive traits. The situation of the enunciation (conference, dialogue, and so forth), as well as Heidegger's previous production, actively contributes to modifying and defining the ordinary context.

This context activates a system of expectations at the lexical, syntactic, rhetoric, connotational (and other) levels, within which, for instance, certain occurrences inventoried in the traditional vocabulary of philosophy, or already introduced, defined and "systematized" in previous works by the same author, will not be unexpected, nor will they be perceived as metaphorical, in most circumstances and at least by a knowledgeable reader.

Within the framework that I have just defined and described, the frequent intervention of extraordinary contexts, called upon by Heidegger's text in order to make certain otherwise incongruous occurrences interpretable, cannot be overlooked. On the contrary, it is a phenomenon of massive proportions. Very often the supplementary context activated is simply the so-called natural (or ordinary) language, when this is unexpectedly "applied" to an occurrence that belongs to the lexicon of philosophy, or else to the domain of that which is questioned in a philosophical text, and which therefore, one would presume, ought to be treated by employing philosophical instruments. Occurrences belonging to natural language will not automatically become metaphorical by virtue of their inclusion in a philosophical discourse. This will only happen as a result of a specific interference with the code (we can call it "the grammar") and the vocabulary that we perceive (but this is always a temporary and local quality, determined by the ordinary context) as properly philosophical.

An example extracted from "Die Sprache" will give us the opportunity to observe (without any commentary at this stage) a metaphorical occurrence of this kind: "[In jedem Falle] gehört die Sprache in die nächste Nachbarshaft des Menschenwesen":[15]

(1)	Language
(2a)	belongs
(2b)	to the closest neighborhood
(3)	of man's being

We can divide this enunciation in three parts and describe them as follows:

(1) philosophical terminology (or object of inquiry);
(2) metaphor (intervention of ordinary language—*gehören*, "to belong," "to have a place," "to be near something"—in metaphorical position; the analogical trait is clearly supported by the ideas of "location" and "proximity"); and
(3) philosophical terminology.

The secondary context[16] is not always connected to the ordinary language. At times it is constituted by a poetic context, that is, quotations from poems or "poetic" metaphors (metaphors usually included in the language of poetry). An extraordinary context is sometimes activated by means of etymological explanations, no matter whether "true" or "false."[17] Within the theoretical framework that I have chosen in order to describe metaphor, there is little doubt that Heidegger's text is full of metaphors.[18] At least, it is full of occurrences that, to be made comprehensible, require the intervention of an unexpected context, next to the ordinary one. As to the quality of those metaphors, a first important distinction must be made between *light* and *heavy* ones. Since philosophical language (and Heidegger's particularly) is neither very formalized nor subject to a rigorous grammar, resorting to ordinary language is frequent and does not usually cause any shock. Many intrusions of ordinary language are therefore indeed metaphorical when applied to a discourse of the philosophical genre, but their force is weak and they tend to pass unobserved, without exercising a significant influence on the interpretation of the text. However, other metaphors have a much stronger influence, especially when occurrences charged with psychological, poetic, or even "pathetic" connotations (such as the metaphor of the abyss) are associated with philosophy's terminology and mode of discourse. If one looks closely at the typology of Heidegger's metaphors, it appears that most of them concern "the place," "the path," the movement of "approaching." One other group concerns the act of "listening." But metaphorical occurrences can be found in respect of all the diverse semantic fields that are active in *Unterwegs zur Sprache*. Greisch[19] identifies and classifies them (not exhaustively, I think) as follows:[20]

(1) "gesture" and "gestation" (*Austragen, Gebärden*);
(2) "trace" and "opening" (of a path);
(3) "own," "proper," "appropriation," and "event" (*Ereignis, Enteignen, Er-äugen*);
(4) "gift," "giving," and "donation" (*Er-gebnis, es gibt*);
(5) "rupture" and "separation" (*Schied*), "duplication" (*Zwiefalt*), and "tear" (*Riss*);
(6) "joint" (*Fuge*);
(7) the "vocative" and the "saying" (*Geheiss, Läuten, Sage*); and
(8) the "semantic" and the "signification" (*Zeige, Anzeige*).

Furthermore, we must take into account the function of Heidegger's metaphors. As far as strong metaphors are concerned, their function appears to be central and important. Since the relevance of the argumentative procedures that are usual in philosophy is very reduced here, "metaphorical flashings"—together with other textual strategies, such as tautological formulas and etymological references—almost entirely support the (so to speak) "positive" weight of Heidegger's discourse. They open a space of meaning that is not immediately saturated (as is normally the case in philosophy) through procedures of modification (defining, structuring, systematizing, dialectizing, and so on). In short, metaphor in *Unterwegs zur Sprache* opens up a possibility of meaning and leaves it in suspense.

Heidegger and Metaphor

Heidegger's text seems to entertain deep and complex relations with metaphor. Deep, because it appears to be intensely affected and even covertly governed by movements of a metaphoric order.[21] Complex, because these movements are not openly accepted by the text itself, but instead subjected to a sort of blackout, disguise, or denial. But what does "to be intensely affected and even covertly governed by movements of a metaphoric order" actually mean? It could mean that the text is subservient to a principle of metaphorical displacement of meaning; that it develops according to the laws of analogy, perhaps in opposition to other, stricter laws, for instance those of logic. Not entirely without necessity, possibly, but—if so—according to a kind of necessity of which a philosopher would know that it is not the only one, and suspect that it is the wrong one for this particular type of discourse. It seems therefore that Heidegger's text abandons itself to a form of specious enticement.

A text, Heidegger's text, proceeds along a certain path. On the ground of its ordinary context, we would have believed that it was advancing in the direction that the philosophical tradition has marked and delimited. But no, we realize that it begins to wander, to lose itself more and more—in vagueness, poetry, mysticism, analogy, tautology, contradiction, the unspeakable. It does not reach its destination, and will never reach it.[22] Why? Because it might have taken the wrong turn, followed the wrong guide: metaphor, analogy, instead of reason and strict logic. But why wrong? If we did not wish to prejudge the issue, we should rather say "a certain turn," different from the one we might have expected. A metaphoric turn, denied by the author, which certainly complicates matters. But there is a further complication. This text, in fact, performs, or endures, something special regarding metaphor.

According to Greisch,[23] "the originality of Heidegger's thought is not the result of a new theory of metaphor." Indeed one cannot find, in his published works, an attempt to establish new theoretical foundations for metaphor. However, Greisch also thinks that Heidegger realizes the inadequacy of the theoretical basis on which the current notion of metaphor is erected.[24] This, on the contrary, seems to me highly unlikely. I believe that Heidegger accepts without problem the traditional notion of metaphor, and consequently condemns it with no possibility of appeal. Metaphor, whether living or dead,[25] is always for him caught in the circle of representation, technique [*Technik*], and metaphysics.

But something else takes place in this text in connection with metaphor, at a deeper level than that of intentions and declarations. This text breaks metaphor. Simultaneously, it breaks up, it breaks down, it stops, it is paralyzed; it suffers and causes suffering.

Grayness

"A certain grayness opposed a certain intoxication":[26] this is how Henri Birault figuratively describes the difference between Heidegger and Nietzsche. If one decided to accept this description, one would be tempted to classify it (a bit hastily?) and therefore contain it under the label of "style" or character: a fiery temper, a flamboyant writing (Nietzsche) against a cautious and slow disposition, an earnest and at times even boring writing (Heidegger).[27] Birault has no doubts. Heidegger's text is not only difficult, as it should be in the case of a discourse belonging to the philosophical genre, and therefore to a tradition that, since Heraclitus at least, has very seldom praised (and even less often practiced) easiness and immediate accessibility. It is also rather sparing (albeit not entirely devoid) of those legitimate joys that the act of reading is, in principle, entitled to: pleasures of aesthetic order, linked to the quality of the linguistic fabric, to the beauty and force of the discursive edifice, to its ability to strike and capture the reader's imagination.

A certain amount of dryness could indeed find precedents and justifications in the tradition of a textual production that tends to avoid the brilliance of surfaces and formal attraction, which in particular wishes to do without the rhetorical stratagems to which it could resort in order to captivate the reader. From this point of view, then, Nietzsche's "intoxication" finds itself in a difficult position and poses problems concerning its identity and legitimacy. But things are not that simple. On the one hand, in effect, the aridity of Heidegger's text does not come from an austere determination to only employ, among the resources of language, the strictly conceptual instruments, the most pared down logical articulations. On the contrary, this text apparently (and voluntarily, I should say, albeit with all the implicit reserves that such a comment requires in Heidegger's case) moves in the direction of polysemy, of analogy, of poetry. Whence the impression of grayness, then? What exactly is the reason for the apparent sadness, for the suffering in Heidegger's writing?

As a first step, I shall conventionally define as "suffering" the effect of that which, in Heidegger's text, binds restraint and rigor with abandonment and freedom. Suffering is the result of a peculiarly uncomfortable position in which the discourse obstinately and consistently forces itself, and which it consequently forces upon the reader. In fact, suffering in Heidegger's text appears to be the lot of the reader in the first place: the reader is ill at ease, something is denied to his pleasure.

My second step is the following: The reader, who suffers in Heidegger's text, suffers in connection with metaphor. Something happens, in Heidegger's metaphors, that makes the reader suffer. In fact metaphor itself, in this text, is "on sufferance": It is tolerated (with bad grace), it waits, it suffers, and is a cause of sufferings. It cannot freely deploy itself, it is prevented from accomplishing its trajectory, from finding its ground again. But an objection takes shape immediately: Why should the *philosopher*/reader suffer from this state of things? Isn't philosophy precisely the place where metaphor must *suffer*, suffer a limitation, a compression, must be put "on sufferance" so that another letter can reach its destination, the good letter,[28] the one in which truth declares itself literally, without rhetorical deviations, without seductive and dangerous disguises?

In Heidegger's text, perhaps, metaphor suffers, but not enough. Perhaps it is not dead, not absent, not absent enough to ensure the philosopher's satisfaction. It shows, shamelessly, its suffering. It shows itself, instead of disappearing, instead of hiding. It shows itself, but not in its full glory: It appears in humiliation and sorrow. Condemned, disavowed, and nevertheless present, always there, waiting. Exposed and disowned, deprived of its credentials and even of its name, but unerasable, unsuppressable, impossible to exorcise.

Suffering

> "Pain is the benignity in the nature of all essential being."
> —Martin Heidegger[29]

The philosopher (Heidegger's reader, in the first instance) suffers thus from the *presence* of metaphor! We are somewhat reassured: It is not metaphor's suffering, its indefinite waiting, that bothers the philosopher, but the faux pas or the bad faith of a text that, mixing genres and losing control (or pretending to lose control, perhaps not without premeditation and gain, somewhere, one suspects) allows itself to be invaded by dangerous plants and inebriating flowers, and cannot manage to destroy them, in spite of its stated (but unconvincing) desire to do so. Metaphor is "on sufferance" in Heidegger's text, it suffers, and makes us suffer. The author himself is perhaps not exempted from this strange condition. What if all the uncanny and difficult quality of Heidegger's text were due not simply to metaphor's presence, but rather to a distortion, or malformation, or perversion of Heidegger's metaphor? If what makes Heidegger so unpleasant to read were nothing more than the coitus interruptus of his metaphorical dashes? Perhaps Heidegger's text is "ill," and its illness may have something to do with metaphor. Is it ill *because* of the presence of metaphor? No. If it were simply and openly governed by metaphor, it would be in perfect health. What makes it ill is perhaps this: that it breaks the contract between thinking and representation, it persistently sabotages the work of representation.

In Heidegger's text the link between reason and metaphor is exposed, and simultaneously the central mechanism of philosophical reason is blocked. The analogical movement, controlled and overcome (in the sense of the *Aufhebung*), which ensures the articulations of philosophical discourse, is interrupted, not accidentally and provisionally, but systematically and permanently. The hypothesis surfaces: What if the principle of reason were in the end a "principle of metaphor"?[30] An obligation of metaphor? A metaphorical imperative, legislating that nothing of what is thinkable can be thought without the intervention of an analogical trait? There is—there shall be—no thought outside analogy, outside representation, outside the representational calculability of the world. Metaphor would then be the true (albeit hidden) root of the entire scaffolding of thought, control, and exploitation that constitutes such a large part of this technological, logical, and philosophical epoch. This is precisely Heidegger's hypothesis.

I said, with Birault, that Heidegger's text is difficult, but, more than that, it is unpleasant, hard to endure, repetitive, and boring. The text is slow, heavy, at times even opaque in its density. If this cannot be brought down (only) to a question of style, what sort of reason can we find for this? Quite clearly the reasons will have to concern the specificity of Heidegger's thought, and I have already underlined the one that appears to be the most important one. But there are others that throw some additional light on certain aspects of Heidegger's philosophical writing. For instance, there certainly is a ritual and magic value in the modulation of Heidegger's text. Its rhythm, at times obsessive, reminds us of certain rites, resembles a litany, seems to conjure up a sacred atmosphere rather than provide a demonstration of philosophical theses. This aspect of Heidegger's prose has been underlined by others, not without justification. However, there is another aspect that I wish to stress here: Heidegger's text gives an impression also of mourning. What is being mourned in this text? What name is constantly, obsessively repeated?

Evidently, the name of metaphysics, of representation, of philosophy. Heidegger does not carry through the mourning of metaphysics, or of his own failure to overcome metaphysics. He remains on the threshold of mourning, in a permanent half-mourning. The suffering of his text is therefore imperfect, survival is guaranteed but the cost is the grayness and pain of half-failure, the perpetual coming and going, signaling the impossibility of either leaving once and for all metaphysics' circle of centripetal attraction, or finding peace within it. Hence the writing's insuperable and indefinite mourning.

Control

Heidegger's text, unveiling the essential conjunction of oblivion of the being and the domination/exploitation of the world, abjures philosophy as the will to total mastery of thought and world, and signals at the same time its own inability to accomplish itself as a perfectly controlled system. On another level, however, the degree of control that the text exerts or wishes to exert over itself is very high. If Heidegger's writing is gray, this is also perhaps because it wants to dominate itself too much. In order not to lose itself, it forces itself to be slow, heavy, and opaque. For Heidegger, philosophy loses itself by throwing itself blindly along the paths of reason, calculation, representation; from this point of view, paradoxically, a scientific text is therefore the most lost of all. In order not to lose oneself, one must, on the contrary, lose as much as possible of all reassuring points of reference, though slowly, feeling the pain of loss and even the anguish of risk—and then jump.

"We do not wish to assault language in order to force it into the grip of ideas already fixed beforehand."[31] No logico-scientific structure, no current metaphor, no established idea is adequate to the task: There are no instruments ready for use. One must, on the contrary, open a path, stop repeatedly, come back, start again, move slowly, stop again. "In thinking there is neither method nor theme, but rather the region."[32] There is therefore, strictly speaking, no path to follow, nor even the instruments to open one. There is only one condition of departure, the condition for all questioning: that on which the question rests must have already spoken.[33] An appeal is required, before anything else: "To undergo an experience with something means that this something, which we reach along the way in order to attain it, itself pertains to us, meets us and makes its appeal to us, in that it transforms us into itself."[34] There in no method, no scientific proof, that would be too easy: "If it were merely an assertion, we could set out to prove its truth or falseness. That would be easier by far than to endure the imposition or make our peace with it."[35] Of course one can always write or philosophize following the paths already open for the exploitation and the control of the world, this is actually entirely legitimate. That would be, for Heidegger, a way of losing without getting lost at the same time; one does not lose one's way, since the paths are already marked. This, however, implies the radical loss of the possibility of a more fundamental experience. To feel this loss, to feel it as intolerable, this is the signal of the onset of the other movement, of the other link, the one that one cannot justify because it operates at a different level from that of reason and representation.

Are we confronted with an irrational movement of thought? There certainly is no way of logically proving that we must think in the direction indicated by Heidegger. But is this enough to disqualify Heidegger's enterprise as a sand castle built on nothing else but a bizarre and obscurely destructive drive? Another hypothesis surfaces; I shall mention it very quickly.

We might suppose that, at the end of a path of thought that is still essentially classical (that is, as early as _Sein und Zeit_[36]), Heidegger reaches the point where discourse breaks down; words become inadequate, go missing. This is perhaps the precondition of the "step back": "This breaking up of the word is the true step back [_der Schritt zurück_] on the way of thinking."[37] It is where the word goes missing that we are put in a position to begin to think the essence of language. At that point the interrogation of the linguistic fact becomes unavoidable, and one is led to conduct it in a radical fashion, by revoking (at least temporarily) the faith one might have lent to current representations of language. From this, to the radical questioning of representation as such, is not a large step. The following step would consist, understandably, in revoking the privilege enjoyed by representation in general, as well as by its first acolyte, metaphor, as the initial and necessary premise for a new reflection, for a new thought.

Let's imagine that we can actually comprehend the reasons for the "step back" and the disavowal of metaphor. What happens when we try to "withdraw" or erase metaphor? A ("catastrophic") generalization of metaphor, says Derrida.

But is there one possible "retreat" of metaphor only? Evidently there are more; for instance, there is the retreat proper to the philosophical tradition, where metaphor is withdrawn to make space for concept. This type of retreat is very different from the one to which Heidegger applies himself. It is possible, however, that—in their difference—the different retreats have this in common: that they do not—they cannot—do without metaphor. Of this, Heidegger's discourse is proof. This discourse, even more than philosophy's traditional discourse, and for reasons which are even more essential, wants to do without metaphor, but cannot take place, does not have a place, without it. In its way of avoiding metaphor, therefore, it can only, in part at least, and in a peculiar fashion, reproduce it, once again.

THE STRUCTURE AND FUNCTION
OF HEIDEGGER'S METAPHOR

Heidegger's metaphor has the structure of a "barred catachresis." A catachresis, because there is no proper name for what is intended (or rather, what "wishes to be said," according to a formulation which is closer to Heidegger); barred, because the analogical trait between metaphor and the unspeakable is annulled (by way of negations, or of a simple overflowing and indeterminacy of metaphors).[38]

Let's take a famous example: that of the abyss [*Abgrund*], of emptiness, of falling:

Language [*Sprache*] is: language, speech. Language speaks. If we let ourselves fall into the abyss denoted by this sentence, we do not go tumbling into emptiness. We fall upward, to a height. Its loftiness opens up a depth. The two span a realm in which we would like to become at home, so as to find a residence, a dwelling place for the life of man.[39]

And now, what is an abyss? What happened to the image, the representation that, by way of analogy, gave us a chance to catch a glimpse of sense? We have only the heap of metaphors without "result": Our terrain becomes slippery and we lose foot. Analogy's operation works in vain. Abyss is a metaphor; but Heidegger's metaphor is itself a bottomless abyss.

Heidegger rejects metaphor as the instrument of representation. He uses it, nevertheless, but only as "open" metaphor: The analogical circle is never closed. Sense is left in freedom, which does not help the definition of discourse, but on the other hand opens a possibility that is not granted by a logically well-defined discourse: the possibility of approaching something (no longer an "object") in a nontechnical, nonlogical, nonmetaphysical way. In the specific case of the quoted passage: to be allowed to sojourn in the speaking of speech (and not in our own scleroticized representations of speech).

Another example of "Heideggerian" metaphor is that of the *appeal*, the calling [*Ruf*], and of *proximity* [*Nähe*]: "The calling here calls into a nearness. But even so the call does not wrest what it calls away from the remoteness, in which it is kept by the calling there."[40] What happened then to the metaphor of proximity? What is proximity, if it "keeps something afar"? In another text the empty core of this metaphor is openly declared: "[nearness] remains unapproachable,"[41] particularly when we try and say something *about* it.

The point here, of course, is not to question Heidegger's right to do what he wants with his metaphors; rather, it is to understand the reasons and effects of his choices, and also to ask ourselves if or to what extent such a discourse is still entitled to call itself "philosophical." But first of all we should remember that this approach to what is essential does not want to be seen as philosophical, does not wish to have anything in common with philosophy. If it isn't philosophy, however, it is still a form of thinking that Heidegger pursues, and not poetry. Meditating (as opposed to calculating) thought is the nonobjectifying approach of that which wants to be thought. Meditating thought, however, does not seem to be able to do without the metaphoric "instrument," modified so as not to fall back within representational thinking, which is strictly connected to (and in fact is a form of) calculation: "[M]odern thinking is ever more resolutely and exclusively turning into calculation. . . ."[42] Not to fall back into calculation means also to abandon "the technical precision of concepts that are merely scientifically univocal."[43] This, however, should not condemn thought to the arbitrary. There is, Heidegger is convinced, a form of plurivocality that does not coincide with ambiguity, a rigor that consists in not allowing any easy representation to make our thought prisoner: Broken metaphor seems to function, and therefore to find its (relative) justification, in this direction.

Heidegger's metaphor bars the possibility of a (utilitarian) *destination* of thought, in the sense that the process can no longer be directed toward an aim to which there corresponds a representation. But, according to Heidegger, this barred possibility reestablishes a more authentic and original destiny, the one to which thought itself must correspond. Metaphors of destiny, destination, sending, are in fact present in Heidegger's text very frequently and heavily. However, it could equally be said that what is left is only the empty form, the skin of destination, so much more insistent because of the radical blackout suffered at its point of arrival.

Heidegger's metaphor could also be described as an idle movement, with which suffering is associated. Suffering is symbolized, as
we shall see, by the poetic image of a petrified threshold, of a paralysis: The impossibility of getting to the light and to grace, and of
coming back to the apparent security of before. Condemned to
eternal darkness, with reason and by his own accord, the agent in
this strange motion pines over the absence of a possible light.[44]

Parenthetically, the tone, which we could describe as "pathetic,"
and which is regularly associated with these meditations, is not something secondary in the economy of Heidegger's discourse. *Pathos*,
which abounds in Heidegger's text and is reflected here, in my own
discourse, is probably not a marginal accident, but a structural effect
of a movement of thought which, on the one hand, does not
renounce (and could not do so) taking itself seriously as thought (that
is, trying to convince) and, on the other hand, must fill the obvious
gaps generated by the situation of impasse that I am describing. In the
absence of the classic, rhetorico-philosophical means of generating
approbation (clarity, structuring, force of the arguments, number and
quality of proofs, and so on), a powerful emotional investment, com-
bined with an obscurely sacred atmosphere, holds the reader. But this,
it cannot be sufficiently stressed, is not the last word on Heidegger.[45]

Heidegger's metaphors are very often linked, or organized
around a central metaphorical core (for instance the "place," the
"approach," the "listening," and so on). The structuring effect that
could derive from the disposition of metaphors in constellations or
suites, however, is regularly disarmed by the presence of powerful
"negative" metaphors (the abyss is no doubt the most striking) or
other unsettling procedures (for instance, the investment in word
etymologies) aiming at producing a suspension of representation.
We could consider, by way of example, the theme of the *Ereignis*:
As soon as the semantic core of *Ereignis* runs the risk of appearing

too "positive," the notion of *Enteignis* intervenes, as an unsettling corrective. It is the same procedure at work in the case of barred metaphor: When meaning shows a tendency to solidify in a representational disposition (which happens regularly), it is imperative to put it in circulation again, or rather in sufferance. It is imperative, because "language holds its own origin and so denies its being to our usual notions [*geläufigen Vorstellen*],"[46] and actually to representation generally. We must avoid representation, if we want to think truly.

Nonrepresentational thinking, and not conceptual thinking, even less abstract conceptual thinking, would be (if it could exist, which is not granted) the truly rigorous thinking. Attacking the alliance of metaphor/representation with concept/abstraction, attacking the complicity of *meta-* (metalanguage, metaphor, metaphysics), does not mean, therefore, renouncing the rigor of thought, but precisely finding it again. Thought wants to find again the marvel of its origins, which was generated by the happening of being. The "putting in relation" of everything with everything, the domination of analogical structures and calculation, all this has obscured our perception of the "being there."

Are we, then, in the presence of a metaphysics of the origin, of the authentic (*Eigentlichkeit*), of the lost purity that it is our duty to recover? There is this aspect, too, in Heidegger's thought, but it is not the most significant. Also, it should be noted that, to Heidegger's eyes, the technico-metaphysical detour of our history was not gratuitous and useless, so that the point is not, simply and perhaps violently, to abandon it.[47] The unthinkable epoch which opens at the end of this one, as well as the almost impracticable thought which opens at the end of philosophy, do not constitute simply a return back to the origins. Something new, albeit connected (but how, by what link?) to what happened in the beginnings of our epoch, is approaching.

The idea of nonrepresentational thinking could hide an excellent[48] cover-up, aimed at defending philosophy, as nonscientific and nontechnical knowledge, and attacking scientific and technical powers. How to get out of the powerful grip of logical thought? It is sufficient to deny it the quality of absolute control. It remains to explain, naturally, just why this denial is legitimate, and to make acceptable this denial which, for structural reasons, cannot be logically justified. How? Through procedures that are eminently _rhetorical_, that is, strategies of a psychological, textual or contextual kind, aimed at producing consensus, or an effect of sacred "aura" in which the only truly essential thesis is stated, the one that takes back from the sciences (and from philosophy as traditionally conceived) the power to reach truth (the essence of being), putting it in the hands of the new avatar of philosophy itself: meditating thought. In this strategy, poetry functions at the same time as a point of access and an area where work can be done. All protocols for the access to and control over reality remain firmly in the hands of science, understood as the domain of definitions, experiences, proofs, results. Poetry sustains the new thought and authorizes it as the trustee of its own truth: It functions therefore in all respects as a sacred text, with one difference only, that in this case the commentary is meant to go further than the text on which it exerts itself. I shall come back to this after a more systematic confrontation of Heidegger's writing.

The Structure of "Die Sprache"

I intend to analyze, as an example, the rhetorical structure of "Die Sprache," the first text in the selection included in _Unterwegs zur Sprache._ My aim is to shed some light on Heidegger's discursive strategy and on the role played by broken metaphor and poetry within this strategy.

I will start by giving a description of the main articulations of the text and of the logico-rhetorical resources that are at work in it.

Textual Articulations

"Die Sprache" develops along the following main discursive articulations:

- *Beginning:* Heidegger highlights the close relationship existing between man and speech. Representation attempts to provide a general idea of what language is.
- *Heidegger's "project":* Not to throw ourselves on language in order to capture it, but to bring ourselves to the site of its being, in order to sojourn there. An abysmal link exists between language and reason (*logos*). We must not run away from the abyss. There is a positiveness of the abyss.
- *Traditional and current opinions of language:* These focus on the ideas of expression, activity, and representation. The "exactness" of these ideas is not in dispute. However, something (the essential) is not conveyed by them: language as such. Where can we find it? In poetry. The poem is "the spoken" in its purest state.
- *The poem:* Trakl, "Ein Winterabend." By examining its contents and describing its form "we would still remain confined by the notion of language that has prevailed for thousands of years."[49] Things and world are called by the poem.[50] The point is not to represent or to express, but *to call.* "Difference" is the intimacy of world and things. It escapes representation, as it is neither distinction nor relationship; rather, "Dimension" and "Pain."
- *Conclusion:* Language does not belong to man, but the opposite. However, it needs man. The poetic regime of language is

the most normal, appropriate, fundamental, and essential one. Making sounds and expression is not the decisive element in human speech; the way in which mortals speak is by responding [*das Entsprechen*].[51] One must learn to inhabit language's speech.

Logico-rhetorical Resources

As concerns what I called "logico-rhetorical resources," one notices in this text:

- affirmative and negative *statements*, made without any demonstration ("the instrumental and expressive idea of language drives us away from its essence," "language makes man, not the opposite," "poetry is the site par excellence where the essence of language appears," and so on);
- *statements subjected to critique*, mostly attributed to the philosophical tradition, to ordinary experience, or to scientific discourse;
- *questions* (for example: "What about speech?" "What does speaking mean?" "Why?" "Where?" "What is suffering?");
- *citations of poetic texts* (Trakl);
- *commentaries* on poetic texts cited;
- *light metaphors*;
- *heavy metaphors*;
- *tautologies* (*die Sprache spricht*); and
- *neologisms*, or at least cores of disarticulation and rearticulation of meaning in correspondence with some semantic families (*Unter-Schied*, *Geviert*, and so on).

Metaphors

A simple list of occurrences that, on the basis of the previous discussion, we could call metaphorical (light and heavy), would suffice to give an idea of the quantitative and qualitative weight of metaphor in "Die Sprache." Interestingly for us, as the reader can easily ascertain firsthand, it is impossible not to see that a good deal of the text's argumentative weight clearly rests on a series of *barred* metaphors: among the heavier, we shall discuss in the following pages those connected with the ideas of "path/residence" (distance/proximity), "abyss," and (within the citation-commentary of the poem) "difference" and "suffering."

It should be noted that this text is not at all exceptional from this point of view. On the contrary, it is quite representative of Heidegger's writing, at least within *Unterwegs zur Sprache*.

The Poem

A Winter Evening

Window with falling snow is arrayed,
Long tolls the vesper bell,
The house is provided well,
The table is for many laid.

Wandering ones, more than a few,
Come to the door on darksome courses.
Golden blooms the tree of graces
Drawing up the earth's cool dew.

Wanderer quietly steps within;
Pain has turned the threshold to stone.
There lie, in limpid brightness shown,
Upon the table bread and wine.

—Georg Trakl[52]

What is the function of Trakl's poem in "Die Sprache"? It is clear, for a start, that poetry finds itself there in an element that is different from its normal one. In "Die Sprache" we are not within a poetic discursive space, but in a philosophical type of discourse, in which the poem appears as a textual fragment of another kind.

By what right is it present there? What does Heidegger do, in a philosophical text, with Trakl, or rather, with his poem, since in truth there is very little mention of Trakl himself?[53] Taking into account his explicit declarations, as well as what has just been said, we can exclude the possibility that Heidegger is using it for metaphorico-allegorical purposes (for example, to provide a representation, an illustration of what *die Sprache* may be), as, however, it would only be logical to expect. Heidegger states his position repeatedly in *Unterwegs zur Sprache*: In meditating thought there is neither representation, nor illustration, least of all of a concept or doctrine. However, *die Sprache* is eminently present in poetry. But why, then, this poem and not another one? Does this poem *say* something special concerning language? How, in which language, in which type of discourse? If we are to exclude that the poem may be used metaphorically, how do we justify that Heidegger makes it say what it does not say explicitly, literally? What operation does Heidegger perform on the poem, if it is not (and we know it is not) a case of interpreting, transposing, applying, and explaining images? We know Heidegger's reply to at least some among these questions: In the poem, language presents itself in its maximum degree of purity. The choice of the poem is not arbitrary; great poetry (it is not the poet that counts, but no other criterion is provided to discriminate) rests in a special proximity to the truth of language. The poem says something: what it evokes, thought thinks, or perhaps will think.

Of course, it would not be difficult to respond to those questions with entirely different answers, which perhaps will sound more sensible to some. I will hazard, briefly, the following: Heidegger does not need the poem to draw his conclusions. However, he needs to lean on something that functions as a sacred text, because he has no other means to justify his position, or (as his enemies would say) to ensnare his reader. From a different point of view, nevertheless, even admitting that Heidegger is perhaps not justified in making the poem say what he wants it to say, this does not automatically mean the result of the operation is null and unacceptable from a philosophical point of view. A text generates significant meaning-effects even in the absence of a rational foundation and procedure. It is an absence that, furthermore, should not cause surprise, given that the point of departure of the entire discourse is the revocation of the privilege attributed to logico-representational reason. No text, however, and specifically no commentary, is final, and its effects are never entirely under its author's control. However well founded we may deem Heidegger's attempt to convince us of the *absolute privilege* of both the poem and his own interpretation of it, nothing prevents a further proliferation of possible meanings of the text, beyond the author's intentions. Indeed, this appears to be a necessary movement, if one does not wish to be immobilized by the fascination emanating from Heidegger's text. The poem has generated a philosophical commentary, and this is a fact that leaves behind all doubt concerning the rational foundations of the operation. What especially interests me here, particularly when Heidegger and his relationship to poetic discourse are concerned, is that the poem does not exhaust itself in that commentary, on the contrary, it can very well come to the fore and comment on the operation in which he is engaged, saying something that Heidegger himself could not, and in any case does not, say.

The question (as I have already mentioned) is not one of telling the truth of the poem, or of Heidegger, a truth even more true than Heidegger's. Rather, it is to carry on a commentary that in principle no one is ever allowed to interrupt; to open more possibilities for meaning and, perhaps, to bring to some sort of provisional destination, even against his intentions, some of the paths that Heidegger abandons behind himself. I shall therefore resume the analysis of certain metaphors that are present in Trakl's poem and in Heidegger's commentary, such as the central ones of the "threshold" and "suffering."

Metaphor and Suffering: The Threshold

> *"Pain has turned the threshold to stone."*
>
> —Martin Heidegger[54]

I shall not attempt to reproduce all the extent of Heidegger's analysis of Trakl's poem. I will instead pursue two themes, the "threshold" and "suffering," which seem to concentrate some of the loose threads that I have been weaving so far around the relationship between Heidegger and metaphor. I have already briefly discussed the idea of "suffering"; it now becomes necessary to combine it with that of "limit." I believe I can say, on the strength of the poem and of the commentary, that Heidegger's metaphor is painful because it detains us indefinitely on a threshold (*Schwelle*).

The threshold separates and unites; the threshold is difference, suffering. The suffering metaphor never reaches the interior, where the peacefulness of bread and wine is waiting for it; it stops on the threshold, in the difference. "Normal" metaphor overcomes the threshold that separates the space where meanings rise from that where relations among things take place in an orderly way. Difference is not in itself relationship; it allows a world of relations to take place, to happen, to overcome the pain of separation: This world of relations is the world of metaphor.

Heidegger's metaphor, on the contrary, lives the suffering of the unaccomplished, of the imperfect; it pulls towards darkness, toward the absence of images. To truly think would thus mean, for Heidegger, to loiter in the suffering of the unthinkable, where nevertheless the essential is closer: to endure the threshold, indefinitely and, since immobility is dumb, to come and go on the threshold forever, taking one step in the realm of rising sense, one in the realm of distributed and well-ordained meaning. One could remain this side of the line, in the poetic dimension, or cross it to move into the scientific/philosophical dimension; let oneself go to *song* or to *management* (both, however, can be found on both sides of the threshold). But true thought must suffer the threshold. True thought is neither the unspeakable before song, nor what comes after logic: It is the uncertain balance between song and management—and yet "decided," though not by a will. To come back from management to song, not to stop there, but to go further back. There, however, there is no speech any more; the most advantageous, the most economical point for thought (but, of course, we are dealing with a general economy of loss, not of accumulation) is the threshold. But this is also the most painful point. There is no suffering before the word or after it; there is no pain either in song or in management. If there is any, it is sublimated in song or management. There is, however, pain on the threshold. Not to be able to leave the threshold. To know that, though able to do so, *one cannot leave the threshold.*

To think is to stand at the point of petrified transparency, of absence of reasons and motives, of the incessant flowing of signification. We cannot think without analogy, without representation, *absolutely* without. Nevertheless, we can strive to think to the limit, to the extreme limit of representation, where the "dark paths" begin or end. There is probably no pure thought: neither purely representational nor purely nonrepresentational. However, it is permitted to stretch thought to its limit. This limit is neither to the right nor to the left, but in the middle. On this side of the limit there is no longer thought, but rather poetry (nomination); on that side of the limit there is no longer thought, but rather philosophy (management of metaphors). The task is to approach asymptotically this imaginary line at which nomination ends and representation starts. Or rather, since to remain static would mean to stay silent, the task is to incessantly cross the line, forward and back. Forward to representation (for instance metaphors, albeit always broken), back toward nomination (for instance to etymologism or, more authentically, to the poetic word). In the first instance (broken metaphor) we do not reach our destination; nor do we reach it in the second (etymologism), since the point is not to install ourselves on the terrain of rising meanings, that is, to create or recover meaning, but always to displace it.[55]

The threshold is the "dawning state" of management. We must regress to that limit in order to gain access to and view the whole.

NOMINATION	threshold	MANAGEMENT
poetry	thought	technique
		(philosophy, science)

"Thought" is nothing: It is a threshold, a virtual limit we need to approach the essence of poetry and of technique. If we are within poetry or within technique, we cannot think either. Thought is an hypothesis, a duty. One cannot *found* thought; what one can do is to believe that thought is possible.

Silence and the Word

> "The poet experiences his poetic calling as a call to the word as the
> source, the bourn of Being."
>
> —Martin Heidegger[56]

Metaphor and poetry are often associated, to the extent that the
adjectives "poetic" and "metaphoric" are sometimes used as syn-
onyms. It is evident that such an assimilation is far from acceptable
for Heidegger, who regularly refuses to qualify as metaphorical
occurrences that may appear eminently to be such; who refuses to
link "great poetry" to the dried-up herbarium of metaphor; and
who makes of the latter the instrument of metaphysics in its central
movement.

Let us therefore propose a hypothesis, one which is apparently
paradoxical, but that nevertheless appears almost literally (as we have
seen) in Heidegger's text: High poetry, the kind that shares something essential with meditating thought, has nothing to do with
metaphor. Its apparent metaphors are not what they seem. To stick
to the level of images, representations, in commentary and interpretation, means losing sight of what is most important. But what,
then, is this deeper level that (true) poetry can reach? Is it the same
one that thought reaches? We find a clue to the right path: Heidegger often repeats that poetry *calls, enjoins, names* (*rufen, heißen,
nennen*), and explicitly declares: "The poet himself composes in
virtue of the claim to the names."[57] What, then, is *naming*? "This
naming does not hand out titles, it does not apply terms, but it calls
into the word. The naming calls."[58] What is it that the poem names
and calls? The things, the world. Poetry (the type of discourse
closest to the original dimension of language) *presents* a world. It is
only on the basis of this presentation that *representation, as repro-

duction and generalized placing-in-relation, can take place. "It is only the word at our disposal that endows the thing with Being":[59] Only when the word is there to say it, can the thing be. It is the word that confers presence, that is, being. So, when the word is missing, there is no thing; but it is precisely when the word becomes latent that, in the silence, the essence of speech appears.

How can the essence of something be found in the absence of that very thing? The fact is that when articulated sound is absent, language itself is not absent. There is no hope of reaching a clear notion of what is suggested here: the essence of language is instantly lost, as soon as we try to describe or represent it. We could say that language consists of the articulation of the totality of differences, and thus more of the empty space between elements than of the sum of the elements themselves; this, however, would only be one more representation, as such inevitably leading us in the opposite direction to the one indicated by Heidegger.

In the absence of speech, in the obliteration of all differences, *difference* itself dawns. In the absence of speech, language indicates itself, makes itself visible to itself as appeal. We must avoid thinking that language is the totality of all that is, and can be, said; language entails also (and essentially) the unspeakable. The unspeakable has to do with the essence of language much more than all that is actually said; the unspeakable belongs to language and comes to us when language itself, not man, speaks.

Die Sprache spricht. Language speaks, but why should it say anything special, anything mysteriously essential, at all? Perhaps we ought to interpret Heidegger's thought differently; that is, if there is something to be understood in the relationship between language and being, whatever this something may be, the only place where (but only to a certain extent) we can hope to find it, to understand it, is language itself, and none other. And this precisely where language becomes more opaque, more dense, more intransitive. Hence the privilege accorded to poetry: not, in the first instance, because of a greater proximity to being, but because of a purer self-reflexive presentation of language. Thinking (*Denken*) will attempt, in due course, to extend the effect of such self-presentation in the mode of questioning, of searching, along the path that is its own.

Die Sprache spricht. Language is not (essentially, although from another point of view it most certainly is) expression and communication. It is not man who speaks, but language (*die Sprache*) itself speaks through man. The human being listens to language, which thus takes place, happens (*Ereignis*). The question is not, for Heidegger, one of presenting a new viewpoint on speech; the task is, rather, "to learn how to inhabit the speech of language." Human speech does not rest in itself, but rather in its belonging to language's speech.

Representation, understood as something that, coming before language, founds its ability to name objects and relations, is rejected, for Heidegger does not accept the idea of an original correspondence, based in turn on (faithful) representation, between world and mind. Without language there is neither world, nor mind, nor the kind or relationship between the former and the latter we call representation. Moving toward the roots of language is the same as moving toward being. Between being and language—understood in an ontic sense—there is a difference; however, between being and language as being's opening/retreat (therefore in an ontological sense), there is for us, the mortals, no difference: There is only, in the silence, *difference* itself.

THE THOUGHT OF DIFFERENCE

Difference and Analogy: The Trait

> "The rift-design is the drawing of the essence of language, the well-joined structure of a showing in which what is addressed enjoins the speakers and their speech, enjoins the spoken and its unspoken."
>
> —Martin Heidegger[60]

What is *difference*? We are told that "the word dif-ference is now removed from its usual and customary usage,"[61] that "[difference] consequently no longer means a distinction established between objects only by our representations."[62] Heidegger's difference, whatever it may be, is in any case yet another broken metaphor by means of which a perpetual oscillation between representation and "beyond representation," between speakable and unspeakable, is maintained. This oscillation is the characteristic trait of the last Heidegger. When we try to translate the oscillation into a more logical code we inevitably end up by betraying Heidegger's intention, as the following attempts will show.

"In the naming, which calls things and the world, what is actually named is difference."[63] Nomination is not an isolated act, only concerning the thing and the name: It only takes place within the difference between thing and world. The thing does not exist in isolation: To name a thing means to name (metonymically, we could say, but against Heidegger) its position in relation to the context without which it is nothing, it means to exploit or institute a network of traits.

The analogic trait is perhaps, from one point of view, one the possible specifications of relationship in general (of difference): Analogy, in other words, is one among the possible forms of difference. The trait, however, may very well be more than that: From another point of view, since it cannot be founded, it is "co-origi-nary" with difference and comes before any possibility of "seeing" any difference, any analogy within language and in the world:

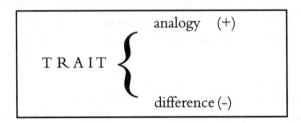

Difference is not simple; at the level on which it is possible to establish classifications (and of course on this level, according to Hei-degger, we miss the essential), difference is at least fourfold: (1) object-world, (2) object-name, (3) name-language, (4) language-world.

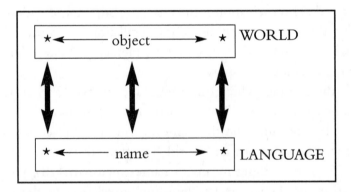

Language, in naming the thing, activates difference: There is no world without a language instituting it as a system of differences. Likewise, a language cannot exist without a world that corresponds to it; what we call here "a world," of course, is not necessarily one and the same with the physical world.

Language does not all the time show this founding relationship: According to Heidegger, it is precisely at the site of its own essence that language disappears, refusing to become speech. In its day-to-day functioning, however, language conceals the founding relationship beneath the system of its actual occurrences, and this—far from being accidental and remediable—corresponds to an intrinsic necessity: "Only because in everyday speaking language does *not* bring itself to language but holds back, are we able simply to go ahead and speak a language, and so to deal with something and negotiate something by speaking."[64] What does "bringing itself to speech" mean? As we have seen, for Heidegger speech reveals its innermost dimension as language there precisely, where we *do not find* the right word for something. An "is" appears where the word goes missing. Here the instrumental function of language is eclipsed, and language becomes visible; precisely when the word is missing, because it is missing, one can catch a glimpse, for an instant, of the shadow of pure difference, of pure relationship, of the *Zwischen*, the suffering of the world.

Difference is pain. But it appeases too: "It stills by letting things rest in the world's favor. It stills by letting the world suffice itself in the thing."[65] Difference appeases the thing as thing by placing it in the world. But language as the sound of peace only echoes in the silence.

The word (and not the sentence) is the constitutive element in language for Heidegger; and, still more precisely, the word *as name* (naming, appeal to being). The word, however, is not a thing; the word is the rapport between the thing and being, what causes the thing to be present in being. "If the word did not have this bearing, the whole of things, 'the world,' would sink into obscurity, including the 'I' of the poem. . . ."[66] Once more, language is thus not (essentially) representation; the essence of language is not instrumental or representational, as language does not primarily have the "function" of faithfully reproducing and classifying a world that precedes it. Only through language is there a world. Things, outside language, do not make up a world; and so they do not exist as things, because only within a world are there things. Language alone, as *relationship* between things and world, allows things and world to appear, makes them show themselves, calls them to presence. The essence of language is therefore—language, the fact that language exists and, by existing, calls into being the world and the things.

Die Sprache spricht: Tautology is, in language, the closest one gets to silence. Tautology is therefore what best (but still very imperfectly) allows us to step back into what precedes representation. And there it becomes possible to perceive the essence of language. Any other means (image, metaphor, definition) reproduces the structure of representation, makes language work as representation and therefore misses its object at the very moment when it (illusorily) grasps it. There can be no object in the relationship between thought and language, if the latter's essence is to be safeguarded, because as soon as there is object, the essence of language ceases to be there.

"*Der Blau ist kein Bild für den Sinn des Heiligen.*"[67] Blue *is* the Sacred: It is not a metaphor for the Sacred. The link blue = Sacred is not metaphorical, but essential. Tautology and nomination, as we can see, play in Heidegger's discourse against metaphor and representation. Here an abyss opens up, into which we are supposed to jump headfirst; here, according to Heidegger, we can hope to have access to truth. "Normal" metaphor deftly jumps over this abyss and finds itself once again on safe ground; Heidegger's metaphor falls into it. But in this fall into the abyss, so Heidegger assures us, we do not become lost.

Poetry is the site where language (thanks to its "poetic," anti-instrumental quality) is closest to the "naming" (and not reproductive) power which is its core. It is therefore toward poetry that one should look for this abyss and for this nonobjectual truth. In (true) poetry language emerges as the dawning of sense. This, as we saw, is for Heidegger incompatible with the operation of metaphor, which is based on a movement of "placing-in-relationship" based on preexisting analogic traits. It follows that, for Heidegger, it is not metaphor that brings into existence the analogic trait, but vice versa. It is not analogy (resemblance) that institutes the analogic trait: For resemblance to become visible, the analogic trait (which is invisible) must already be there. Here, it would be tempting to let oneself go to the mystique of the inexplicable. Once again, we can try to resist the temptation, even if this means running the risk of distorting the deepest intention of Heidegger's text.

We could then suppose that proximity (the trait) is not given from a mysterious and superior place, through the intervention of some mysterious agency. Nor is it merely the result of the relationship among the elements present. Rather, we could see it as the effect of all relations; as the world, which cannot be entirely "in presence," and which in turn is only a world within the opening of a language. A language that, as original saying, is, according to Heidegger, the relationship of all relations.

Where do analogic traits come from? It is a gift: *es gibt.* They are there, buried in the heart of presence; there is no point in asking whether they come before or after naming. Poetry calls things, by naming them, into difference. "Where has it ever been *seen* that there is the same relation between the sun and its rays as between sowing and seeds?" asks Derrida.[68] Nowhere; the sun, within a certain world, in a certain language, is trapped in a network of relations that allows some room for the analogic trait on which that particular metaphor rests, whether it is ever uttered as actual occurrence or not.

And metaphor? Is it then something posterior to the system of relations? Or is it precisely what constitutes that system? How does a system of relations become constituted?[69] From Heidegger's point of view there is no doubt, as we have pointed out, concerning metaphor's constitutive secondarity. As for myself, I cannot help feeling that Heidegger's world, for instance, the world at least of *Unterwegs zur Sprache*, is largely (though possibly not "originarily") constituted by a fluid system of relationships instituted by a few metaphors; which, however, does not in any way solve the problem at hand. The question must remain open for a while longer.

Poetry and Thought

> *"Both poetry and thinking are distinctive Saying in that they remain delivered over to the mystery of the word as that which is most worthy of their thinking, and thus ever structured in their kinship."*
> —Martin Heidegger[70]

The kinship between poetry and thought is not identity. The poetic act does not display an unlimited power to clarify the relationship of being and language: "The poet must relinquish the claim to the assurance that he will on demand be supplied with the name for that which he has posited as what truly is."[71] It is, however, ". . . a genuine renunciation, not just a rejection of Saying, not a mere lapse into silence."[72] In any case, poetry does not think explicitly the relationship that is the essence of speech, and even though it may happen to state it, it cannot do so in the manner that meditation does: "The verse calls the difference, but it neither thinks it specifically nor does it call its nature by this name."[73] Meditating thought will therefore have its place here, its legitimation and its charge: to swim up the stream of the resonances of poetic saying, toward the *gift* by which there is language and there is a world.

Meditating thought does not trust traditional representations, nor does it try to shape new ones. As Greisch[74] correctly notes, Heidegger never disputes the "exactness" (_Richtigkeit_) of the analysis of language provided by Western "philosophy of language," and of the conclusions to which it comes. The only question that interests him concerns their representational status, their metaphysical essence; that is, the question of their link with the specific form of conceptual and "representational" thinking.

Thought opens up a space of sense that is not technically organized. What difference is there between thinking and poetry? Poetry can only _call_ by name, thought thinks: It questions nomination. Its instruments (negation, tautology, activation of the _etymon_ and of semantic families) serve[75] the purpose of taking us up the current of signification in the general direction of the source of the appeal: Being. Poetry and thinking rely on the secret of the word, but the secret of the word cannot be found in _a_ word, in a representation, in a concept. It resides in language, which is not the sum of all words. The secret of the word is the ability of language to present a world—not to label a preexisting world, but to make it be—a world that, among other things, enables the use of labels.

Heidegger's broken metaphor upsets the relations among labels, returns language to its original weight, to its constitutive opacity and impenetrability. The vague meaning, barred designation, bring us closer to language as such and not as an instrument for calculation or representation. Language becomes once again an unexplored country. The "project" is, thus, to return language to its extraneity, to its _Unheimlichkeit_, in view of truth. The essence of the world is language, the essence of language is opening, the opening is truth. We, the human beings, are already in the language, in the world, in the truth. Language-world-truth, this is the fundamental rapport: One does not exist without the others. But it is this precisely that eludes us in our daily experience: We do not see how deep we are immersed in language-world-truth, we think of language-world-truth as something external (language = instrument of communication; world = the whole of all objects or perceptions; truth = objective relationship between language and world), and we remain foreign to its unity.

Is it useless to *look for* truth, since we already are in it? One has to *know* that truth is always already there, although it is never at hand. And this is not an instantaneous knowledge: We must *go* there, where we are already. To achieve this aim, the intervention of thought is necessary. Once more, we are not asked to find refuge in a mystical experience of annihilation of apparent reality. And it should be noted that thought's own requirements have nothing to do, of course, with those proper to the fields in which the question concerning objective truth is relevant, since it remains pertinent elsewhere. But as far as thought is concerned, things are otherwise: Thought is condemned to look for a "useless" truth, in which we already are.

Truth is, first of all, action, although not necessarily *our own* action.[76] To think is first of all the commitment by being for being, which translates in a gift of language: "[F]irst of all it is needful that language vouchsafe itself to us."[77] A large component of listening, of submission, is required, since one has to be obedient to what thought has to think.

The essential act of thinking is not questioning: ". . . the authentic attitude of thinking is not a putting of questions—rather, it is a listening to the grant, the promise of what is to be put in question."[78] The essence of acting (*Handeln*) is not in fact the will, but the accomplishment (*Vollbringen*).[79] Thought accomplishes the relationship of being to the essence of man. In order to accomplish this founding relationship we must get away from grammar, from logic, and from the technical interpretation of thought. It is precisely this liberation of language from the ties of "grammatical" constriction, in view of a more "originary" articulation of its element, that is the preserve of thinking and poetry.

Poetry rises in the act itself of the poetic irradiation of language, and—far from mastering it—is entirely subjected to it: "The poet does not keep the names a secret. He does not know them."[80] _Thinking_ wants to go upstream in the direction of this irradiation, to reach the site of the source, of the origin, of the essence, which is also that of destiny and of the unknown.[81] However, thinking, too, is forced to resort to language; how can it resist the flux of language, go upstream, say an origin that is necessarily beyond words? By breaking words and what they represent.

True _poetry_ is the rise of a world, the disclosure of a place accessible to truth, the opening of a dimension and of a path. _Philosophy_ (which is not thinking), on the other hand, is perception of analogies, management of metaphors, elaboration of a field that has been poetically opened up, general establishment of relationships within a world. In every type of discourse there will be, in varying degrees, both poetry and philosophy. The maximum degree of poetry is found in the highest poetic creations; the maximum degree of philosophy is found perhaps in science and technique.

Poetry: nomination, creation, opening of a world
Philosophy: metaphor, analogy, management of the world.

But without poetry nothing can be said (there is no language), without philosophy nothing is intelligible (there is no relation and language is useless). Philosophy, metaphor, analogy, management of the world, technique, forgetfulness of being, all this constitutes one and the same chain, which Heidegger "attacks" in each one of its links. Poetry, country, opening of a world, gift, all this belongs to the domain of the primordial and of the essential toward which, according to Heidegger, thought must direct itself.

As we saw, meditating thinking finds itself on the side of poetry, but distinguishes itself because of the sense, or rather the direction of sense. In poetry sense dawns; in thinking one moves upstream, toward the origin of sense, perpetually (since this origin is not a place one could finally reach). To do that, one must break the crystallizations of sense that make it accessible and easily manageable. And along the path there are for thinking, as well as for poetry, insuperable obstacles and arrests, where the name becomes the signal of the unspeakable: "We can only name it," says Heidegger of the *Ereignis*, "because it will deign no discussion."[82]

However, a fundamental question remains unanswered: Why must we wish to make the effort to struggle up the stream of signification? Why move back, why the *Schritt zurück*? The origin of the "other movement" is unjustifiable and probably (from a certain point of view at least) inadmissible. One must already be caught in a very particular bond (*Bindung*), says Heidegger himself, in order to feel the necessity of the "other movement": "Must we not be bound by a different standard before we can gauge anything in that manner? Of course."[83] We must therefore surrender to a "harsh law": There simply is no ultimate justification for the most essential movement of our thought.

Heidegger's Operation

> "No, nothing is clear; but everything is significant."
> —Martin Heidegger[84]

We have now reached, once again, the limit of the unspeakable in
Heidegger's text. This limit corresponds, in my discourse, to the
point of maximum "listening" and of greatest abandon to the
requirements of that text. An act of rebellion, a centrifugal movement, is presently required. In order to put all this into perspective,
to counterbalance the inevitably mystical effect of Heidegger's text, I
find it both pertinent and useful to take on, albeit provisionally and
without subscribing to it, a point of view that could be described as
external (or as external as possible) not only to this particular text and
its requirements, but also in general to philosophy and to the vested
interests, so to speak, of its agents. From this point of view, it is not
difficult (as I have already briefly indicated) to see what Heidegger's
"operation" really might be. It could be described as follows:

- to produce a strange and unfamiliar atmosphere (intervention
  of a poetic and sacred aura, pseudoetymological action on
  words, and so forth);
- to question our habitual representations, without actually
  refuting them through argumentation, rather rejecting them as
  devoid of any essential truth; and
- to introduce a new idea, in an obscure and fragmentary
  manner, protecting it in advance from any possibility of direct
  confrontation with generally received ideas, stating from the
  very beginning its constitutive unthinkability.

The aim of the operation has nothing to do with the text's
explicit contents and stated objectives. It can be described, instead,
as the establishment of the superior status and value of both the discourse itself and its producer. This, in turn, should be assessed
against its historical background, taking into account the crisis of
the relationship (one of domination, necessarily) between philos-

ophy and science,[85] philosophy and politics, philosophy and society, and so forth. Taking into account, in short, the end of philosophy as the true discourse on the totality of being (which still represents the project of *Sein und Zeit*), we understand why philosophy must look for new paths in order to reaffirm itself, or simply to survive. Heidegger, from this viewpoint, does precisely that, bestowing to poetry the quality and function of a sacred text. Philosophy (under its new name, "thinking") becomes therefore, if not the depositary of truth, at least the guardian of the paths that open up the (unspeakable) truth of (true) poetry. Appropriate "blackout" procedures prevent any verification of poetry's "truth," as well as of the relevance of Heidegger's "meditation" as a path towards that truth.

Ergo, philosophy always manages to find a place where it can take it upon itself of enunciating (or, at least, of approaching) the deepest truth (the essence). And, generally speaking, the chosen place is not just any place at all: It must regularly coincide with the site of the foundations, and thus grant an exclusive privilege to access and control the entire field of whatever can be said and thought.

The clearest example is the very theme of *Unterwegs zur Sprache*, language, and the fashion in which Heidegger deals with it. Linguistics, physiology, anthropology, all offer "valid" (that is, irrefutable by philosophy) viewpoints on language, but they are structurally blind to the essential. The essential truth about language is hardly utterable, and it is murmured in poetry. Poetry and thinking entertain the closest of relationships, founded on their parallel listening to the profound word that sets us on the road toward the essence of language. Thought, Heidegger's meditation (the last embodiment of philosophy), has access (submitting to it) to the truth of poetry and, albeit unable to state it directly, can offer it a chance to resonate in a more "thinking" fashion. Hence the privilege of the thinker and his discourse.

The critical position I have just presented is at the same time valid, or at least not easily refuted, and of no utility outside a sociological approach, which is most certainly meaningful and interesting, but cannot be smuggled in as the final explanation of the texts in question. Any discourse, or discipline, can be analyzed on the basis of the vested or class interests of its representatives, and of the need for self-affirmation inherent in the discourse itself. But this does not say it all, and probably not even what is most important, as far as the possible effects (which are always local and always different) of such a discourse or discipline. Whatever we make of the political position and status of Heidegger as a man and as an intellectual, of the effects of such a position and status in his discourse, and of the means through which this discourse confirms itself, Heidegger's meditation truly introduces us to a different and more "essential" dimension of language, to unheard-of effects of sense. And there is probably no "less mystical" way of making this dimension explicit. Whether this dimension is actually viable and up to what point, whether it allows the thinker anything more than a coming and going of broken metaphors, whether therefore it is desirable to have access to it, all this remains subject to a decision with no justification; or rather, a decision that can only remain foreign to the field of logical reasons and justifications.

Grayness or Bliss?

The path I have been following is certainly not the only one a reader may follow in order to provide an interpretative frame for Heidegger's text. Numerous are those who preceded me (and no doubt even more numerous those who will follow me) in this task, and the results can be very diverse. Before concluding this chapter, I wish to settle one more debt[86] and, at the same time, put into perspective my conclusions by comparing them with those of an author who preceded me on this path, and whose approach I largely share.

Jean Greisch, in an article published in 1973,[87] from which I have already quoted, opened the question of the relationship between Heidegger and metaphor. He underlines, on the one hand, the great weight, for philosophical discourse as such, of the question of metaphor's ontological dimension, and, on the other, the crucial importance of clarifying the status of metaphor in Heidegger's text. Starting from these premises, Greish carries out a remarkable exploration of his problematic field, to which my own analysis is in part indebted, and which I shall not reproduce here. I will limit myself to two footnotes:

(1) As I have previously signaled, Greisch rightly insists on the fact that Heidegger directs his critique of philosophy and of the common perception of language not against the contents of a determined discipline or preconception, but rather against their metaphysical and representational essence. I think, however, that Greisch misses one point that deserves careful attention: Heidegger not only does *not* criticize *a* certain manner of representing language, but—even more importantly—he does not suggest at all that a more adequate one exists. He strives to escape representation *in general,* wishing to think language (precisely as any other object of his meditation) without having recourse to representation, or to metaphor, which necessarily belongs to the former. Representation and metaphor are neither good nor bad; they are simply and inevitably at one with the epoch of metaphysics. In other terms, Heidegger is not on the lookout for a *nonmetaphysical representation* of language. He wants to experiment with the unheard-of possibility of

thinking language beyond (or before) representation, which means for him beyond (or before) metaphor. There is, for him, no "true" metaphor[88] at all; and if metaphor is nonetheless present in his own text, this fact cannot be dismissed as if nothing happened, or easily justified on the basis of a distinction between types of metaphor.

(2) As far as the practice (as opposed to the theory) of Heidegger's metaphor is concerned, Greisch seems to hold a similar idea to the one I have presented (barred metaphor). He describes an iconic aspect[89] of Heidegger's metaphor, in the sense of a presentation of the nonrepresentable, of the invisible, in an element which is foreign to it. In the icon the trajectory is not completed: The point of departure is a representation, but a destination is never reached; destination is barred because of the insurmountable excess of that which ought to be represented. Once again, thus, the conclusion is that Heidegger is rejecting traditional metaphor in favor of a metaphor of an iconic type, which is more appropriate to meditating thinking.

I can only state, once more, that I personally find this interpretation slightly optimistic. It actually goes in the same direction as Ricoeur's, with his distinction and opposition—within Heidegger's text—between living metaphor and dead metaphor, and it misses one central aspect of the problem, that is, the fact that Heidegger's situation (not only in connection with metaphor, by the way) is, to a large extent, more one of impasse than of free choice, and often painful impasse at that.

In a very interesting more recent book, Greisch, resuming his work on Heidegger and more specifically on *Unterwegs zur Sprache,* elaborates on some of his conclusions in the previous article. The distance that now separates his approach from mine is evident from the very title of his book: *La parole heureuse.*[90] Greisch, as a matter of fact, does not share with Birault a feeling of "grayness" when reading Heidegger; on the contrary, he opens his book on a controlled but rather cheerful note:

> If Heidegger's philosophical word can be said to be a "joyful" one, in a thoroughly essential sense of this adjective, this is not, in the first place, because it provides an answer to problems against which others fought in vain, but because it is throughout a search for that word and, in the end, an experience of that joyful word.[91]

To be certain, this is not a proclamation of the triumph of philosophy or of thinking. Nevertheless, it would be very comforting indeed to know that, at the end of a very difficult quest, there is, for the thinker, too, a possibility of accomplishment, of a joyous experience. And, once again, this experience would have to do, in an essential manner, with metaphor: not, of course, with "old" metaphor, the one Greisch, in homage to Aristotle, calls *epiphor*[92] and declares obsolete; but with a new metaphor, which belongs to a "nonmetaphysical" conception of language, and which deserves the new name of *diaphor.*[93] This term signals a transformation of metaphor in the direction of the icon ("it becomes, in fact, inevitable to talk of an 'iconic augmentation' of reality"[94]) and of diachrony: "Diaphor is metaphor thought from the perspective of difference, in other words, metaphor understood within the 'diachrony' of the poem."[95] Now Heidegger, according to Greisch, conceives of and practices metaphor as diaphor, and there is no incompatibility at all between it and meditating thought.

It is quite clear what is at stake in the operation masterfully carried out by Greisch: In one go, he is able to rescue meta/diaphor, Heidegger, and philosophy itself, granting them a space and discursive means that have nothing in common with those of everyday life, of science, and even of all the disciplines of the intellect, except poetry (which, however, from an Heideggerian point of view, can certainly not be said to belong to the "disciplines of the intellect"). It is in fact a poetic citation, and precisely from Saint-John Perse (concerning _Oiseaux_, the painting by Georges Braque), that carries almost the entire weight of Greisch's demonstration:

Oiseaux, sont-ils de faune vraie. Leur vérité est l'inconnue de tout être créé. Leur loyauté sous maints profils, fut d'incarner une constance de l'oiseau . . . du réel qu'ils sont, non de la fable d'aucun conte, ils emplissent l'espace poétique de l'homme, portés d'un trait réel jusqu'aux abords du surréel.[96]

Greisch is explicit on this: "Nothing, perhaps, better defines the ontological stake of diaphor, than this commentary by Saint-John Perse";[97] and, in fact, we are told very little more concerning the actual status and viability of diaphor. If, therefore, "diaphor is the last word in the comprehension of the joyful word,"[98] I can only keep in this matter to my opinion: There certainly is for Heidegger, as for all those who write, some joy in writing, in words that sing and touch as only poetry can. But Heidegger's thinking cannot be joyful, it is actually excluded from the very possibility of joy, conceived as an experience of accomplishment, precisely because of its stubborn insistence on residing at the limit, in the no-man's-land that is generated by the rejection of representation. I fully accept that Heidegger's discourse is "not a treatise."[99] This also depends on the "eccentric" (in relation to the philosophical tradition) position and shape taken in it by metaphor. But in Heidegger's text I can also read some degree of suffering; and indeed, a work of thought, which is not, cannot, and does not want to be poetry, can only suffer, to an extent, not only from its renunciation, but also from its incapacity to enunciate itself in a more luminous and accomplished manner.

NOTES

1. Martin Heidegger, *Unterwegs zur Sprache* (Pfullingen: Neske, 1959; henceforeward US). In addition to the German original, I will also use the following English translations: for "Die Sprache," "Language," in Heidegger, *Poetry, Language, Thought*, trans. Albert Hofstadter (New York: Harper & Row, 1975); for "Der Weg zur Sprache," "The Way to Language," in Heidegger, *Basic Writings*, ed. D. F. Krell (London: Routledge, 1993); and for the other essays, Heidegger, *On the Way to Language*, trans. Peter Hertz and Joan Stambaugh (New York: Harper & Row, 1971).

2. Heidegger, *On the Way to Language*, p. 104. US, p. 211: ". . . müssen wir freilich zuvor das rechnende Vorstellen fahren lassen."

3. "In," "before": This—as my reader will realize—is also, always, and already a *position of metaphor*. Metaphor precedes us in our attempt to read metaphor in Heidegger's text.

4. Jean Greisch, "Les mots et les roses. La métaphore chez Martin Heidegger," *Revue des sciences philosophiques et théologiques* 57 (1973; henceforth MR): 437: "Il faut d'abord apprendre à supporter l'intransigeance d'une pensée qui exige qu'on suive son propre itinéraire pour comprendre ce qu'elle veut dire."

5. Heidegger, *On the Way to language*, p. 166; US, p. 44: "Das Blau ist kein Bild für den Sinn des Heiligen."

6. Ibid.: ". . . Animal face / Freezes with blueness, with its holiness"; US, p. 44: ". . . Ein Tiergesicht / Erstarrt vor Bläue, ihrer Heiligkeit."

7. Ibid., p. 101; US, p. 207: "Wir blieben in der Metaphysik hängen, wollten wir dieses Nennen Hölderlins in der Wendung «Worte, wie Blumes» für eine Metapher halten."

8. Martin Heidegger, *The Principle of Reason* (Bloomington: Indiana University Press, 1991), p. 48; *Der Satz vom Grund* (Pfullingen: Neske, 1957), p. 89. It is therefore clear why Heidegger's thinking must resist the hermeneutic postulate of the "general metaphoricity of language" and also, for reasons that we shall see in the discussion of Heidegger's notion of "poetic nomination," be suspicious of Gadamer's thesis that "showing" is already interpreting (Hans-Georg Gadamer, *Truth and Method*, London: Sheed and Ward, 1979).

9. Ricoeur, for instance; as we have seen in chap. 2, Derrida is more cautious on this subject.

10. See US, p. 59; Heidegger, *On the Way to Language*, p. 178.

11. See in this regard Heidegger, *The Principle of Reason*, pp. 48ff.; *Der Satz vom Grund*, pp. 89ff.

12. Paul Ricoeur, *The Rule of Metaphor*, trans. R. Czerny (Toronto: University of Toronto Press, 1997), p. 284; *La métaphore vive* (Paris: Editions du Seuil, 1975; henceforth MV), p. 361. Greisch shares the same opinion; see Jean Greisch, *La parole heureuse. Martin Heidegger entre la parole et les mots* (Paris: Beauchesne, 1987; henceforth PH), pp. 441, 445, 449, 455.

13. I will soon continue the discussion on this point, and I shall try to show that for Heidegger the original energy of language is not metaphorical, but *poietic*; and that he does not reject dead metaphor only, but metaphor *tout court*. However, should it transpire that even he cannot altogether avoid metaphor, this would have a crucial impact on the whole of his "thinking gesture."

14. The point here is not to presuppose the underlying unity of an acting and deliberating subject, but only to postulate the empirical (and thus also fortuitous, arbitrary) unity of a textual corpus and a signature. Within this corpus we recognize traits that are distinguishable to us because we tend to isolate them as directly presenting or concerning the author's will.

15. US, p. 11; Heidegger, *Poetry, Language, Thought*, p. 189.

16. For the purposes of this discussion, the words "supplementary," "extraordinary," and "secondary" are used interchangeably in connection with "context."

17. Concerning Heidegger's use of etymology, see chap. 4 of this work.

18. As we shall see in more detail in "The Structure of 'Die Sprache,' " in the present chapter.

19. PH, p. 303.

20. Of course, it is not always possible to reproduce the system of semantic cross-references and connotations, which belongs to a specific language, in a different one.

21. This is also the opinion of Greisch (MR, p. 445): "Car la métaphore fonctionne pleinement dans son discours, et le travaille en profondeur, plus peut-être qu'aucun discours philosophique antérieur." ("Because metaphor functions fully in his discourse, working it in depth, more perhaps than any previous philosophical discourse.")

22. Derrida writes concerning Freud something that I deem relevant with regard to Heidegger too: "the irresolution of the scene of writing that we are reading is that of a *Bindung* which tends, stretches itself and ceaselessly posts (sends, detaches, displaces, replaces) to the extreme, without conclusion, without solution, without acting, and without a final orgasm (rather a series of orgasmic tremors, of enjoyments deferred as soon as obtained, posted in their very instance), along the line of greatest tension, at the limit of the beyond of the PP [pleasure principle], without simply stepping over the line. . . . One takes pleasure only to lose it—and to keep it *comes back, amounts* [*revient*] to the same" ["*et le garder revient au même*"] (Jacques Derrida, *The Post Card* [Chicago: University of Chicago Press, 1987], p. 396; *La carte postale* [Paris: Aubier-Flammarion, 1980], pp. 423–34). I shall develop these themes all along the present chapter.

23. MR, 434: "l'originalité de la pensée heideggerienne ne consiste pas dans une nouvelle théorie de la métaphore."

24. Ibid.

25. Heidegger, however, never explicitly makes this distinction, to my knowledge.

26. Henri Birault, *Heidegger et l'expérience de la pensée* (Paris: Gallimard, 1978), p. 10: "une certaine grisaille contre une certaine griserie."

27. This in not the place to carry further the comparison between Heidegger and Nietzsche. However, I wish at least to suggest that the difference signaled by Birault could have to do with metaphor. Very summarily: While Nietzsche thoroughly accepts metaphor, Heidegger (apparently) rejects it as vehemently. This results from a different ethical attitude: Nietzsche is a philosopher of will, Heidegger of resignation. Of course, from Heidegger's point of view, it is Nietzsche who remains a prisoner of metaphysics, precisely because of his intention to ride the truth metaphor actively. For Heidegger truth always controls us in advance of any intention, and abandon to metaphor only confirms the submission.

28. It is evident that I am here implicitly quoting from the "Séminaire sur *La lettre volée*" by Jacques Lacan (in *Ecrits* [Paris: Editions du Seuil, 1966]), and "Le facteur de la vérité" by Derrida (in *La carte postale*).

29. Heidegger, *On the Way to Language*, p. 183. US, p. 64: "Der Schmerz ist die Gunst des Wesenhaftes alles Wesenden."

30. Ibid., p. 86: ". . . the sufficient reason which rationalizes beings as the results of reason, reason's effects, and therefore satisfies our conceptualizations [*Vorstellen*]." US, p. 191.

31. Heidegger, *Poetry, Language, Thought*, p. 190. US, p. 12: "Wir wollen nicht die Sprache überfallen, um sie in dem Griff schon festgemachter Vorstellungen zu zwingen."

32. Heidegger, *On the Way to Language*, p. 74. US, pp. 178–79: "Hier gibt es weder die Methode noch das Thema, sondern die Gegend. . . ."

33. See US, "Das Wesen der Sprache"; *On the Way to Language*, "The Nature of Language."

34. Ibid., pp. 73–74. US, p. 177: "Mit etwas eine Erfahrung machen, heißt, daß jenes, wohin wir unterwegs gelangen, um es zu erlangen, uns selber belangt, uns trifft und beansprucht, insofern es uns zu sich verwandelt."

35. Ibid., pp. 76–77. US, p. 181: "Wäre es nur eine Behauptung, dann dürften wir uns daran machen, ihre Richtigkeit oder Falschheit zu beweisen. Dies wäre um vieles leichter, als die Zumutung auszuhalten und uns in sie zu finden."

36. It is interesting to note that in *Sein und Zeit* Heidegger only seems to grant poetry a preontological sense, and no privilege. Jean-Michel Palmier's interpretation (very coherent, in my opinion, and supported by the evidence from the texts) is that, since the language of metaphysics makes the overcoming almost impossible, Heidegger had to turn to poetry. *Situation de Georg Trakl* (Paris: Belfond, 1972), pp. 506–507. Beda Allemann, however, thinks that "right from this point in time [i.e., *Sein und Zeit*], where nevertheless there is no mention whatsoever of a common provenance of thinking and poetry, the presuppositions of a future dialogue of thinking with poetry are ready to become manifest" (*Hölderlin et Heidegger* [Paris: Presses Universitaires de France, 1987], p. 115).

37. Heidegger, *On the Way to Language*, p. 108; US, p. 216. Here, evidently, Heidegger is busy commenting on poetic texts, and is not talking of his own enterprise.

38. Gerald Casenave offers an idea that is not very far removed from mine: In Heidegger's text, according to him, thinking reaches—thanks to the irruption of metaphor—a more fundamental level of experience, which it (thinking) seeks to systematize in a new discursive field, which in its turn will have to be broken by metaphor, interminably. "Heidegger and Metaphor," *Philosophy Today* (summer 1982): 140–47.

39. Heidegger, *Poetry, Language, Thought*, pp. 191–92. US, p. 13: "Die Sprache ist: Sprache. Die Sprache spricht. Wenn wir uns in den Abgrund, den dieser Satz nennt, fallen lassen, stürzen wir nicht ins Leere weg. Wir fallen in die Höhe. Deren Hoheit öffnet eine Tiefe. Beide durchmessen eine Ortshaft, in der wir heimisch werden möchten, um den Aufenthalt für das wesen des Menschen zu finden."

40. Ibid., pp. 198–99. US, p. 21: "Das Herrufen ruft in eine Nähe. Aber der Ruf entreißt gleichwohl das Gerufene nicht der Ferne, in der es durch das Hinrufen gehalten bleibt."

41. Heidegger, *On the Way to Language*, p. 104; US, p. 211: "[die Nahnis] bleibt das Unnahbare und ist uns am fernsten, wenn wir «über» sie sprechen."

42. Ibid., p. 84; US, p. 189: "das heutige Denken immer entsch-

iedener und ausschließlicher zum Rechnen wird. . . ." Also, a little further:
"To the modern mind, whose ideas about everything are punched out in
the presses of technical-scientific calculation . . ." (ibid., p. 91; US, p. 197:
"Für das heutige Vorstellen, das überallhin durch das technisch-wis-
senschaftliche Rechnen in seine Formen ausgestanzt wird . . .").

43. Ibid., p. 192; US, p. 75: ". . . aller technischen Exaktheit des bloß
wissenschaftlich-eindeutigen Begriffes. . . ."

44. I will take up again the elaboration of these themes later in this
chapter.

45. I will have often the opportunity to stop and take up points of
view that one could call "demistifying" on Heidegger. The validity of such
points of view, however, does not exclude at all the relevance and acceptability of an entirely different, more "respectful," type of approach.

46. Heidegger, *On the Way to Language*, p. 81. US, p. 186.

47. Ibid., p. 96: "But such detachment must not be forced, because the
tradition remains rich in truth." US, p. 202: "Die Loslösung duldet jedoch
keinen Gewaltstreich, weil die Überlieferung reich an Wahreit bleibt."

48. Albeit marginal, of course, within the framework established by
the movements and bodies of knowledge that effectively dominate this
epoch.

49. Heidegger, *Poetry, Language, Thought*, p. 196. US, p. 19: "in die
Vorstellung von der Sprache gebannt, die seit Jahrtausenden herrscht."

50. Ibid., p. 200. US, p. 22.

51. Ibid., p. 208. US, p. 32.

52. Ibid., p. 210. US, p. 17:

> Wenn der Schnee ans Fenster fällt,
> Lang die Abendglocke läutet,
> Vielen ist der Tish bereitet
> Und das Haus ist wohlbestellt
> Mancher auf der Wandershaft
> Kommt ans Tor auf dunklen Pfaden.
> Golden blüht der Baum der Gnaden
> Aus der Erde kühlem Saft.

Wanderer tritt still herein;
Schmerz versteinerte die Schwelle.
Da erglänzt in reiner Helle
Auf dem Tische Brot und Wein.

53. This has earned Heidegger some critical scolding. See, for instance, the already quoted Palmier, *Situation de Georg Trakl*, p. 530. The same author, however, considers "absolutely true" Heidegger's interpretation of Trakl's poetry (p. 545).

54. "Schmerz versteinerte die Schwelle." Georg Trakl, quoted by Heidegger, *Poetry, Language, Thought*, p. 195. US, p. 17.

55. On the question of etymologism, see also chap. 4.

56. Heidegger, *On the Way to Language*, p. 66. US, p. 169: "Der Dichter erfährt den Dichterberuf im Sinne einer Berufung zum Wort als dem Born des Seins."

57. Ibid., p. 144. US, p. 225: "Der Dichter selbst dichtet aus dem Anspruch auf die Namen."

58. Heidegger, *Poetry, Language, Thought*, p. 198. US, p. 21: "Das Nennen verteilt nicht Titel, verwendet nicht Wörter, sondern ruft ins Wort. Das Nennen ruft."

59. Heidegger, *On the Way to Language*, p. 141. US, p. 221: "Das verfügbare Wort erst verleiht dem Ding das Sein."

60. Heidegger, *Basic Writings*, p. 408. US, p. 252: "Der Aufriss ist die Zeichnung des Sprachwesens, das Gefügen eines Zeigens, darein die Sprechenden und ihr Sprechen, das Gesprochene und sein Ungesprochenes aus dem Zugesprochenen verfugt sind."

61. Heidegger, *Poetry, Language, Thought*, p. 202. US, p. 25.

62. Ibid.

63. This theme is developed in the essay "The Nature of Language," in *On the Way to Language*, pp. 57ff.; "Das Wesen der Sprache," in US, pp. 159ff.

64. Ibid., p. 59. US, p. 161.

65. Heidegger, *Poetry, Language, Thought*, p. 206. US, p. 29: "Er stillt, indem er die Dinge in der Gunst von Welt beruhen läßt. Er stillt, indem er die Welt im Ding sich begnügen läßt."

66. Heidegger, *On the Way to Language*, 73. US, p. 177.

67. Ibid., p. 166. US, p. 44: "Blue in not an image to indicate the sense of the holy."

68. Jacques Derrida, *Margins of Philosophy*, trans. Alan Bass (Chicago: University of Chicago Press, 1982), p. 243; *Marges de la philosophie* (Paris: Editions de Minuit, 1972), p. 290.

69. Of course, we should never lose sight of the fact that Heidegger would refuse to think of difference in terms of a "system of relations"; in this respect, I am aware that I am forcing the text in the extreme. However, as indicated in my introduction, I have no intention to escape the oscillatory movement (between repetition and confrontation) of my text.

70. Heidegger, *On the Way to Language*, pp. 155–56. US, p. 238: "Beide, Dichten und Denken, sind ein ausgezeichnetes Sagen, insofern sie dem Geheimnis des Wortes als ihrem Denkwürdigsten überantwortet und dadurch seit je in die Verwandtshaft miteinander verfugt bleiben."

71. Ibid., pp. 146–47. US, p. 227.

72. Ibid., p. 147. US, p. 228.

73. Heidegger, *Poetry, Language, Thought*, p. 205. US, p. 27.

74. MR, pp. 436–37.

75. The verb "to serve" is legitimate here as long as it resonates in the sense of "service," and even "sacrifice," but not in the sense of "usefulness" or "instrumentality."

76. On these topics, see in particular Heidegger, *Letter on Humanism*, in *Basic Writings*.

77. Heidegger, *On the Way to Language*, p. 72. US, p. 176.

78. Ibid., p. 71. US, p. 175: "Daß das Fragen nicht die eigentliche Gebärde des Denkens ist, sondern—das Hören der Zusage dessen, was in die Frage kommen soll."

79. Heidegger, *Letter on Humanism*, p. 260.

80. Heidegger, *On the Way to Language*, 79. US, p. 184.

81. Ibid.: "Worin du hängst—das weisst du nicht" ("Wherein you hang—you do not know"—Stefan George).

82. Heidegger, *Basic Writings*, p. 414. US, p. 258: "Wir können es nur

noch nennen, weil es keine Erörterung duldet; denn es ist die Ortshaft aller Orte und Zeit-Spiel-Räume."

83. Heidegger, *Poetry, Language, Thought*, p. 197. US, p. 20: "Muß uns, damit wir solches Messen vermögen, nicht schon ein anderes Maß binden? Allerdings."

84. Heidegger, *On the Way to Language*, p. 64. US, p. 167: "Nein, nichts ist klar; aber alles bedeutend."

85. "Philosophy is haunted by the fear of loss of esteem and validity, if it is not itself a science," states Heidegger himself. (*Letter on Humanism*, p. 29.)

86. Of course, I have not yet finished paying my debts to Jacques Derrida and Paul Ricoeur.

87. See MR, p. 441.

88. Ibid., p. 455.

89. Ibid.

90. This title is a modified quotation from the title of Jacques Bouveresse's work on Wittgenstein, *La parole malheureuse. De l'alchimie linguistique à la grammaire philosophique* (Paris: Editions de Minuit, 1971). Greisch, however, repeatedly suggests a comparison between Heidegger and Wittgenstein that does not irrevocably oppose them (which would be futile, given the radical difference of their respective positions and styles), but rather reveals some unexpected common traits.

91. PH, p. 7: "Si la parole philosophique de Heidegger peut être dite «parole heureuse» dans un sens tout à fait essentiel de ce mot, ce n'est pas d'abord parce qu'elle apporterait la réponse à des problèmes contre lesquels d'autres se seraient vainement battus, mais parce qu'elle est de part en part quête de cette parole, et à la fin, expérience de la parole heureuse."

92. PH, pp. 198-210; Aristotle's definition of metaphor as *epiphora*, that is, "transport," is almost tautological.

93. PH, pp. 394-404; the term is not Greisch's invention. As the author himself indicates, it has been used by Philip Wheelwright and others.

94. PH, p. 401: "il devient en effet inévitable de parler d'une «augmentation iconique du réel»." See also Ricoeur, *The Rule of Metaphor*, pp.

189–91 (MV, 240–42). Ricoeur discusses in these pages Paul Henle's thesis, who in turn borrows from Charles Sanders Peirce the concept of icon.

95. PH, p. 400: "La diaphore, c'est la méraphore pensée à partir de la différence, autrement dit, la métaphore comprise dans la «diachronie» du poème." The term "diachrony" too, in this context, is a reference to Ricoeur.

96. Saint-John Perse, *Birds*, trans. J. Roger Little (Durham, 1967), pp. 15–16 (quoted by Greisch, PH, p. 402): "These are birds, true fauna. Their truth is the unknown quantity in each created thing. Their loyalty, under many profiles, was to embody the constant: bird. . . . But with the reality of their being, not with the tale of any fable, they fill the poetic space of man, borne on a stroke of reality to the borders of surreality."

97. PH, p. 402: "Rien ne définit peut-être mieux l'enjeu ontologique de la diaphore que ce commentaire de Saint-John Perse."

98. Ibid.: "la diaphore est le dernier mot de la compréhension de la parole heureuse."

99. MR, p. 436.

4

OF PHILOSOPHY

"It does what it wants, but it only wants what it can; it is free, and not sovereign."

—Paul Valéry[1]

I shall now widen the discussion, as promised on the threshold of this study, to the object that is simultaneously the closest to and the furthest from this inquiry: philosophy. The closest, because it is its most pressing and constant raison d'être; the furthest, because it is, among its objects, the least easily accessible and the most difficult to grasp and to deal with.

I will not attempt to legislate on the status, rights, and limits of the discipline; I shall, however, propose some points of view on the matter, if only to verify their validity. In particular, I will begin by

193

"locating" philosophical discourse among the research disciplines, genres of writing, and modes of discourse that appear to be its most immediate neighbors, or—sometimes—competitors. The question of the difference here takes on a vital meaning: I believe that philosophy cannot avoid facing constantly the problem of its distinction from literature (and poetry), so-called ordinary speech, and human sciences. This does not mean that it is in its power to decide its own status: this "decision"[2] depends to a large extent on the conditions of the field in which philosophy today operates.

PHILOSOPHY AMONG THE MODES OF DISCOURSE

Modes of Discourse

By "mode of discourse" I mean a type of linguistic production that takes places according to specific rules and forms which permit its definition and distinction from others.

Any "discipline of knowledge," any "literary genre,"[3] can be viewed, in some respects, as a "mode of discourse," inasmuch as it shares with the other modes of discourse, albeit distinguishing itself from each of them, a common dimension: that of language. This, however, is not a dimension like any other. It is obvious that the linguistic dimension enjoys a specific privilege; our assumption is that it is the most vital one for those disciplines or genres that carve out their space, as discourses, in the linguistic element. And without taking the trouble actually to provide a demonstration, I shall accept as axiomatic the notion that language spans and forms, in different fashions, all aspects of a speaker's "being in the world," experience and behavior. As Greisch states: "[L]anguage is therefore more than a simple reflection of the objective perception of the world. Language does not only mediate between self and other, it also mediates between self and the world."[4] To consider these disciplines as "modes of discourse" should therefore provide access not only to the external forms of their articulation and transmission within the linguistic community, but also, more essentially, to a central level of their constitution and functioning.

This does not necessarily mean that all modes of discourse are commensurable with each other, but simply that all take place in the finite (albeit not homogeneous) space of the speakable. The limits of this space and its internal subdivision are neither established a priori, nor absolute; the space of the speakable is indeed constantly modified, although at any one point in time it is only in relation to this space, such as it presents itself, that every mode of discourse, existing or merely possible, situates itself.

Speaking of "modes of discourse" gives us therefore the opportunity to enter a dimension in which philosophy can be envisaged as one type of linguistic articulation among others, and different from all others. This can offer certain advantages, but also present some risks. Of course, I am not suggesting that *every* difference should be flattened or reduced to a mere matter of degrees and fashions. There are many ways in which the perspective that I am presenting here would simply make no sense: in general, to compare philosophy and science, as disciplines, or—to be more specific— philosophy and physics, for instance, would make no sense at all, because every discipline lives inside its own, incomparable universe of meaning. However, to compare philosophy and science, or even physics, as modes of discourse, is perfectly possible, if that means to study certain aspects they have in common and manage differently: such as, for example, the resources of language, the attention of the public, institutional links, and so on.

From the point of view of the "modes of discourse" it is possible to say, generalizing widely, that no mode of discourse can dispense itself from either of the following: (a) making sense, or (b) opening up its own space of signification. A mode of discourse is recognizable through the fact that it produces "text" (this term is going to be used in the very general sense in which deconstruction, for instance, employs it) in forms that make its productions discernible from others that do not belong to its field. An oppositional (or even competitive, agonistic, and conflictual) dimension is therefore automatically inscribed in the constitution of the diverse modes of discourse.

The philosophical mode of discourse, as any other, looks for, appropriates, and attempts to retain and expand its space among the other modes of discourse. If one considers philosophy as a "mode of discourse" among others, one can attempt to situate it among its nearest neighbors on the basis of a series of "variables." For the needs of the present discussion, I will align here, next to philosophy, five other modes of discourse: (1) science (I refer here to "hard" science, such as physics or biology), (2) social or human sciences (for instance sociology, anthropology, psychology, or history), (3) literature, (4) poetry, and (5) ordinary speech. First, some preliminaries:

- Any discipline, any genre, any form of expression is more than simply a "mode of discourse." Each one has aspects that are not strictly discursive and that are essential to it. However, I shall not deal with those aspects here.
- The modes of discourse to which I refer, including of course philosophy, are treated here as ideal types, not as real examples. It is clear that, in the real world, the various discourses do not always or necessarily match the type I present here. The type has the characteristics of a (hypothetical, not statistical) average.

- These modes of discourse have been chosen because of the particularly intense relationships (of neighborhood, exchange, or competition) they entertain with philosophy.
- It seems useful to deal separately with literature and poetry, because of the distinctive traits that separate them, although in the practice of some contemporary writing they show sometimes a tendency to blend.
- Ordinary speech can only be conceived of as a mode of discourse, inasmuch as it can be distinguished from other types of exploitation of the resources of language.
- Among the possibilities of interaction or interference among modes of discourse, there is imitation; literature, for instance, is a largely mimetic mode. This must be understood not only in the sense that it reproduces reality, but also in the sense that it can imitate, include, or reproduce other modes of discourse. On another level, human sciences have a tendency to imitate the ways of hard sciences.
- I can obviously not boast direct and profound competence in each of the modes of discourse I have mentioned, nor did I try to acquire one indirectly. That could very well constitute the precondition for a separate and entirely different work. However, for the limited needs of the present analysis of the modes of discourse, I shall simply rely on the level of knowledge, concerning the functioning of the modes of discourse, available to the average educated reader. No claim to objectivity or completeness is therefore made or implied. Let us say that the my aim is to clarify my own perception of the state of affairs as to the discourses that share some kind of border with philosophy.

Analysis of Variables

I shall now proceed with a comparative analysis of the selected modes of discourse, based on certain variables that all modes of discourse have in common. The list of relevant variables is not exhaustive; I will only deal with those that are pertinent in the light of the present work. The variables in question are parameters apt to quantify (at least comparatively) dimensions or ingredients that are present in the functioning of the modes of discourse.

For the present analysis the following categories can be isolated: rationality, formalization, truth, verification, ethicality, institutionality, selection of producers, selection of the public, accessibility, definition, closedness, openness, finality, aims, freedom, interaction with reality, and analogy/metaphor. I shall offer a definition of each category and try to apply it to each of the chosen modes of discourse. The definitions are not to be taken absolutely, but only within the limited scope of an inquiry on modes of discourse. I shall not deal, therefore, with "truth" in general, but only with the meanings of this word that are pertinent when observing the functioning of the modes of discourse.

Rationality, that is, the more or less strict compliance with the rules of Western logic (noncontradiction, *principium reddendae rationis*, and so on): It is clear that the modes of discourse differ greatly from this point of view: poetry, literature, and ordinary speech can to a large extent dispense with such compliance; science, on the contrary, makes it its banner; human sciences and philosophy may challenge it, but it remains to be determined up to what point they can truly set themselves free from it.

Formalization, that is, the intrinsic necessity, actual existence, and practical application of rules, symbols, and definitions (as well as other semantic depositories) that modify the so-called natural language (both syntax and lexis) in order to make it uniform, stable, univocal: We find here the same positive progression (- to +) we noted for the previous variable: poetry, literature, ordinary speech, philosophy, human sciences, science. Contemporary poetry and literature abide less and less by the genre rules that previously, by standardizing and imposing poetic or literary forms, would function in a way similar to that of formalization for scientific discourses.

Truth, that is, the intrinsic necessity, actual existence, and practical application of a requirement of control over the text based on a normative principle external to it and independent of the producer:[5] Such a principle exists for all modes of discourse; indeed, I believe that, although it may be applied in very diverse ways in the various modes of discourse, it is crucial for the autoconstitution of each of them. In ordinary speech it is probably embodied, in widely varying degrees, in a general requirement of verifiability of statements, in a very loose sense. In hard and human sciences, more or less stringent procedures exist for the verification of statements. In literature and poetry, a principle of "fictional truth" may be in place, whereby fiction must be able to temporarily superimpose itself on the reader's world, short of which the specific intention of these modes of discourse is not fulfilled.

Verification, that is, the intrinsic necessity, actual existence, and practical application of systematic procedures aimed at satisfying the truth requirement in an "objective" fashion, on the basis of a comparison between textual segments and "real" (that is, extratextual) data: This principle, on the contrary, does not apply to all modes, but only to science, less stringently to human sciences and very loosely to ordinary speech. Philosophy, as we shall see, is excluded by definition from the possibility of verification as defined here.

Ethicality, that is, the intrinsic necessity, actual existence, and practical application of a superior principle that, freely accepted as a duty, guides the entire activity aimed at the production of the text: Such a principle can exist for any discourse, but must exist (in other words, it is constitutive) only for philosophy, human sciences, and science.

This superior principle *may* be embodied by the truth requirement itself in the case of human sciences and hard science; but only for philosophy is this compulsory. As for hard and human sciences, the ruling superior principle may be represented by efficacy in the real world, possibly measured in terms of verifiability or usefulness. As for literature, poetry, and ordinary speech, obviously certain ethical instances may be active in those discourses, but this is not required for the constitution of the mode of discourse itself. A principle of pleasure, for instance, may very well occupy the place of an ethical instance in the act of the production of the text and within the structure of its aims.[6]

Institutionality, that is, the embodiment of a mode of discourse in institutional structures that underpin and delimit it: Institutional structures are not always and necessarily social institutions in the strict sense; the publication of a text through determined channels, for instance, is a phenomenon belonging, in some respects, to the order of the institutional.

Here there is certainly a positive progression, from ordinary speech (degree zero), to literature and poetry (light institutionalization: publishing houses, universities, conferences, periodicals, and so on), to philosophy, human sciences, and sciences (progressively heavier institutionalization: universities, careers, laboratories, financing, and so on).

Selection of producers, that is, of those who are entitled to produce (or, at any rate, do produce) text, which is recognized as belonging to a specific mode of discourse: The selection of authorized producers (achieved by various means, such as identification of relevant gifts, vocation, training, and so on) is increasingly strict, in the following progression: ordinary speech (no selection other than through knowledge of the relevant language or variety; any speaker is authorized as producer of the mode of discourse identified as "ordinary speech"), literature and poetry, philosophy, human sciences, and hard sciences (strict selection, nowadays entirely institutionalized).

Selection of the public, that is, of those who are supposed to be in a position to read the text of a specific mode of discourse, or in any case do read it: A negative progression (restriction of potential public) can be observed, moving from ordinary speech (language speakers, text producers, and public all coincide), to literature, poetry, philosophy, human sciences, and hard sciences.

Accessibility, that is, the degree to which the text can be correctly interpreted by readers who are not producers: The progression is the same as in the previous case. Ordinary language is accessible to the producers of all other modes of discourse, while the text of hard science is, in practice, only accessible to its producers or to potential producers of similar text.

Definition, that is, the degree of precision in establishing, on all levels, the limits of a discourse: Ordinary speech has normally no procedures in place to define its own limits; literature, as well as poetry, has such procedures, but can easily override them; philosophy has limits that it constantly tends to exceed, sometimes actually managing to displace them, albeit not without pain; human sciences and hard sciences are finely defined, always having, at any given time, rather strict field limits. No mode of discourse, however, has unmovable limits.

Closedness, that is, the degree of resistance exercised by a discourse against the importing of text, rules or producers coming from other modes: The same progression noticed in the previous case is applicable; ordinary speech, literature and poetry, philosophy, human sciences, and science (the closedness is here almost absolute, at least on the surface of the text; there always is, however, some importing of models, terminology, and attitudes: No discourse is totally closed).

Openness, that is, the degree to which a discourse is disposed to become acclimatized in other discourses, or other discourses are able to welcome it: It is not surprising to find, in comparison with the previous variable, the opposite progression; science (the more a discourse is formalized and securely in the hands of professionals, the less exportable it is), human sciences, philosophy, poetry, literature, and ordinary speech (segments of ordinary speech can find a place almost everywhere, depending on the context). Once more, however, some degree of openness appears to be inevitable for all modes of discourse.

Finality, that is, a global, stable, and effective orientation of a discourse in a specific direction: This is very strong in science, human sciences, and philosophy (where in general the discourse must have a precise direction); less so in literature and poetry; and usually close to zero in ordinary speech.

Aims, that is, a determination of finality in terms of limited objectives, which should be recognizable and accessible; or, in any event, the existence of objectives of this type, even independent of any global finality: The progression from less to more here is different; from poetry and literature (there can be no aims here: should specific aims be active and overcome other considerations in the constitution of the text, we are dealing with something else, for instance propaganda), philosophy, ordinary language (usually there some kind of practical purpose here, at the very least an aim to establish and reinforce communication, or to stop it), human sciences, and science (there are always specific aims in this discourse, albeit not necessarily of a practical nature).

Freedom, that is, the degree of flexibility in the relation between producer and discourse, particularly as regards the compliance with the various rules that are involved in the production and consumption of text: The positive progression appears as science, human sciences, philosophy, poetry, literature, and ordinary speech. Doubts may arise concerning the comparative degree of liberty between literature/poetry and ordinary speech. Obviously literature and poetry can choose to break all rules, which ordinary speech would do only in very special circumstances; on the other hand, the producer of ordinary speech is in general the most free in terms of number and weight of constraints to which he is subject in the production of text. This is, in fact, the discourse requiring the lowest level of competence.

Interaction with reality, that is, the degree of interactive exchange with the world external to the text, and the relevance of such exchange in view of the production of the text itself: This variable does not coincide purely and simply with verification. What is at stake here is the need, for a certain discourse, to relate constantly to the "real" world. The following positive progression exists: poetry, literature (both these modes of discourse can create their own world apart), philosophy, human sciences, science, ordinary speech (here the contact with day-to-day, "real" concerns is almost permanent).

Analogy/metaphor, that is, the presence in the text of meaning-displacing mechanisms that require the intervention of extraordinary contexts (see chapter 1): This parameter will be analyzed in more detail in the next section.

Modes of Discourse and Metaphor

From poetry, to literature, to philosophy, to human sciences, to science, one can ascertain—at least according to a very widespread view—a progressive deterioration of the metaphoric content in the constitution of the modes of discourse. On the other hand, there is a positive counterpart to the waning of metaphor, in the shape of an increase in formalization, codification, definition, and generally in rational structuring. From poetry to science, there is more structure; that is, more "stricture," more restrictive definition of objects, loss of transversal mobility, less vagueness, less freedom. In a word: less metaphor.

If we wanted to assign relative values to apparent degrees of metaphoricity, the result would be something like this:

- Ordinary Speech: +1. This is the level of metaphoricity that one could, conventionally, define as "normal."
- Formalized Scientific Language: 0. Metaphor is here, in principle, banned and replaced by precise definitions, abstract concepts, and a terminology capable of covering the entire field of its objects.
- Poetic Language: +n. Here, the only limit to metaphoric displacement—and then only if the producer decides to accept it—is the requirement to make sense.

It would be wrong, however, to think that the metaphoric function is totally foreign to some modes of discourse. Even in science metaphor is present, in more than one way: not only in the genesis of terminology (which, by the way, is a permanently active and never insignificant procedure), but also in the use of models.[7] According to Ricoeur, "the model belongs not to the logic of justification or proof, but to the logic of discovery";[8] as a heuristic instrument, therefore, it represents an essential element within the processes of acquisition and organization of scientific knowledge. Furthermore, metaphoric representation may possibly constitute an essential part, if not of demonstration (which can be entirely for-malized), at least of scientific explanation. According to Mary Hesse, for instance, "the deductive model of scientific explanation should be modified and supplemented by a view of theoretical explanation as metaphoric redescription of the domain of the *explanandum.*"[9]

Finally, metaphor certainly has a decisive function in the history of science: The widening of the field, the discovery, the enlarge-ment or amendment of the paradigm/model are the moments where metaphor seems to become most active. As soon as a theory becomes more stable, metaphor is (in principle) expelled, or steril-ized through definition-formalization, and it becomes easy to lose the trace of its effective intervention in the genesis of theory itself.

Modes of Discourse and Ethics

There is a degree of ethicality that is represented by the action, in or on the text, of values and principles foreign to the grammar of a mode of discourse. Science reduces the ethical instance (in the sense of the relevance of values) by means of formalization, automatic procedures of text production, conventional bounds, and relative rigidity of language; it is, however, not necessarily devoid of guiding principles of an ethical nature. First of all, science cannot bestow upon itself the linguistic freedom of poetic practice, that is, reduce itself to pure form, lest it lose something essential to its own consti-tution. It obeys, therefore, imperatives that, albeit perfectly rational, are nevertheless foreign to its discourse and unjustifiable from a purely logical point of view. First is the "imperative of knowledge" itself; that is, the principle that acquiring knowledge is in itself an aim worth pursuing. It is true that often justifications of a utilitarian or pragmatic type (which, too, however, belong to the field of values) can intervene, but I do not believe that alone explains the central drive in scientific activity. This inner engine appears to be of a typically ethical nature: We *must* know, irrespective of the practical value of the knowledge we acquire.

Poetry can reduce the ethical instance, for example, using formalization, procedures of automatic or associative writing, and opaqueness of linguistic material. However, very often it openly carries values. Sometimes it is even supposed to accomplish a superior gnoseologic function (as in Heidegger), under the command of a force that is obviously of a moral type: One *must* "correspond," answer the call, say what can only be said poetically.

Philosophy, as we shall see, cannot eliminate the ethical instance, since it constitutes its most specific trait (search for the founding truth), and also because it does not have at its disposal those procedures science, for instance, can use in order to freeze both the "ethical ardor" (truth with ethical index) and the "heath of imagination" (metaphor).

Modes of Discourse and Truth

Every mode of discourse has a different relationship to what I called "truth," which obviously does not correspond exclusively to the traditional notion of truth (*adaequatio*), or to the notion of formal truth only. One can distinguish, on a first level, three determinations of the notion of truth in the element of discourse: (1) experimental verifiability of the correspondence between a text segment and a world segment (material proof); (2) compatibility of a text segment with the whole of the procedures and data internal to the text (formal proof); and (3) in general, coherence between a text segment and the whole of the language permitted and shaped as required by the mode of discourse to which it belongs. With respect to this first level, that is, to what we may call factual or formal truth, we observe that the following situation obtains:

- *Science* accepts and requires: (1) experimental verification, (2) compatibility with the whole of its internal procedures and data, and (3) coherence with the whole of permitted language.
- *Philosophy* accepts and requires (2) compatibility with the whole of internal procedures and data and (3) coherence with the whole of admitted language, but not (1) experimental verification.
- *Poetry*, on the contrary, neither requires nor accepts any of those three determinations of truth.

Science applies strict control procedures to both the external level of the proof and the internal one of the form of discourse. In poetry, on the contrary, the function of expansion (the same that Ricoeur mentions) requires that all three conditions of truth control be let go. In philosophy there is no factual proof, but the discourse must "hold" on the formal and structural level. We could say, with Chaïm Perelman and Lucie Olbrechts-Tyteca, that philosophical discourse belongs (together with religious argumentation, moral or artistic education, and jurisprudence) to the domains where argumentation can only be rhetorical, since neither are judgements purely formal, nor have statements such a content that experience suffices to justify them.[10]

There is, however, another level of pertinence of truth, which no mode of discourse can escape. Any discourse, in fact, complies with a validation principle that determines not so much the belonging of a text to a mode of discourse (which can be achieved in a purely formal manner), bur rather its validity as a *type* or *exemplum* of its genre or discipline. This validation principle, pursued by the producer and activated by the reader, is different for each mode of discourse, and even for each internal subdivision of each mode of discourse.

For instance, for the literary text the general validation principle would be the ability of the text to "set up a world" (I mean by "world," here, the whole set of the relations in which a reader is included). This has nothing to do with the correspondence with the real world (although, of course, a literarily produced world can represent, mimetically, the real one). It concerns, rather, the mechanisms that, in the reader, trigger what we could call "the world effect":[11] not necessarily an effect of realism or naturalism in the usual sense, rather an effect of inclusion of the reader in a dimension (known or unknown, normal or abnormal, possible or impossible) of the "world." Only when this happens is fiction successful and the mode of discourse produces a text that is not merely acceptable from a formal point of view, but also a carrier of truth, the kind of truth that is constitutive for this discourse and makes a specific actualization exemplary. If this does not happen, the text still produces effects and situates itself in relation to its reader, thus taking place in his world; however, it does not itself function as a supplementary or temporary world for the reader.

PHILOSOPHICAL DISCOURSE

> *"It is just as deadly for the mind to have a system as to have none at all. So one has to make up one's mind to have both."*
> —Friedrich Schlegel[12]

I propose to offer some ideas on philosophical discourse, having regard to its relative difference from neighboring discourses that enunciate themselves in different ways. I shall momentarily place in parentheses the idea that philosophy has of itself, as well as the very remarkable differences existing among the various types of discourse that have been and are being practiced under the name of philosophy.

Why present a discourse on philosophy, if not normative, at least descriptive? Perhaps because, as I have already signaled, in the practice of philosophy a self-examination of the conditions of possibility and legitimacy of its own discourse is necessarily enshrined, and certainly also because of the competition of the neighboring modes of discourse. Every discourse, however, can find itself in need of producing its own letters of accreditation, not as an individual discourse but as a mode of discourse: This is what I would call the philosophical moment, the most fundamental and the least founded component of a mode of discourse.

What, then, first of all and in the most general terms, is philosophy? An almost infinite series of acceptable answers can be proposed, and for instance: a fictional genre; a scientific discourse, with its own specific rules; a discourse founded on intuitive and non-demonstrable certainties; a purely logical discourse; a discourse on the philosophical tradition; a discourse on the foundations of any possible knowledge; a discourse on the relationship between language and the world.

I could go on at length. Let us say that, probably, any one of these interpretations of philosophy has been envisaged and practiced, but none is observable or has been practiced with an absolute degree of purity. I shall discard none, nor shall I attempt to find the lowest common denominator to all. I will propose, instead, a model that seems to offer an adequate description of some important (or even essential) aspects of philosophy as it is practiced today, in the shape of some specific textual productions.

First of all, some preliminary considerations and terminological remarks. By *world*, I shall mean the whole of things, events, and relations that constitute the widest frame of reference of a mode of discourse or of all modes of discourse (it is not the same world in all instances, of course). Without these three elements (things, events, relations), there is no world, but only varying degrees of chaos or emptiness. Vis-à-vis the world, one may feel surprise, which translates into questions. Questions generate discourses, which can follow paths leading to solutions of the order of proof (empirical, experimental, or logical), although not always.

Philosophy is, at a first approximation, a type of discourse concerning questions regarding the intelligibility of the world or portions of world, to which it is not possible (or it is believed to be impossible) to answer according to methods requiring objective validation. This model, however, would be incomplete without the intervention of an ethical element, which seems crucial in activating this mode of discourse: Philosophy is also, for the producer, a matter of duty.

Let us then venture a provisional definition. Philosophy: the discourse that satisfies the *moral obligation* to look for and state the *truth* on matters that, in the perception of the producer, cannot properly be dealt with on the basis of the ordinary verification criteria of daily life, or on the basis of the extraordinary verification criteria of science.[13]

Philosophical Truth and Ethics

> *"To let ourselves be told what is worthy of thinking means—to think."*
> —Martin Heidegger[14]

Philosophy has no privileged relationship with truth in general; it has instead, as any other mode of discourse, a certain relationship with a certain "truth regimen" that is specific to it. Truth in the domain of philosophy can have at least two meanings:

- *A "weak" meaning*, such as the one described above: *adaequatio rei et intellectus*. Congruence with observable reality, adherence to historical, verifiable data. Also, the formal truth of what is demonstrable by means of defined procedures internal to the discourse. This truth, which is capable of and subject to proof, is the only one we may call, by convention, "real" or "objective."
- *A "strong" meaning*: affirmation and creation of truth. Proposition of that which is (de jure or de facto, temporarily or permanently) undemonstrably true, autoproclamation of what must be true. This truth is not subject to proof. It concerns a series of very diverse phenomena, such as "common opinion" truths (which indeed are sometimes very weak; but the strong/weak opposition must be understood here in relation to the degree of "active imposition on reality"—as opposed to passive acceptance—in the forms and within the limits of a specific mode of discourse), beliefs, value systems, and all "theories" in the stronger sense—those whose scope is too large to subject them to factual proof, or to make such proof truly final.

The practice of philosophy seems to be linked, to a large extent, to the pursuit of truth of the "strong" type. It has, instead, very little to do with truths of the first kind. However, it is unlikely that the two types of truth exist in a pure and isolated state; a mixed state, with varying proportions of each, seems more common. Indeed, any "strong" truth will tend to look for some sort of factual confirmation, and often truths of the "weak" sort inscribe themselves within either a larger theoretical system, or a wider belief system (both instances of "strong" truth).

In the fields of the sciences, human sciences, and philosophy a tendency to reduce "strong" truth to "weak" truth is endemic (sometimes under misleading appearances), as if there were only one type of truth, that is the correspondence to objective data (to reality). Hence come endless misunderstanding and impasses. Of course, we might agree that only one type of truth exists (the first one) and that all the rest is error. This, however, would mean not to take into account all the discursive instances where an occurrence of truth appears that is not identifiable as belonging to the first type. It is a fact that "strong" truth may be illusory, dangerous, metaphysical, or false: But the point is that several modes of discourse rely on truth of the second kind. And, as far as philosophy is concerned, it would have no raison d'être, as an independent mode of discourse, if the possibility and necessity to produce statements regarding the truth of that which cannot be *proven* true or false were not inscribed in our world.

A crucial difference between philosophy and other modes of discourse, concerning truth, is therefore the following one: In the philosophical discourse, there is no avoiding (strong) truth. The pursuit of this sort of truth is the ultima ratio and the only justification of this discourse. Philosophy cannot survive simply on the strength of formal requirements, which means that philosophical discourse can neither content itself with being pleasant, beautiful, or well proportioned, for instance, as is the case sometimes for poetry, or exploit utilitarian justifications, as science can do (this is primarily because philosophical discourse can seldom prove a direct efficacy on the real world). It is therefore only philosophy's relationship, not exclusive but privileged, with "strong" truth that constitutes and distinguishes it.

Philosophy, however, is not "useless": On the contrary, it carries out a vital function, connected to the rational elaboration of strong truths, within the economy of the space of the modes of discourse as they present themselves in a given moment in history, and it generates effects that go well beyond its disciplinary boundaries. This does not mean that such a function is an "absolute of the human mind,"[15] or that there will always be a philosophical discourse; even though it is very difficult for us to imagine a world entirely void of "strong" truths to be pursued or created in the discursive forms that belong to philosophy, one cannot a priori exclude this possibility.

Philosophical truth (a specification of what I called "strong truth") is strictly linked to the ethical impulse, in the sense that it can only be pursued and "found" under the impulse of a moral imperative. Truth in philosophy, in effect, cannot be founded on a real state of things, it can in no way be verified, it cannot found itself on the authority of a sacred text, and cannot simply coincide with the good and correct form of a discourse (this condition may well be necessary, but not sufficient). Nothing can justify it, and nothing can justify the act of looking for it.

I would say, therefore, that in philosophy that is true which, without reason, imposes itself and yet is freely accepted by the thinker, and subsequently demands to be supported by an order of reasons, by a rhetorical apparatus, by a certain discursive structure. The order of priority, however, is not chronological: There is not, first of all (and outside the discourse), a truth that imposes itself and, thereafter, a discourse which supports it: it is within the discourse itself, _in fieri_, that a core of strong truth dawns, around which the discourse organizes itself.

"Without reason" is to be understood here in this sense: there is no conclusive justification, in terms of logical or objective proof, of what is stated. This does not mean that there are no reasons at all. However, they come (logically) after, not before: that is, after the act of imposition and acceptance of a core of unjustifiable meaning that constitutes _truth_.

Were the thinker not "free" to accept or reject what presents itself to his mind and imposes itself on it, whether under the influence of physical constraints or emotions external to his judgement, there would be no philosophy, but some form or other of material or spiritual subservience. Without the effort to sustain truth by all available discursive means within the order of rationality, such as it is constituted in a given field at a given moment, we would have blind belief or faith instead of philosophy. This effort is linked to what Perelman calls "the principle of responsibility," upon which his "new rationalism" is founded, which does not rest on absolute evidence but on the free consideration of the whole formed by all arguments presented.[16] In fact, it corresponds, probably, to what Aristotle understood under the heading of "rhetoric," that is, the technique of persuasion by means of proof and argumentation.

Philosophy thus, even though not useless, occupies itself with things that (at least in the limited sense of immediate and direct utility) are useless to social life and are not subject to the usual means of verification. This can only be justified on the basis of a moral principle (to look for truth is good in itself); furthermore, proof can only be, in the end, the effect of a conviction of an ethical sort ("this is the truth, I am sure of it"), supported, of course, by the internal congruence of the discourse and its pertinence within the general field of the rationality of the epoch.

Some questions surface immediately (they will not, however, find an answer here): Why and how does "the truth" impose itself? If that which imposes itself on me does not at the same time do the same on everybody, what about the alleged universality of philosophy? But can philosophy truly give up its aspirations to universality? Why do we call that which imposes itself "the truth"?

Let us go back for a moment to the question of ethics. I have ventured that the instance imposing something on a free subject, who is not dictated to by any external constraint, is an imperative of the ethical order. It is, however, important to note that, although the initial impulse of truth in philosophy is of the ethical type, this clearly does not prevent truth from finding its place within movements and mechanisms of a nonethical type (such as, for instance, social, rhetorical, political, religious, and so on). Furthermore, the specificity of ethics is far from clarified and defined. Perhaps ethics is the result, at a very deep level of sedimentation, of the various kinds of interaction (social, political, linguistic, and so on) taking place in a community. The reference to the ethical impulse, therefore, can only have the validity of a shortcut. The crucial point is that the producer of this mode of discourse, though a philosopher, cannot explain the reason for the most significant movements of his own thought. They are, however, not unjustified: They have a status similar (though not identical) to that of beliefs or values, they belong to the ethical order.

Two examples of this are Heidegger and Derrida themselves; can one justify the "step back," or deconstruction? I do not think so, for the reasons I have outlined above: the foundation, the origin of the movement cannot be justified, perhaps because there is neither foundation nor origin. Perhaps also (I come back to this, at the risk of boring the reader) because it is in the interest of the thinker or deconstructor that they remain hidden, or at least implicit? Perhaps; but this point of view, however legitimate, does not seem determining.

Forthcoming Thought

> "J.—One site is metaphysics.
> D.—And the other? We leave it without a name."
>
> —Martin Heidegger[17]

The two types of philosophical production I mentioned most frequently in the present work, those of Heidegger and of Derrida, both present themselves (despite all the differences separating them[18]) to a large extent as strategies for the management[19] of a complex space of thought, far more complex than the one that is customary in the philosophical mode of discourse. The complexity of this space seems to be due in good measure to its constitutive duplicity; that is, to its unfathomable discord between limitation of means and infinity of the project, present and future thinking. To think, for both these authors, means, inextricably, to manage a heritage of which it is impossible to get rid[20] and to prepare the possibility of the entirely other, of the unthinkable; to repeat and to overcome metaphysics; to deconstruct and . . . the *pars construendi* of this project has no proper name yet. But thinking has a sense, a direction: it takes place as the preparation[21] of a mode of thinking that is forthcoming. It is "forthcoming," but at the same time it is there already, it generates writing: This writing is, then, perhaps, the place of encounter and combat between two kinds of thought in one text.

thought 1 ⟶ WRITING ⟶ thought 2
(past—present)   (future)

As I have tried to show in the previous chapters, the two kinds of thought (1 and 2) are only (partially and momentarily) compatible thanks to an enormous effort of constant remobilization of all the available instruments and signifiers, which belong to metaphysics. The (modified) operation of metaphor turns out to be indispensable to the precarious management of all the displacements of meaning required by the operation. If it is true that, according to

Heidegger, one cannot speak of being (which is not a thing) *more metaphorico,* neither can we talk about it literally; we are forced, therefore, to speak of it "almost" or "ultrametaphorically." The quasi metaphor takes the place of more orthodox procedures, which aim precisely at stabilizing sense. The philosophical writing of Heidegger or Derrida is therefore constantly and necessarily in a position not only of instability, but also of infraction vis-à-vis the rules of traditional philosophical discourse.

In the light of the preceding analysis, we could say that, for Heidegger and Derrida at least, there is a radical conflict, at the heart of the text, between the central imperative and the ability of the discourse to carry it out without at the same time depriving itself of all means of validation. This conflict by no means prevents the text's existence and proliferation. This confirms two things: on the one hand, that the unverifiable "strong" truth of the discourse (its central imperative) is its force and motivation sine qua non; on the other, that philosophical discourse (but we should perhaps say *ex*-philosophical, to do justice to Heidegger's and Derrida's specific positions) must shroud its truth in all the procedures that are available to it, in order to make it acceptable and, if possible, dominant within the existing discursive field.

Truth, in the typically philosophical form of a moral imperative, drives discourse, which responds as best it can, with the available resources, in forms that, in all instances, must allow it to maintain its generic identity, albeit pushing it to the extreme limit. In this game, and particularly when it is a little risqué, it is not the author who decides the results, but the response, immediate or delayed, of the field, which, however, is also itself as a whole modified by it.

Precisely because it concerns "borderline" discourses, the proposed examples (the "forthcoming" thought of Heidegger or Derrida), seems to illustrate very well some of the characteristics and dynamics of the mode of discourse we call philosophy. It follows that what constitutes it in the first place is not a structure, a syntax, a vocabulary, or a field of objects, but instead, on the one hand, the triggering of a specific spring in the moral order (truth) and, on the other, the requirement of self-identification, which activates a dialectic of acceptance and rejection (but never *total* acceptance or rejection) vis-à-vis the archives of the genre.

Nonrepresentational Thought

> "... *in die Vorstellung ... gebannt. ...*"
>
> —Martin Heidegger[22]

It is true that, as Birault[23] notes, the entire work of Heidegger can be viewed as a "destruction" of the identity of thinking and philosophy. This sort of "destruction," however, remains strictly *philosophical*, not in the sense of the philosophical tradition but in the sense of what we proposed to call the philosophical mode of discourse, of its forms, its limits, and its aims.

I believe that Heidegger's example can tell us a great deal concerning philosophical discourse, its strengths, its constraints, and its impossibilities. More specifically, I now wish to take a little further my reflections on Heidegger's attempt to conceive and practice a nonrepresentational thinking, an attempt that initially takes the form of a rejection of representation. Let us start again from the beginning, and examine, for instance, the following statement:

We must / think / in a way / that is nonrepresentational.
    1   2   3   4

Let us analyze its components, giving space to the questions and objections that each triggers:

(1) *We must*: It is clear that this statement rests on a moral, counterfactual requirement. Why must we?

(2) *Think*: The statement revolves around thinking; we must think, philosophy has the duty to think, and this sort of thinking is possible. But what does "thinking" mean?

(3) *In a way*: There are several ways, they are not equivalent, we must choose one, we can choose one, the best one. Is it possible to choose how to think?

(4) *Nonrepresentational*: This is a way that is not founded on representation, has nothing to do with it, has no need to refer to something else is order to think something properly; one that therefore wishes to reach the thing itself, with no detours, without forcing upon it a form that is foreign to it. Is there such a thing as nonrepresentational thought? What is it?

If, keeping in mind the preceding discussions, we try to explore the notion of representation, we should probably start by defining representation, in an admittedly banal way, as the image that presents a thing in the absence of the thing itself. For instance, I think about an apple and I see it (with "the eyes of the mind," so to speak). The mental image is a representation; but the word "apple" itself is a representation, as is a photograph or drawing or verbal description of an apple.

Perhaps it is not entirely correct to conceive representation as a "mental image"; if, for instance, I think of something such as "freedom," what do I see? Probably not freedom. There are therefore ideas with which a representational image is not associated. Of course we can associate images with freedom, but none will represent it exhaustively (covering all possible instances of freedom) or even individually (fully representing one instance only). It remains true, nevertheless, that I can consider the word, the sign, the symbol, or the definition or description of "freedom" as a representation, even though this idea has no representational image. Relinquishing the notion of "mental image," therefore, does not change the essence of the problem. The crucial point is that everything that allows us to identify an apple or freedom, to think of it and to speak of it, is a representation, and never the "thing itself." This way of reasoning, a little simplistic in its appearance, brings us nevertheless to the core of the problem: Freedom is nothing for us without representation, and neither is the apple. We have no direct access (that is, simultaneously productive of meaning and independent from signs) to reality. Language, art, science: all is representation. The origin, as Derrida (to whom I refer for this kind of meditation) says, is always already secondary, repetitive, *representational*, that is, already and forever lost. How could we then think without representation, once the possibility of a direct access to things or to the essence has been barred, or exclusively consigned to language, to signs, concept, and metaphors?

But, first of all, *why* think without representation? We have already seen the reasons why Heidegger embarks upon such an adventure. Essentially, he thinks of representation as the acolyte of metaphysics, and of metaphysics as the oblivion of being. This certainly establishes a rational chain of argumentation, but not a rational *primum movens*. It is useless to go up the chain to find the justification of what, in the end, will remain an unjustified imperative. I have dwelled enough on this.

Let us therefore concede that there is no necessary and sufficient reason to justify the intention to overcome representation, and come back to the previous point: Is it possible to do it? Several clues seem to suggest that it is not possible to expel representation from the place of the origin, which it occupies and bars from direct access. This, however, does not mean that it is impossible to attack it from another side. One could, for instance, try to suspend or restrain representation, to delete or overcome it a posteriori. An extremely formalized language could be a way of suspending representation, by activating a powerful, well-woven system of relationships and procedures. Of course, what is achieved there is not exactly the elimination of representation in the sense of obtaining a direct access to things, to truth. Instead, the analogical functioning of discourse by associations is reduced to a minimum. The representational drift is blocked, by way of fixing all the elements of the discourse in a rigid relationship with their references, whether intra- or extradiscursive.

According to a widespread idea, the closer one moves to abstraction and theory (science, philosophy), the more the representational dimension fades out; not that scientific and/or philosophical language is more proper, that is, more directly connected to its object that poetic language. It would simply be less representational (relying less, for instance, on associated images) and more rigorous (more strictly trapped in a net of defined relations). The representational aspect, on the contrary, would remain strongly present in everyday language, as well as in poetic language. It is in this process of restriction of representation that metaphor, its most powerful and insidious instrument, must fall: Hard sciences, human sciences, and philosophy have all attempted to proceed along this course, with more or less success, as we know.

Clearly, this cannot satisfy Heidegger's need, which is far more radical; the procedures I mentioned above, indeed, can very well reduce vagueness in discourse, but they can certainly not purloin it from metaphysics. At a deeper level, as we have seen, formalization, abstraction, calculation, representation, and metaphor are all accomplices in the same game. The point, therefore, is not one of regulating in a different way the flux of discourse, but rather one of *thinking differently*. The practicality of this other mode of thinking remains to be demonstrated; but we cannot expect Heidegger to provide a demonstration.

Thought As Productive Fiction

> *"Assuming that thinking will succeed one day. . . ."*
> —Martin Heidegger[24]

Poetry exists, science exists, philosophical discourse, too, exists. Does thinking exist, at least as understood by Heidegger? Plainly, there is Heidegger's text. Is this sufficient proof of both the existence and the practicability of the *other thinking*, such as Heidegger wants it? In many respects Heidegger's text seems to invoke thought, rather than truly exercising it. Thinking is not there yet; we have seen above good reasons why forthcoming thought cannot yet be present, and how that even contributes to constitute the specific quality of this text. However, we must come back to the question of the two thoughts and interrogate in greater depth their respective status. Let us open once again *Unterwegs zur Sprache*.

Thought 1 is not exactly a region that we should leave; it is, rather, the *path* itself that must take us to thought 2. Conversely, thought 2 is not *another* place that we should reach; the task is, for us, to arrive where we already are: "To turn back to where we are (in reality) already staying: that is how we must walk along the way of thinking which now becomes necessary."[25] We can therefore neither jump in the other thought, nor build it patiently piece upon piece, as a castle. A "jump" is indeed required, but not to project ourselves into another place. Patience is also necessary, but not to build another home for thinking; on the contrary, precisely *not* to do it. Calculating thought wants to throw itself on a representation in which to rest, on which to found itself; we must not attempt that. We must jump out of representation, as much as possible, and not fall back into it again.

We do not know thinking that is not representational, and not only that: Nothing tells us that, for us, in accordance with the way in which our relationship to language happens, such thinking can exist. All we know, different from representational thinking, is a suspended thinking, which rests neither in representation nor in anything else. What is, then, the other thought? Perhaps a *fiction*: the hypothesis that a different type of thought exists. The central imperative of Heidegger's thought has, for the time being, only this form: We must pretend that something different from science (or philosophy) and poetry exists. We must set out toward a place that probably does not (yet) exist.

What is the purpose of such fiction—to found a possibility of a future discourse that will be neither poetic nor scientific nor philosophical in the traditional sense? Perhaps. But there is a far more immediate and pressing aim: The fiction of a forthcoming form of thought generates and justifies present writing. It is therefore a productive fiction, and even exceptionally prolific, since it does not contemplate the possibility of its own realization, and therefore of the end of the intermediary writing that is forever en route toward it.

Should we conclude that all this happens strictly and only in the interest of the philosopher, who needs for himself a space of distinction and, if possible, a privilege, to install in it his own discourse, different from all others, and his own legitimate authority, and make them last as long as possible? It would be tempting to do so: To this temptation human sciences (sisters/enemies of philosophy) yield so much more easily, inasmuch as it is in their interest that the end of metaphysics, and of philosophy itself, should be declared. They would then take over, which is already happening. However, it is not absolutely necessary to draw such a conclusion.

Not only does Heidegger's discourse remain an excellent example of the mode of discourse that I call philosophical, it also provides an illustration, and in my opinion a convincing one, of the specificity of this mode of discourse, and of its unique function in the general space of discourse. I have described philosophy as the mode of discourse that manages the relationship between language and a type of nonobjective, nonverifiable truth. I believe that this function is indispensable, in the economy of the modes of discourse such as we know them; it affords them, in effect, the occupation of spaces of meaning that science would prefer to abandon as unsafe, and art cannot elaborate rationally. Philosophy, instead, can elaborate them in flexible forms (much more flexible than those of science, but still rational) which prevent them from sliding into the oblivion of the unsaid, and make them discursively accessible.

These "spaces of meaning" concern either theoretic structures that are too ample for verification; or the pockets of nonthought in current discourses; or the possibilities of extension, revocation, replacement, or radical modification of the limits (logical, syntactical or whatever) that scientific discourses force themselves to respect, and must abide by, in order to be productive in their specific way. Any mode of discourse can, therefore, at one time or other, cross such spaces, sometimes even explicitly: this is another aspect of what I call the "philosophical moment." However, it is the specific vocation of philosophical discourse to collect, organize and exploit them. The local and historical situation in which a determined philosophical discourse is produced and addresses itself [26] determines the ways in which the selection, collection, organization, and exploitation are executed. We might presume that in philosophy, as in any other mode of discourse, there is never complete freedom or total constraint. Philosophy cannot free itself entirely from the subjection to the (mostly implicit) structures it brings to discourse. But the fact itself of bringing them to discourse means to stir the bottomless foundations of discourse: It means leaving (as much as possible) the dimension of "weak" truths and entering that of "strong" truths.

This does not "justify" philosophy; no mode of discourse can "justify" itself, that is, bring itself back to its ultimate foundation, to a final intention and reason. Philosophy, not unlike science or poetry, exists and, for as long as it lasts (which is perhaps not forever), the fact itself of its existence tells us that it has a space to fill in the domain of what can be said and thought.

Heidegger's Reader

I wish to examine now, in view of a description of the functioning of the mode of discourse that we call philosophy, the rapport between Heidegger's text and its reader.

Heidegger's thought eludes a purely logical appreciation. However, it does not (and cannot) avoid presenting itself as "proposition," and can, therefore, not disregard the reader's judgement. But of what kind shall the reader's evaluation be? Heidegger can suggest to the reader a particular type of evaluation, he can try to convince him of the pertinence of one sort of appreciation (of reading) over another one, and he does just that. However, more than Heidegger's direct suggestions, it is the structure itself of his text, a certain relative and contingent weight of his writing, that tends to limit or select "possible" and "adequate" readings.

The text presents itself (also) as a system of needs, which the reader can take into account or disregard. If he takes it into account and judges consequently, this means that to a certain extent he lets himself be convinced by the text, that he accepts to "do it justice," to follow the slope that the text, more or less subtly, provides.

What does it mean "to do justice" to a text? Why can one not read a text "objectively," for what it is, without labeling it, without having to either accept or reject anything in advance? Perhaps, first of all, because a text is *not* an object, is *nothing*; nothing readable, at least. A text, on its own, does not exist; among the conditions of its existence there is also, and first of all, the framing effected by the reader before reading, and the continuous framing carried out during reading. Both, operating normally at the unconscious level, direct the actualization of contexts and, in short, the production of meaning, which however has already always started before the beginning of reading, and partially always escapes the judgement of the reader.

Every text attempts to direct reading. However, what the text *explicitly declares* concerning the way in which it ought to be read does not necessarily coincide with the way in which the text desires and strives to be read. Heidegger's text presents itself as the fruit or the promise of a different form of thought and declares, or suggests, that it can only be correctly read in a new, unheard-of fashion. Is it really necessary to envisage a new type of discourse in order to be able to identify and read Heidegger's text, to do it justice and to judge it? Is this what the text truly requires from its reader?

I would say that the text of the late Heidegger, below the surface of his explicit declarations, wants to be read in a way that is religious, ethical, and aesthetic. It is religious because it presents itself as a sacred text, or as a legitimate commentary to a sacred text, and demands an unconditional adhesion in advance. It is ethical because it presupposes, to let itself be read, an engagement of an ethical nature, a recognition of the validity of the aims that are proposed for thought and for the reader. It is aesthetic because the intervention of poetic texts, and in general a certain poetic aura that often accompanies them, as well as the rejection of logical categories, all tend to favor a "reading as echo," through assonances and vague (also in the sense of the Latin *vagus*) associations.

If, therefore, we conclude that Heidegger's text wants to be read from a religious-ethical-aesthetic point of view, what are the consequences? That Heidegger's discourse, from the point of view of philosophy, is worthless? That it has the same value as a poetic text, with the disadvantage that it refuses to offer itself for what it is, and therefore stands in a false and untenable position? Once more we are called to deliberate on the validity of Heidegger's text, to decide whether to accept and read it, and how. And once again, instead of doing so, I shall ask the following questions: What is the "validity" of a text, for a reader? That depends on the reader. It is comprehensible, and even conceded by Heidegger in advance, that a scientist or the man in the street should find Heidegger's text illegible, useless, and even dangerous. Who or what, then, is the reader that this text calls and selects? We must make a distinction: The reader desired by the text might be different from the one the text seems to invoke.

Heidegger's text seems to call upon a *pure reader*, but I believe it wishes to convince a *reader-philosopher*, which should cause some surprise, given the attitude of its author toward philosophical discourse, at least in its traditional form. The strategy is quite classic. There is no pure reader, just as there is no pure speech, or unspecified mode of discourse: The pure reader is a fiction dear to the reader-philosopher, who is (like any reader) impure and, among other things, driven by the precise (and more often than not undeclared) interests of his corporation. Nevertheless, because of the habits already inscribed in this mode of discourse, to appeal to the pure reader is a good strategy (albeit insufficient on its own) to capture the reader-philosopher. Heidegger dreams of (phantomatic) nonlogical and nonrepresentational thinking, and, to think it, a (phantomatic) thinker who is nothing else but the idea that any philosopher has of himself.

Of course, it is not necessary to accept the radical alternative posed by the text ("follow me, or go somewhere else"). We could certainly do something else: displace, disturb, read otherwise, parasitize the text. In order to do so, we must dispose of another focus and, furthermore, choose to obey the appeal coming from it. This choice, in turn, may very well found itself on reasons, but at the very end we will find, on the side of the reader, too, corresponding with the same logical void that generates writing, an ethical motivation: One *must* read in this way. The reader-philosopher accepts as the only principle of his reading an imperative of the same type as the one the author-philosopher accepts as the only principle of his writing, that is, the ethical attraction of a truth without foundations.

This seems to open the way to all sorts of abuses;[27] in fact, the principle of decision is uncontrollable. But not so the rest of the chain, which is subject to flexible criteria of validation and even revision. This seems essential for philosophy: the desire (in its turn unjustifiable) to pursue and manage that which is least manageable, and which incessantly evades verification.

A desire to push truth and control beyond the limits of what can be verified and checked is constitutive for philosophy; hence the impossibility of finally satisfying this desire. Heidegger's "threshold" is the limit resisting this desire: We *must not* abandon the threshold; that is, we must not cease trying to push control beyond representation and metaphysics. We must not, out of impatience, abandon the threshold and lose all control. We must not attempt to regain the sort of total control that only metaphysics (illusorily) promises.

Prisoner of its imperatives and of its limits, of its desires and of its needs, the philosophical text is never pure. To reproach to Heidegger the different strategies and movements at work in his text would be as pointless as reproaching to the captain the winds and currents that shake the ship: He does not control them. One can only control a text to a limited extent: Writing, or reading, always means, essentially, abandoning oneself, sometimes with some resistance, to a drift. Writing is a compromise, and producing a philosophical discourse necessarily involves an illusion. If one wishes to write, no matter whether literature or philosophy, it is not required to be strongly aware of it; but awareness becomes necessary if one wishes to understand what writing (and in particular "writing philosophically") means.

Etymology, Quotation Marks, Rhetorical Question

Among the procedures that, albeit not directly involved with metaphorical displacement, are used in philosophical discourse in order to achieve "effects of meaning" and modify the ordinary context, we can mention the recourse to etymological references, the usage of quotation marks, and the intervention of rhetorical questions.

Heidegger's *etymologism* has been harshly criticized by many, who have pointed out mistakes in the etymological explanations proposed by the philosopher, and more generally questioned the admissibility of such instrument in the framework of philosophical discourse.[28] We know, for instance, that Heidegger was mistaken concerning the etymology of *Eignis*, which (so the specialists declare) has nothing to do with *eigen* (own); the derivation is rather from *aügnen* (to increase). But even if he had not gone wrong, why look for philosophical truth in the meanders of the genealogy of words? Heidegger's answer could be that, by going back to the origin of language, one would find not a more precise concept of its nature, but more telling[29] indications of a relationship to being that metaphysics has hastily hidden away under its network of representations. The "initial" dimension of philosophizing languages (Greek, German), more than any conceptual development, places us thus in the proximity of truth.

From this point of view, however, the etymological mistake ought to be viewed in a very serious light, particularly when it points toward a path that serious historico-linguistic studies disqualify; unless, of course, the thinker obstinately believes himself in possession of a more immediate and more true intuition of language than the experts in etymology. But even in this case, the use of etymological instruments ends up proving nothing more than is already believed. Why bother using it, then? First of all, it is clear that within the framework of Heidegger's discourse there is no question of "proving" something.[30] The use of etymology has the same function as commentary on poetic texts or the intervention of metaphors; it aims at allowing language to come to us.[31] If we accept this point of view, the fact that language does not tell us anything to confirm the theories of the various scientific disciplines should not surprise us.

From the standpoint of the present work, we maintain that Heidegger's etymology (as well as Hegel's) functions much as metaphor: It renders an occurrence "unusual" that would normally be perfectly common, and immediately recontextualizes it;[32] not, however, to the point of complete redefinition. The difference from metaphor is that the etymological explanation provides in explicit terms the extraordinary context that is necessary for the recomprehension of the occurrence, and can therefore better control it.

The use of *quotation marks* generates, on the other hand, an effect of decontextualization without resolution (except, of course, in the case when they are used only to signal something, for instance a metaphor: "Translation 'kills' the poem"). In the sentence "Deconstruction is only in first approximation the 'operation' of a 'subject,' " the quotation marks around the words 'operation' and 'subject' extract them from the immediate ordinary context of philosophy and leave them in suspension. Of course their immediate context gives them a meaning, but only a partial one. The result of quotation marks is a modification of the context by deletion of sense, rather than by addition.

The *rhetorical question* is one that admits one answer only, or heavily invites a certain answer. Are there questions in philosophy that are not rhetorical? Even without doubting the good faith of philosophers, we can still question the possibility, for those who write and those who read, of leaving or radically modifying the context in which they write or read. "Before philosophy's questioning, there is the assent of thought":[33] There is a truth and an imperative one cannot resist. Does that not decide in advance the destiny of questioning? On the other hand, any question (of this kind) that can be answered intelligibly is, to an extent, rhetorical. The answer (and even when it is not the one the questioner expected) indicates in effect that the question has been understood, and therefore that a context "comprehending" both question and answer is active: Thus, the possibility of the answer that has been actualized was there already, before being uttered. The question "with no answer" does not escape the rule, it is actually one of the best examples of a rhetorical question: A silence loaded with meaning is often precisely the expected answer. The philosophical discourse, with its long maieutic tradition, has always been particularly good at exploiting the possibilities offered by the "canalizing" question.

There is, however, one type of question (or answer) that is truly not rhetorical: It is the question (or the answer) that one does not understand, for instance because it is uttered in an unknown language, or by a madman, or in any case in the total absence of a common context. This sort of situation can even be used on purpose, for instance to analyze the phenomenon of the total interruption of sense. It can, furthermore, always be "reduced to reason," made sense of, for instance by learning the foreign language in question, or by having the particular sentence translated. But philosophical discourse, like any other discourse, only proceeds on relatively stable and well-known terrain: The entirely new would be entirely out of context. There is, however, the possibility of employing in the argumentation the whole range of "sensible questions," going from the truly "rhetorical" to the "difficult," without forgetting those "with no answer," or which are "provocative," "apparently incomprehensible," and so forth.

It remains true that there is no virginal question, whether in philosophy or elsewhere, and that a question is never the first step: "The authentic attitude of thinking is not a putting of questions—rather, it is a listening to the grant, the promise of what is to be put in question."[34] Truth comes first.

Philosophy and Metaphor

In the functioning of the philosophical mode of discourse, the role of metaphor is not secondary. In a sense, we can say that metaphor is the essential instrument of philosophy, which confirms Heidegger's ideas. However, contrary to his opinion, I believe that metaphor remains essential even in thought that strives to overcome metaphysics and representation. This is for the excellent reason that, for philosophy, at least as it is constituted today, there is no possibility of truly overcoming representation.

Furthermore, I do not believe that other modes of discourse have this possibility, except as a chance to "moderate" the metaphorical movement. Indeed this possibility is given to philosophy, too, together with the ability to make metaphor function "differently." As

I have sought to show, it is possible, for instance, to overturn it, to jam its mechanism and make it work in reverse, or to stop it at the highest point of its trajectory. But the one thing one cannot do is do without it: It comes back.

The philosophical discourse, because of the type of objects it handles and the mechanism that animates it, invokes metaphor. Concepts (and in general the rigidity of scientific languages) and the more open forms of poetic or literary discourse are unable to manage the spaces of meaning and the requirements facing philosophy. Metaphor, on the other hand, plays the principal role, because it is flexible and malleable enough to satisfy both the requirement of extension of sense and that of control of discourse, which are the two central engines of philosophy. This, however, only concerns a rather superficial level of the philosophical text; at this level only one can legitimately speak of metaphor as an instrument, and of the author as somebody who can choose his instruments. At a deeper level, this way of looking at it makes no sense, as there is no choice. The most crucial core of the philosophical operation (the one I indicated as "strong truth") has neither place nor being of its own, and is only accessible indirectly by way of representations and metaphorical displacements. All the meaning of philosophical discourse resides in the controlled approach to the "hard" cores, and can be achieved exclusively by way of metaphor (in the wide sense).

Strong truth, from its unfathomable origin, reverberates on the whole of the text: All the important articulations of philosophical discourse are, more or less openly, metaphorical in nature. Philosophy, from one end to the other, lives off metaphor; but metaphor is not the shameful side of philosophy, unless philosophy is seen as the pure element of conceptual thought that it has never been. Philosophy is the discourse exploiting all metaphorical possibilities of language, bridling them through rational procedures of control, which become stricter or looser depending on circumstances. Seriously restricting metaphor would mean, for philosophy, condemning itself to eternal repetition of what it has already been able to systematize, and therefore renouncing its vocation. It is metaphor, in fact, that disorganizes and reorganizes the world by activating analogical traits previously unperceived, as it has the capacity to disorganize the conventional order and to reorganize reality according to new schemes.

Paradoxically, truly and radically to abandon metaphor (assuming that this is possible) would mean to deprive oneself of all means to sustain philosophical discourse, to renounce reason and lose sense. This also is a possibility in the general field of discourse, a possibility that poetry sometimes explores, following other paths and driven by different motives. But this possibility is not viable for philosophy; even the discourses that more closely approach the limit of the loss of sense, of total obscurity, such as Heidegger's or Derrida's, do not cross it in truth. They cannot and wish not to cross it.

It is possible to explain in this way—as a consequence of the double necessity of "overcoming" metaphysics without renouncing meaning—not only the presence of metaphor, but also the excess of metaphor that we see in Derrida's and Heidegger's texts. Metaphor, albeit in disguise or broken, resurfaces and fills the spaces of movement and articulation of sense that more traditional procedures of control, having been in part expelled or dismantled, are no longer able to manage.[35]

Metaphor comes back, but in truth it never went away: Heidegger's and Derrida's discourses, heterodox but still strictly philosophical, can only reveal, like litmus paper, the inevitable presence of metaphor at the heart of philosophy.

To conclude this section with a concrete example, I shall now examine the way in which a particular philosophical discourse, Derrida's deconstruction, while (both in its object and in its own form) going beyond philosophy's borders in the direction of the neighboring literary-poetic discourse, manages—at a price—to keep the innermost movement of philosophy (that is, theory) alive. The example is especially telling, since it reveals the connection between metaphor and theory, and its consequences.

STRATEGIES OF DECONSTRUCTION, OR THE ENDLESS DEATH OF THEORY

Deconstructive practices take place also within nonphilosophical discourses; of particular interest to us is literary-critical discourse. What, if any, is the specific role of philosophy in literary criticism, from a deconstructive point of view? And what is the role of metaphor? What does all that tell us about philosophy?

Two Metaphors

Two opposing sets of metaphors often (albeit not always consciously) subtend the endeavors of the literary critic or theorist, and sometimes emerge in the process of defining the meaning, the objects, the methods, and the limits of what we usually call "literary theory" and "literary criticism": that is, whenever a conscious effort is made to understand, on the one hand, the nature and the structure of the literary or poetic text, and, on the other, the different ways in which the literary and poetic text can, should, or happen to be approached.

I would describe these two groups of metaphors as follows: (1) metaphors referring to the poetic/literary work as an organic, living body, on the one side; and (2) metaphors depicting the poetic/literary text as a structure of relations, spaces, and differences, on the other. On a first level, the opposition concerns the metaphor of the body/organism against the metaphor of the system/structure. It is interesting to note, however, that this alternative (rather anodyne in itself) regularly tends to slide into a stronger dichotomy sustained by a powerful (if unperceived) system of ethical values, in which the full = the body = the living is opposed to the differential = the empty = the dead. And it is not unusual to discover, associated with these, metaphors representing the critic as the one who kills the text by dissecting or violating it, as opposed to metaphors representing the critic as the one who respectfully and faithfully brings it to life or keeps it alive.

These two sets of metaphors (in short: *life* versus *death*) are somewhat special; in their irredeemable opposition nothing less than the meaning and the value of literary theory and criticism (and certainly much more than that)[36] is at stake. These two images (supposing that we can reduce them to that) often seem to command the choice of position with respect to the literary work, or to the relationship with the literary work, more powerfully than any rational argument. Precisely for this reason, the simple, overwhelming, and (perhaps) deceptive clarity of the fundamental opposition itself (life/death) needs to be carefully reconsidered.

Literary theory in general is sometimes confronted with broad reproaches that have their origin in that primary opposition; and deconstruction in particular, in many people's minds, clearly seems to dwell on the side of emptiness, of death. Its strategies (which many see as cold and senseless procedures, marked by the disdain for any practical result, and by the masochistic glorification of an intellectual "cul-de-sac") seem to justify the worst of the fears that always accompany all analytic endeavors: fears of irreparable damages inflicted on the living body (of the literary work, in this instance) that is being submitted to analysis.

Let us note, by the way, that speaking of *text* (as opposed to poem, work, novel, and so on) seems in itself a dangerous indication of preference for the deadly structuralist/poststructuralist procedures. And having pronounced these two names, I shall add that, in general, structuralism and deconstruction, in spite of all differences, are often associated together as the worst representatives of what is perceived as the "danger of theory." They are seen as similarly insensitive and cold (with similarly chilling and deadly effects) in their ways of approaching the fragile and precious life of the literary work. It will perhaps be useful to stop for a moment and give further consideration to the implicit reasons for (and the shortcomings of) such an assimilation or amalgamation.

Structuralism and Deconstruction

When we try to provide ourselves with a simple, clear idea of what structuralism and deconstruction are and of what they can contribute to the critical approach to the literary object, we inevitably run the risk of forgetting their larger (that is, properly philosophical) implications, and of reducing them to models, applications, or appliances. The student or the critically minded reader comes to the field of literary criticism and theory and expects to find a series of interchangeable tools (Marxist, psychoanalytic, sociological, structuralist, deconstructive, and so forth) with which to "access" the literary text.

This metaphor is only useful up to a point: Structuralism and deconstruction (as well as Marxism, psychoanalysis, and so on) can hardly be compressed into easily operable applications without losing much of their impact. In fact, they are not simply methods, and they do much more than just process textual material. They actually interfere with and change the world around them, mainly by modifying its coordinates.

Simply as methods of literary criticism, and if methods are to be judged from their immediate "results," structuralism and deconstruction are very poor instruments, since they almost regularly lead to some form of degeneration of their original thrusts: to inert formalism and superficial technicism in the case of structuralism; or to vagueness, nihilism, and uselessness in the case of deconstruction. But the impact of both, inside and outside the literary field, is far greater than one resulting from the mere application of fixed procedures to texts.

The fact that the scope of both structuralism and deconstruction goes beyond the limits of literary criticism, not to speak of the even narrower limits of specific *methods* in literary criticism, does not mean that their effects in literary criticism are of no value. It rather means that structuralism and deconstruction, although they can certainly be used and be considered as two methods, in literary criticism as well as in other fields, are first of all two different ways of perceiving, understanding and enacting the theoretic gesture in general. By "theoretic" gesture I mean the one by which, and in the frame of which, knowledge is made possible, gained, validated, accumulated, revised, discarded, and so forth.

This must be kept in mind at all times, in order to avoid reducing the two theoretic gestures to two mere sets of tools and procedures, and in order to perceive in their functioning implications that exceed the order of the immediate applicability. In effect, once the philosophical frame of structuralism and deconstruction has been excluded from consideration, any chance of understanding the reasons and the direction of what is going on in those gestures is forever lost, even if we were left with the perfectly understandable handbooks of two perfectly functioning text-munching machines.

In many ways, and particularly when they are seen as methods, structuralism and deconstruction can be considered as equals; that is, as two different (albeit not totally discontinuous) intellectual attitudes, two different positions on the same plane of the theoretical approach to knowledge. I would now like to raise the question of a possible difference of level, with regard to theory (its notion and its practice), between structuralism and deconstruction; a difference that inevitably tends to fade when one deals with, so to speak, *applied* structuralism and, even more, *applied* deconstruction. In fact, the risk of losing sight of the difference of level between structuralism and deconstruction is indeed one of the more immediate and less visible effects of the incorrect (or at least insufficient) perception of them as simple methods.

I should add at this point that I will not argue for the superiority of the one over the other, for instance of deconstruction over structuralism. I am interested in showing that structuralism and deconstruction (not as methods—this would be self-evident—but as theoretic movements) function in different ways and at different levels, not only and not essentially because they apply different tools to the same object, but because they create two entirely different types of objects and because the theoretic movements that they generate and exploit are radically different. This difference of level also generates a difference in the range of effects that structuralism and deconstruction produce.

To summarize the two different kinds of intellectual gesture, I would describe them, very generally,[37] as follows: Structuralism aims at *exploiting* the possibilities of a given and well-defined system. Deconstruction aims at *exploring* the limits of any given (but never closed) system. Structuralism is essentially *description and explanation*, whereas deconstruction is essentially *question*. I would go so far in this direction as to argue that for structuralism, there are basically no problems and no questions, apart from those generated and controlled within a closed system. For deconstruction all problems and questions may get out of control, which in itself is proof that no system is ever closed, and therefore that any system can be subjected to a radical interrogation concerning its borders, the sealedness of its limits.

Structuralism does not question the oppositions on which it founds itself: It either accepts or creates them. For example, it does not challenge the basic setup of the subject/object relationship. It sees itself as (and *is* in fact, to a point) the discourse of science about a certain object; for instance the literary object, which is one among many others. Anything, from a structuralist point of view, can be constituted as an "object," following an act of delimitation of the field and of definition of relevant factors and correct procedures. Deconstruction, on the other hand, questions all conceptual dichotomies, and in particular the very ones on which it (no longer entirely and securely) founds itself. Both movements can be understood only by reference to philosophical positions, or, rather, to "dispositions of philosophy": structuralism, and for example structuralist literary criticism, is philosophy at work in delimitating and analyzing a particular class of objects, for example the literary text. Deconstruction is philosophy questioning itself everywhere, even outside its own territorial limits, for instance within the literary text. The two activities seem to be mutually exclusive: In fact they are not absolutely exclusive, but distinct enough to be discernible and to place the theoretical activity of structuralism and deconstruction on two different levels.

In this respect (and, by the way, all this has a lot to do with *respect*; that is, the relation with a given order of priorities, the acceptance or rejection of a state of things) structuralism belongs to the tradition that (through both idealism and empiricism) strives to regulate the relation between subject and object that is called *theory*, and links it inextricably to the metaphorical field of *vision*. For example (and, once again, simplifying in the extreme), we could say that from the structuralist point of view the literary object (like any other object) may initially be positioned outside the field of vision of the reader/subject, but can in principle always be included in the theoretical field through operations of the mind aimed at the discovery and production of structures. This setup or disposition is never really questioned; nevertheless, it constitutes the foundation not only of structuralism, but also of that necessary part of structuralism that is at work everywhere in criticism and in theory, even beyond the recognizable legal borders of structuralism itself.

Deconstruction questions any given opposition, it even questions the very *position* from which only theory is possible (for instance, the position of the subject as external to the object): the "old name"[38] of this position is philosophy. It can therefore be argued that deconstruction sees the theoretic relationship (that is, philosophy) as a problem in itself, as the first and most important problem of theory. This problem regularly seems to be one of *limits*.

Deconstruction is haunted by the problem of limits, and attempts to deal with it as radically as possible. There is always, at the heart of theory and criticism, a problem of borders and of inclusion. For instance, in the case of literary criticism and theory, deconstruction would question the very distinctions in which those activities find their initial impulse, and ask: What is the difference between literature and theory, between literature and criticism? And, if theory and criticism belong essentially to philosophy, if not in terms of corpus, mode of discourse, guild, and genre, at least as disposition of the mind, What is the deep difference (if any) between literature and philosophy? On the other hand: What if philosophy were, after all, *inside* literature, one possible form of the literary text? Where does the one end and the other begin? These are the kinds of questions that distinguish deconstruction from, for instance, structuralism.

HEIDEGGER AND DERRIDA ON PHILOSOPHY AND METAPHOR

But not only the type of question, also the type of answer is different. For deconstruction, as everyone knows, no answer is final, all answers are strategic; that is, only locally and temporarily valid. In the case of the relationship between literature and philosophy ("Which is *in* which?"), both answers, both positions are possible. Strategically, one can and will be made temporarily dominant: *Literature* can become strategically dominant, for instance to expose the desire of philosophy to constitute itself in the absolute seclusion from the nonessential, the nonserious, and thus to deconstruct its dream of total control over itself and over the other; or *philosophy* can become strategically dominant, to show certain regularities at work in any discourse, in any kind of discourse, and even outside the proper discourse of metaphysics, even in literature or in art.

The difference between structuralism and deconstruction is not a difference in depth, nor does it derive from totally different philosophical traditions: On the contrary, Derrida himself recognizes some continuity between structuralism and deconstruction.[39] The very term "poststructuralism" (often applied also to deconstruction) implies not only an intention of overcoming, but also, and very correctly, a measure of continuity, of common belonging to the same tradition and to a destiny that, somewhere (in spite of a radical bifurcation), remains the same. At times, as we have seen, this common belonging of structuralism and deconstruction to philosophy, to theory, is even perceived as predominant, and it is very often this perception that justifies, in the name of "life" and against the dangers of hypertheoretical approaches, the coupling of structuralism and deconstruction in one and the same movement of rejection. But there are points of view from which the two machines and the two gestures are radically different, function in totally opposite directions, and refer to different and incompatible theoretical horizons.

Force and Form

> *"Form fascinates when one no longer has the force to understand force from within itself. That is, to create. This is why literary criticism is structuralist in every age, in its essence and destiny."*
>
> —Jacques Derrida[40]

It is interesting to note that one of the very first essays published by Jacques Derrida ("Force et signification," in 1963) deals precisely with a certain uneasiness with respect to the then dominant structuralist approach to the literary text.[41] Structuralism, and in particular, in Derrida's terms, "ultrastructuralism" (which is a sort of extreme generalization, at times with "degenerative" results,[42] of structuralist principles), by focusing on the teleological, simultaneous presence of its object, and by reducing it to a spatial structure (that is, to its *form*), misses in the literary work nothing less than the essential, something that Derrida—for want of something better—calls *force*.

Deconstruction in its early stages seems therefore already to include a critical approach not only to structuralism, but also to literary criticism in general, inasmuch as it must include a structuralist component. And Derrida's criticism concerns precisely the fact that structuralism, by forcing a model (in this case the geometric model) onto the text, loses sight of the specific, vital quality of the literary work.

At the same time, Derrida recognizes that a certain loss of force and life is unavoidable in literary criticism, be it officially structuralist or not. In fact, all literary criticism, as soon as it includes a theoretic movement, is (up to a point) structuralist, *precisely* because it must include a reduction of *force* to *form*. Reading with the intent of doing more than merely enjoying the text, reading with the intent of understanding not only the message delivered by the surface of the text, but also other and less explicit (but not less important) meanings, all this is already, in part, "structuralist."

On the other hand, criticism is not (and never will be) science. It belongs to the uncertain realm of the middle: to the obscure region of the limit between pleasure and duty, creation and repetition, control and drifting. Something (and not anything) has to be said about a text; something meaningful, understandable, enlightening, and new must be added to the text itself. But this "something" will never be able to exhaust the text. This might be (in utterly general terms) the specific role and limitation of any critical approach to the literary text; and this might be the reason for the constitutively precarious situation of criticism, which forces it to be always somewhat structuralist, but prevents it from fulfilling entirely the structuralist intention.

In "Force et signification," while criticizing the excessive reliance on structure and geometry (for instance—it is Derrida's example—in Jean Rousset's structuralist criticism), Derrida could be seen as exalting force, beauty, everything that, in the literary work, is mysterious and incomprehensible, inaccessible to science and to its categories. In fact, his text can only be understood by taking into account the strategic value of any deconstructive statement. The revaluation of *force* at the expense of *form* is a strategic "step back": Derrida is not trying to reach the ultimate truth of the matter, and to rescue literature from theory, but to destroy the appearance of ultimate truth that is created by the reliance on the notion of structure, and therefore to keep theory alive in its relation with the literary text.

What is force, in fact? *Force*, when opposed to *form*, seems to belong to the metaphorical field and the orbit of *life* in its cosmic opposition to *death*: This "appeal to life" is certainly visible in Derrida's text, as one of its effects. But deconstruction does not rest in the comfortable opposition of fundamental metaphors. In fact, in Derrida's text the opposition between force and form does not signal the end of the critical work; on the contrary, the opposition demands an act of deconstruction, in the course of which *force* itself (described as "a certain pure and infinite equivocality which gives signified meaning no respite, no rest, but engages it in its own *economy* so that it always signifies again and differs")[43] becomes a deconstructive factor.

What kind of critical-theoretical activity (supposing that this is what it is) is deconstruction, then? Deconstruction does indeed belong to theory, *is* a theoretic mood, remains a theoretic effort, even in spite of its own pertinacious and perfectly justifiable denial, even in spite of its own strategic rejection of the classical opposition of "theory versus practice." It remains a *motion of theory*, even if it is *not a theory*.

It is not without reason that deconstruction strives *not* to be a theory. It cannot become a theory without dying as a motion of theory. Deconstruction fights death; nevertheless, it has (indeed like any other philosophical approach to the world, I would argue), a lot to do with death. But not particularly, I surmise, with the death of its "objects," for example the literary work, whose life and radiance little depend, in general, on critical/theoretical efforts; rather with the life and death of theory itself: in other words, with *its own* unavoidable, inconceivable and endless death.

Precisely this (that is, this particular relationship between theory and death) might be the special quality of deconstruction and its specific difference from other philosophical positions. Deconstruction relates to its own life and death in a different way, as we shall see in a moment.

Metaphor, Theory, and Supertheory

Death, life; force, form; grasping, penetrating, dwelling: always metaphors. Why have all these metaphors at all, when dealing with theory? Why can we not say what theory is in a purely abstract, purely intellectual way, without detours, illustrations, or metaphors? One possible answer is that maybe there is no way of avoiding metaphor in theory, because, in fact, theory *is* metaphor: It is a certain type of metaphorical displacement of the available resources of meaning.

At the heart of theory and of our relationship with theory there is metaphorical displacement, in at least two important ways. (1) Theory produces a special kind of metaphorical displacement of the meaning when it is "applied" to a text, or to an "object" in general; it translates, shifts meanings toward a new explanatory configuration. (2) A theory, a theoretical system or cluster, is seizable and manageable only metaphorically, it is accessible only when it is possible to draw a visible, sensible (albeit not necessarily complete) model of its invisible (or even inexistent) structure.

This is the reason why the two metaphors mentioned above (text as full, living body and text as interplanetary space made up of emptiness, attraction, repulsion, difference, nothingness) are essential to the comprehension of the theoretical machines that they represent, or betray, and in general to the understanding of our relationship with the text.

In this perspective, a theory is a metaphor used to understand the world, and it in turn needs a metaphor to be understood, and even to be born. There is no possibility of isolating either one of the two terms without the other; this is clearly a circle, and this circularity is the main problem of theory, from a philosophical point of view, as I have stressed in the first chapter of the present work. From other points of view, however, it is no problem at all: The operative circularity between metaphor and theory nourishes any theoretic endeavor, and becomes an obstacle only when it is thematically approached as such, with the radicality proper to philosophy.

When it is thematically and radically approached, the problem becomes really complex and can no longer be reduced to a mere question of "style," if metaphor is not only one among many rhetorical figures, but also (in the larger sense of "displacement of meaning") all the different ways in which the discourse is ordered, strategically shaped, and disposed in order to say something and to convince: in other terms, if metaphor coincides with language in general. And if theory is not only a model, but also philosophy in general, all instances in which the power of metaphor is used to create and control truth effects. The relationship between "metaphor" (meaning) and "theory" (control) is then nothing less then the philosophical question par excellence. One aspect of this problem, as the reader will recall, is that it is no longer certain whether theory can really "use" metaphor. Beyond a point, which becomes rather uncertain, theory is itself used, driven by metaphor; will this circularity, then, perhaps finally and totally engulf philosophy's dream of theoretical control?

I shall once again abandon this question and suggest instead another, less terroristic one: Would it be possible to put together a supertheory capable of unifying and explaining the different metaphorical operations produced by the different theoretical movements and systematizations (for example, the two opposing metaphors/theories: text as body, text as net of differences)? A supertheory of theory? A model capable of encompassing all theoretic possibilities?

The question is less idle than it may seem. Deconstruction, more than a specific theory, is in my opinion a dynamic element in the path leading toward (but not nearly approaching, and for essential reasons) such a supertheory of all the possible theoretical effects. The path is not simply long: It is in fact endless. The old (and almost empty) name for such a supertheory would be, once again, as it has always been, philosophy. Today perhaps, admittedly, a philosophy in its last throes; whose agony, nevertheless, according to some, is not yet about to end.

A central element of this global (if imaginary) systematization of the theoretical effort should be the acceptance of the fact that metaphor resides at the heart of theory, and also that metaphor is essentially more a *displacement of meaning* than a meaning, and as such it can never be entirely controllable. As a consequence, first of all, let us posit a pragmatic rule, a sort of regulatory principle saying: Do not throw yourself blindly in any particular metaphor (for example—it is always the same example—"life," "death"), or do it only for exploratory purposes, to see where it leads. Don't trust a metaphor blindly, and not even a theory, because theory is always somehow metaphor, and metaphor has always to be either partly unseizable, partly ineffective, or guilty. In Derrida's terms: "Metaphor is never innocent. It orients research and fixes results."[44]

In other words, all the metaphors that we find in theory are not wrong, but the dogmatic interpretation of each one of them leads to "error." In this case, what I call error is at the same time the very force of metaphor (and of theory): its visibility, its explanatory quality, the fact that it helps understand. Indeed, we might say that there can be no understanding at all without it. But the problem is that, in any metaphor, part of the meaning must remain hidden, unseizable, absent. The petrification of a metaphor into a given meaning or set of meanings is an excess of the very "seizability" that is essential to metaphor. But, in turn, this is an effect of the even more fundamental quality of "unseizability" that accompanies all metaphorical processes. Because of its own instability, any metaphorical process tends to stabilize in an image. When a metaphor becomes perfectly clear, the unseizable parts of meaning are eliminated, and hence the grasp is total. And it is there precisely that the metaphorical effect ceases to be a displacing force and becomes an inertia, a black hole; a theoretic effort becomes a theory; a quest ends in a model. For example, the spatial model, in the case of structuralism: "When the spatial model is hit upon, when it functions, critical reflection rests within it. In fact, and even if criticism does not admit this to be so."[45]

Apart from the pragmatic principle (or the moral imperative) mentioned above, the relationship of theory and metaphor could also be approached from a different angle. And once again, the approach requires a metaphor; once again, as we shall see, life and death are involved.

Fidelity and Transgression

The strategy of deconstruction is certainly an accentuation of difference, of space, of time, against all kinds of metaphysical fullness of whatever body. But deeper than that, it is an act of fidelity to the necessity, to the fragility and to the infinity of theory, and therefore (paradoxically) it must include an element of infidelity to itself: Deconstruction cannot trust itself and its own metaphors entirely. Its mistrust starts right from the beginning, when it rejects the very possibility of providing itself with rules, theorems, principles, hence of "deciding."

Deconstruction is not (but can become, sometimes with unfortunate results) a *method* for reading texts. First of all, deconstruction is a strategy of exasperated but controlled attention to the fact that, before the text (before the world), total awareness is not possible, complete control is never reached, full presence of the meaning, of the intention, of the truth, is out of range. Deconstruction does not dictate rules; on the contrary, it always also looks for the unruly. Its only regulatory principle is a double one: that any intelligible text must simultaneously belong, in one form or other, to *the same* (the *logos*, the past, the only way in which we can reasonably think and make ourselves understood), and that no text can exclude from itself *the other* (the unseen, the illogical, the difference, the noise).

Deconstruction is at the same time faithful and unfaithful, reactionary and revolutionary, stuck in the possible and stretched toward the unthinkable. By denying itself access to a totalizing system, deconstruction confesses its own finiteness and mortality, but postpones indefinitely its own death; and this is precisely what makes it best suited, in a certain particular moment, and not forever, to the theoretical endeavor, to the endless life/death of theory. Not forever, because even deconstruction inevitably tends to solidify into a set of metaphors, into a position, a theory, a method; and any theory, sooner or later, becomes repetitive and unproductive, and (maybe only temporarily) dies.

Deconstruction is the ambiguous position from which one half-resists and half-accepts one's own language, metaphors, past. This position requires a complex strategy, one important aspect of which is what Derrida calls "paleonymy" (the art of old names): the strategic use of old names, of old words, of words taken into the network of the language, but deformed, distorted, obliged to mean something different, to differ from themselves. Deconstruction is always a strategic act, and strategy is certainly a problem of space, but also and first of all of time; time, as the dimension of change, is essential to deconstruction. A strategic act requires time, is not conceivable in the absolute, but only as a moment in a sequence of moments. In this sequence a change or even a complete reversal of positions is possible: No moment is final, no meaning is fixed.

As a consequence, the notion of strategy in deconstruction presents one obvious difference from its normal usage: there are no final aims, objectives, or positions to conquer. But even this statement is not final: on the other hand, as a matter of fact, in different contexts, there may indeed be positions to conquer and to maintain. We only need to think of current debates in universities, where deconstruction has risen to powerful institutional positions, is being attacked and is resisting attack. This is not specific to deconstruction, and deconstruction cannot avoid it: Intellectual positions and institutional positions should not be totally confused with one another, but definitely there is a relationship, and an evolution of this relationship, between the two.

However, the position of deconstruction with regard to theory (that is, with regard to a specific way of pursuing the truth) and with regard to metaphor (that is, with regard to language, its limits, its traps, and so forth) is specific and makes deconstruction different from other positions, and this difference can be best perceived through the metaphor of strategy. This means, for instance, that the position from which, and the movements within which, the statements of deconstruction are uttered are more important and crucial than those statements and their contents themselves.

Even the metaphor of strategy, then, is strategic and temporary. Deconstruction can only momentarily be seen as a strategy, that is, as a series of acts unified by a certain intention. There are important aspects of deconstruction that are not conveyed, that are even utterly betrayed by this metaphor or "old name." At times, deconstruction can also (and better) be described, for instance, as a drama that happens entirely *within* the text itself; in which opposed forces not governed by any intentional agency come to grips with each other.[46] From this point of view, the literary object deconstructs itself by showing/hiding its belonging/nonbelonging to multiple and contradictory dimensions, and finally contributes to deconstruct (which does not mean to destroy) the distinction between the opposing dimensions themselves.

Deconstruction anticipates the partial failure of any one of its own statements, which does not make them meaningless, but, rather, strategically operative. A typically deconstructive statement, such as, "There is nothing outside the text," is valid only dynamically, as part of a strategy, and does not exclude the validity, in a different context, or from a different point of view, of the very opposite statement: "Everything is outside the text." Once again, the real problem here is not the truth or the falsity of the statement itself; the real problem is that the strategy, in spite of the extreme caution and prudence with which it is carried out, is not entirely controllable, being in fact always much more a motion of the language, the partly controlled liberation of a fold, of an anfractuosity of language, than a movement of an intentionally determining subject.

Deconstruction is always more a matter of questions than a matter of answers. As everybody knows, there are at least two kinds of questions: "internal" questions, which require, allow, and direct an answer; and "external" questions, which pursue an impossible answer. That is, questions whose deep intention is not to find an answer, but to keep the questioning alive, because of reasons escaping the rational order, and essentially in fulfillment of an ethical need to look for truth even beyond the possibility of an answer. The kind of questions that deconstruction asks are basically of the second type, namely, questions with no answer. When an answer is offered, often it consists in excluding the ability of a particular answer to provide a solution to a particular question, and thereby in keeping the questioning open.

Life and Death

The question of death, of mortality, as I have already indicated, concerns theory in a very central way. Let us think for a moment of death, ideally, not as an interruption, but as the accomplishment of a process. Let us imagine life as the desire to rest, to die. All that which is vital wishes to die, but not before its own time; it wishes to die, and can rest (like Samuel Beckett's voices), only after the exhaustion of all its given possibilities.

The peace that is calling from the end of life asks the living/dying to exhaust the possibilities, to try all the differences; not because difference is good in itself, but because the path of difference is the voyage of life toward death. Death is then no longer the absolute opposite of life; it is its accomplishment, its "summa." As far as theory is concerned, it is the total and instantaneous recollection of all possible combinations of thought.

This, perhaps, (beyond all reasons and interests, and without excluding them) is what drives theory: the unreasonable, unjustifiable compulsion to occupy and control with the means of reason all the available and all the possible spaces of meaning. Not only for the sake of power, but also and even more for the sake of peace; so as to be able, having said all there is to say and explained all there is to explain, finally to rest; which, of course, is impossible.[47]

Through its metaphors, theory endlessly approaches super-theory, its own accomplishment, end, and death. Petrified metaphors, perfectly working models, can never exhaust all possibilities; they become static, each of them a trap for the meaning. It is each time a bad end, a false death for theory. A new metaphor will soon be born.

Real beings always reach death before all possibilities have been exhausted. In particular, death is always untimely for human beings, because their species seems to know no limits to its own possibilities. But the process of human knowledge, of which theory is a part, can afford an endless death, must take advantage of this, and is trapped in it. Deconstruction is, among many other things, a powerful reminder of the endless death of theory.

The general theory of theory, or the general metaphor of theory, if anything like that existed, would be at the same time a theory and a metaphor and therefore also, in a circular way, the theory (or the metaphor) of the infinity of the effort, of the unseizability of metaphor, of the impossibility of theory.

Everything, therefore, seems to revolve around metaphor. Indeed Derrida often gives the impression of exalting metaphor, which is true, but not absolutely true. For deconstruction (and this is easily said and repeated, but much less easy to think and, so to speak, to put into practice) nothing is absolute, nothing is pure, everything has to be seen from a strategic point of view. The recognition of metaphor and the proliferation of metaphors are part of the strategic deconstruction of metaphysics. But any metaphor can in turn become a body, a metaphysical body of absolute presence and fullness of meaning, of truth, and thus it automatically becomes the new "target" of the deconstructive strategy, not because it is a metaphor, but because it no longer is a metaphor: It has been transformed into a solid body, a final body of celestial purity and perfection.

Philosophy, as we have seen, has long fought against metaphor, but for different reasons or for precisely the opposite reason; namely, that it saw (and still sees) metaphor as a danger for its own body (be it textual or spiritual), for presence, for truth.

In deconstruction (and, according to deconstruction, everywhere), any truth, any presence, any meaning is metaphorical, partially absent, partially improper. Metaphor cannot be avoided; and even the solidification of metaphor is necessary to a certain extent, because there is no intellectual understanding without representation, without image.

But beyond this uncertain limit, any metaphor becomes an obstacle, not to some superior or deeper truth, but simply to other metaphors, to more possibilities, and to the final, inconceivable peace of the accomplished exhaustion of the possible, which remains the mortal aim of theory.

NOTES

1. "Elle fait ce qu'elle veut, mais elle ne veut que ce qu'elle peut; elle est libre, et non souveraine." So says Valéry of language; quoted by Arion L. Kelkel, *La légende de l'être. Langage et poésie chez Heidegger* (Paris: Vrin, 1980), p. 610.

2. This is the "nonvoluntary decision (*décision non volontaire*)," which is not made by a subject, mentioned by Derrida in connection with Heidegger's "*Aufriss*" ("*entame*" in French). Jacques Derrida, "Le retrait de la métaphore," *Po&sie* 7 (1978); henceforth RM): 122; "The *Retrait* of Metaphor," *Enclitic* 2, no. 2 (1978): 29.

3. Of course one could widen the notion of "mode of discourse" to include in it nonlinguistic productions, such as those of the figurative or musical artistic disciplines. For the present discussion, however, I shall only take into consideration those discourses that share with philosophy the immersion in the linguistic element.

4. Jean Greisch, *La parole heureuse. Martin Heidegger entre la parole et les mots* (Paris: Beauchesne, 1987; henceforth PH), p. 181: "La langue est donc plus qu'un simple reflet de la perception objective du monde. Elle n'est pas seulement médiatrice entre moi et autrui, mais entre moi et le monde."

5. See below the definition of *producer*.

6. I shall come back to this.

7. See Max Black, *Models and Metaphors* (Ithaca: Cornell University Press, 1962), p. 219: Black analyzes the functioning of scientific models and identifies three types of models at work in science: (1) scale models, (2) analogical models, and (3) theoretical models.

8. Paul Ricoeur, *The Rule of Metaphor* (Toronto: University of Toronto Press, 1977), p. 240; *La métaphore vive* (Paris: Editions du Seuil, 1975; henceforth MV), p. 302.

9. Mary Hesse, "The Explanatory Function of Metaphor," in *Logic, Methodology and Philosophy of Science*, ed. Y Bar-Hillel (Amsterdam: North-Holland, 1965); quoted by Ricoeur, *The Rule of Metaphor*, p. 242; MV, p. 304. On the question of models, see also Jean Molino, "Métaphores, modèles et analogies dans les sciences," *Langages* 54 (1979): 83–102; and Silvana Borutti, "Le virtù ermeneutiche dei modelli," *Materiali filosofici* 15 (September–December 1985): 62–88.

10. Chaïm Perelman and Lucie Olbrechts-Tyteca, *Rhétorique et philosophie. Pour une théorie de l'argumentation en philosophie* (Paris: P.U.F., 1952), p. 39.

11. It is probably in a similar sense that Heidegger says that language allows man "to figure a world" (*Gesamtausgabe* 29/30, p. 409; quoted by Greisch, PH, p. 160).

12. Quoted by Tzvetan Todorov, *Symbolism and Interpretation* (London: Routledge and Kegan Paul, 1983), p. 7.

13. This (pushing the desire for truth beyond its "objective" limits) can be seen in connection to the "will for totality" that Ernst Cassirer (in an entirely different context and with a different intention) describes in *Language and Myth* (New York and London: Harper and Brothers, 1946) as the animating principle of all theoretical activity. If this is true, there would be a common theoretical intention between science and philosophy, which however would exert itself in different ways.

14. Martin Heidegger, *On the Way to Language*, trans. Peter Hertz and Joan Stambaugh (New York: Harper & Row, 1971), p. 155; *Unterwegs Zur Sprache* (Pfullingen: Neske, 1959; henceforth US), p. 237: "Sich das Denkwürdige sagen lassen, heißt—Denken."

15. However, I am not prepared to declare that it is not: I am simply leaving this question suspended.

16. Perelman and Olbrechts-Tyteca, *Rhétorique et philosophie*, chap. 5: "La quête du rationnel." The consequence of this is that only rhetoric can provide us with an understanding of the nature of the "philosophical proof" (ibid., chap. 6: "De la preuve en philosophie").

17. Heidegger, *On the Way to Language*, p. 42; US, p. 138.

18. In Greisch's words, "the specifically 'itinerant' character of Heidegger's thought is of another order than grammatology's *exhorbitant errance*" ("le caractère spécifiquement 'itinérant' de la pensée de Heidegger est d'un autre ordre que l'errance *exorbitante* de la grammatologie" [MR, 435 n.]). Derrida himself, as we have seen, rejects the idea of a "direct continuity" between his own thought and that of Heidegger.

19. Of course Heidegger, once more, would not approve of this terminology.

20. Neither should we wish for it. See Heidegger, *On the Way to Language*, p. 96; US, p. 202.

21. "Perhaps we can in some slight measure prepare for the transformation in our kinship with language" (Martin Heidegger, *Basic Writings* [London: Routledge, 1993], p. 425; US, p. 267).

22. US, p. 19; Martin Heidegger, *Poetry, Language, Thought*, trans. Albert Hofstadter (1971; reprint, New York: Harper & Row, 1975), p. 196.

23. Henri Birault, *Heidegger et l'expérience de la pensée* (Paris: Gallimard, 1978), p. 170.

24. Heidegger, *Poetry, Language, Thought*, p. 208; US, p. 31.

25. Heidegger, *On the Way to Language*, p. 84; US, p. 190: "Wir müssen erst da-hin zurückkehren, wo wir uns eigentlich schon aufhalten."

26. "Every proper language . . . is sent, hence fateful," says Heidegger. "There is no such thing as a natural language, a language that would be the language of a human nature at hand in itself and without its own destiny. Every language is historical. . . ." (Heidegger, *Basic Writings*, p. 422; US, p. 264).

27. Heidegger is aware of the danger and indicates the need to resist

any abandonment to what he calls *"das Unverbindliche"* (US, p. 123; *On the Way to Language*, p. 30).

28. PH, pp. 154–55: "The etymological method displaces indefintely a question that it cannot truly resolve. . . . Etymology's paths lead nowhere, at least in philosophy . . . one plays games with language, and such games are always dangerous." ("La méthode étymologique déplace indéfiniment une question qu'elle n'arrive pas vraiment à résoudre. . . . Les chemins de l'étymologie ne mènent nulle part, du moins en philosophie . . . on joue avec le langage, et de tels jeux sont toujours dangereux.") Greisch concedes however that the game can have some heuristic value.

29. The aim is, in fact, to find not the "true" but the "old" sense of the words: "Here we are thinking of the old sense of command . . ." (Heidegger, *Poetry, Language, Thought*, p. 206). "Hier denken wir den alten Sinn von Befehlen . . ." (US, p. 28).

30. Greisch: "The 'primitive meaning' has no normative value, but only an indicative function" ("Le «sens primitif» n'a pas de valeur normative, mais uniquement une fonction indicative [Hinweis, Wink]") (Jean Greisch, "Les mots et les roses. La métaphore chez Martin Heidegger," Revue des sciences philosophiques et théologiques 57 [1973; henceforth MR]: 449). Kelkel: "Heidegger's thought becomes commemorative of the original meaning of words, not so much in order to restaure a lost meaning and origin, but rather in order to recuperate its own power of poietic utterance" ("La pensée de Heidegger se fait commémorative du sens originaire des mots non tant pour restituer un sens et une origine perdus, que pour recouvrer sa propre force de parler poiétique") (*La légende de l'être. Langage et poésie chez Heidegger*, p. 540).

31. Jacques Derrida, *Glas* (Paris: Galilée, 1974), p. 187, right column: ". . . il faut laisser s'élaborer silencieusement le glas de la langue. . . . Et puis vous croyez et voulez faire croire que vous êtes le maître de ce travail de la langue: elle ne s'élabore plus, elle ne bande plus." *Glas*, trans. John P. Leavey Jr. and Richard Rand (Lincoln and London: University of Nebraska press, 1986), p. 166, right column: ". . . it is necessary to let silently elaborate itself the *glas* of the tongue. . . . And then you believe

and want to make others believe that you are the master of this work of the tongue: the tongue no longer eleborates itself, no longer bands erect."

32. Ricoeur: "When Hegel hears *taking-true* in *Wahrnehmung*, when Heidegger hears *non-dissimulation* in *a-lêtheia*, the philosopher creates meaning and in this way produces something like a living metaphor" (*The Rule of Metaphor*, p. 292). I would add that while practicing dubious etymologism, he "redistributes" meaning.

33. Birault, *Heidegger et l'expérience de la pensée*, p. 364.

34. Heidegger, *On the Way to Language*, p. 71; US, p. 175.

35. A quotation from Blumenberg seems here particularly relevant: "Metaphysics has often seemed to us a metaphorology taken literally; the dissolution of metaphysics calls metaphor to take back its rightful place" (Hans Blumenberg, *Paradigmi per una metaforologia*, trans. M. V. S. Hansberg [Bologna: Il Mulino, 1969], p. 183).

36. It could perhaps be argued that the opposition between these two metaphoric fields informs all instances of the relationship between an understanding subject and a meaningful object, however complicated or uncertain this relationship may become through the elaboration (or deconstruction) of the very notions of "subject," "object," and "meaning."

37. The following generalization is indeed very extreme. I am aware of the existence of many variations in the structuralist gesture, not all of which will easily fit my description. But I agree with Derrida when he hints that "ultrastructuralism" shows something which is present in any kind of structuralism. See "Force and Signification," in *Writing and Difference*, trans. Alan Bass (Chicago: University of Chicago Press, 1978).

38. See Jacques Derrida, *Dissemination*, trans. Barbara Johnson (London: Athlone Press, 1993), pp. 3ff.

39. ". . . we take nourishment from the fecundity of structuralism . . ." (J. Derrida, "Force and Signification," in *Writing and Difference*, p. 4).

40. Ibid., pp. 4–5. "La forme fascine quand on n'a plus la force de comprendre la force en son dedans. C'est-à-dire de créer. C'est pourquoi la critique littéraire est structuraliste à tout âge, par essence et destinée" (Jacques Derrida, *L'écriture et la différence* [Paris: Editions du Seuil, 1967], p. 11).

41. On Derrida's position on structuralism, see also "Structure, Sign and Play in the Discourse of the Human Sciences," in *Writing and Difference*.

42. "What is most serious is that this 'ultrastructuralist' method, as we have called it, seems to contradict, in certain respects, the most precious and original intention of structuralism" ("Force and Signification," in *Writing and Difference*, p. 26; *L'écriture et la différence*, p.43).

43. Ibid., 25. ". . . une certaine équivocité pure et infinie ne laissant aucun répit, aucun repos au sens signifié, l'engageant, en sa propre économie, à faire signe encore et à différer" (*L'écriture et la différence*, p. 42). The notion of *force* is here, I believe, the forerunner of what, at that time, did not yet (and indeed never will) have a proper name: *la différance*.

44. Ibid., p. 17. *L'écriture et la différence*, p. 30.

45. Ibid.

46. See, for instance, Jonathan Culler, *On Deconstruction* (London, Melbourne, and Henley: Routledge & Kegan Paul, 1983), p. 216.

47. The question whether or not this compulsion is exclusive to theory and makes it different from science, politics, art, and other spheres of activity, is central to the problem in hand, but must remain unanswered for the time being.

IN PLACE OF A CONCLUSION

"*Interrompre, ici, par décision et coup de tête.*"
—Jacques Derrida[1]

The temptation of every (impossible) conclusion, symmetrical to that of every (endless) introduction: to start again, refine, modify, add; to carry on, indefinitely, along the path that it has been so difficult to open up in the first place, and which could not lead to the treatise or the encyclopedia, even less to the system. But we must restrain ourselves; conclude, and stand back, without which true continuation and advancement would not be possible. To conclude at all costs, therefore, let me offer some remarks that should help either to clarify or underline the sense of what precedes, or to signal its essentially incomplete character.

261

HEIDEGGER AND DERRIDA ON PHILOSOPHY AND METAPHOR

On the border of an interrogation of philosophy today, I have isolated two cases (Heidegger and Derrida) that seemed significant
because of their specific character, at the same time extreme and
provocative, and (within the dynamics of a specific mode of discourse in a specific epoch) radically "normal." However, I also chose
them (it is almost superfluous to confess it now) because of an
appeal, and of an answer to it that I believe I can only justify by
saying that I thought it right to pay attention to that appeal, and to
answer it: ". . . such listening to the grant for what we are to think
[*die Zusage des zu-Denkende*] always develops into our asking for the
answer."[2] I read this as meaning that, under any accumulation of
questions, an answer to the appeal is waiting from the beginning.[3]

Nevertheless, to pay attention, to answer, does not mean to
accept and to repeat blindly; in my case, the answer is often loaded
with doubt and sometimes rather close to rejection. This oscillation
may have irritated some readers; but the rigid alternatives of approbation and rejection do not belong to this work's repertory of
effects, and I tried to avoid forcing the choice, as much as possible,
knowing that it is not entirely possible.

Concerning what he calls Heidegger's "first philosophy," Greisch
claims to aim at "a rigor of analysis that places itself beyond a double
mistake; the mistake of a purely tautological discourse, or on the
contrary the mythopoietic charms of a reason abandoning itself to
poetry."[4] I, too, have tried to avoid this double misunderstanding,
and in particular to avoid closing on a mystical-dogmatic note. I
believe that Heidegger's discourse is at times openly and fiercely tautological, but I also believe that tautology is never absolutely devoid
of sense, and that Heidegger's tautology is actually loaded with it.
That he sometimes abounds in mythopoietic enchantments and is
very close to the (virtual) limit of poetry, if it were not for his delib-

erate slowness, his control, and his "suffering." And that Heidegger
knows and says all this very ably, at least to the—inevitably limited—
extent a writer is able to know and say.

This limited and specific ability to know and to say takes, within
philosophical discourse, the shape of *speculation*.[5] In the close contact with Heidegger's text we discover that speculation is above all a
matter of *pace* and of *rhythm*. The *speculative pace* is the limping one,
a painful coming and going of thought that restrains itself on the
threshold of pleasure. The *speculative rhythm* is the insistent, obsessive
repetition that results from it. Speculation is, therefore, the infinite
postponement of pleasure, of representational and conceptual
accomplishment. The *end of representation*, that is, the end of metaphor, is in fact also the end of speculation. The accomplished, per-
fected system, which no longer deems itself metaphorical, is no
longer speculative.

Heidegger speculates; he theorizes and invests, anticipating a
future gain. Does he invest in or against metaphor? In and against, at
the same time. "To speculate in metaphor" can also mean this: to
invest in and against, in one's own interest. A coitus interruptus in
one's own interest? Yes, in the long term. To restrain oneself, to keep
one's drives in check, the drive to domination, the conceptual drive.
Why? So as not to have on one's hands a cumbersome bundle. Perhaps also for the pure pleasure of dominating the drive (*Bemächti-
gungstrieb*). Perhaps also in order better to in debt one's descendants,
better to bond them to oneself by making them inherit as infinite as
possible a legacy; by generating for them (and for oneself) the greatest
possible quantity of controlled energy. To speculate on and in the
descendants; to speculate on and in one's descendants' speculations.

What does all this mean? That it is a good idea to make things as
complicated and obscure as possible, lest readers should stop won-
dering too soon? Not just that: also, not to abandon in the hands of

the descendants too cumbersome a bundle, which sooner or later would force them to discard it. But certainly also to leave in their hands a bundle just big enough to make it difficult for them to abandon it; to unlimit the bundle, and the debt; to get oneself, and the descendants, into debt, into an endless future path; to make oneself unavoidable, uncircumventable, for a long time.[6]

It is not at all necessary that all this should be intentional, and even less that it should be interpreted as a symptom of lack of intellectual integrity. Writing, inasmuch as it wishes to stay, is never innocent, and its effects depend neither on the author's intentions, nor on his degree of moral integrity. The philosophical mode of discourse requires that all the "truth" be told, which it is possible to tell without utterly and completely losing control. The fate of what has been said depends only on the state, and subsequent modifications, of the field within which it is interpreted.

The *trait* is probably the most mysterious character in this story, and it somehow sums up all the enigmatic atmosphere that, under the species of the "indecidable," of the *Ereignis*, and so forth, reigns in it. The trait is not namable itself, either literally or metaphorically: What are we doing, then, when we name it, when we talk of the "trait"?

It is neither a thing, nor a being, nor a meaning. However, there is meaning in all this. It is not necessary to have at hand a specific sense in order to have *some* meaning.

The *pathos* of the ineffable is always ready to jump on such a golden opportunity to kneel before mystery. However, the theory of the philosophical mode of discourse provides the tools to analyze these margins of undecidability without risking transforming them into sinister idols. They are, simply, the nonmetaphorical limits of a metaphorical impetus; the (provisionally) external border of a discourse that accepts no limits, except those that derive from the need to stand up as discourse, to permit its own reading. Philosophy wants to say it all, but it cannot, and sometimes it says more than the state of the field can authorize or tolerate. This "saying more" says almost nothing intelligible within the field (that is, intelligible *tout court*), but it signals the groundless foundations of the field itself. This quasi-analogical and allusive reference to the faceless magma that "precedes" language does not necessarily mean that deconstruction is a myth of the origins, or a negative theology. I should say, however, that it includes echoes of both, which does not seem at all shameful to me. Not only is philosophy close to poetry, it is also not far from theology and from myth, though its intention is profoundly different.

The "evasion from the field" is the defining element of philosophy today, and probably not only today. Philosophy is, essentially, no more metaphorical than previously. Sometimes, however, it can only be, today, *catastrophically* metaphorical, as Derrida has taught us, to safeguard its perilous and necessary balance on the border between the sayable and the unsayable. The management of this border, as awkward as it may be, is nothing mysterious. Nothing of what is said, or felt, or intended, is perfectly unsayable: We say it, as best we can, and that (usually) makes some sort of sense. However, nothing of what is sayable is perfectly said once and for all: We can and we must say it again, perfect it, repudiate it, carry on.

NOTES

1. Jacques Derrida, *La dissémination* (Paris: Editions du Seuil, 1972), p. 67. "To break off here, clear-headedly and for kicks" (*Dissemination*, trans. Barbara Johnson [London: Athione Press, 1993], p. 58).

2. Martin Heidegger, *On the Way to Language*, trans. Peter Hertz and Joan Stambaugh (New York: Harper & Row, 1971), p. 75; *Unterwegs zur Sprache* (Pfullingen: Neske, 1959; henceforth US), p. 180.

3. US, p. 175: "Jeder Ansatz jeder Frage hält sich schon innerhalb der Zusage dessen auf, was in die Frage gestellt wird" (Heidegger, *On the Way to Language*, p. 71: "Every posing of every question takes place within the very grant of what is put in question").

4. Jean Greisch, *La parole heureuse. Martin Heidegger entre la parole et les mots* (Paris: Beauchesne, 1987), p. 15: "Cela réclame une rigueur de l'analyse qui se situe au-delà d'une double méprise; soit la méprise d'un discours purement tautologique, soit au contraire les enchantements mythopoietiques d'une raison s'abandonnant à la poésie."

5. The reader will hear in what follows the echo of Derrida's "To Speculate—on Freud," in *The Post Card: From Socrates to Freud and Beyond*, trans. Alan Bass (Chicago: University of Chicago Press, 1987).

6. Derrida and Ricoeur, among others, often use, talking of Heidegger, the adjective *incontournable*. See also, for a critical counterpoint, Jean Bollack and Heinz Wismann, "Heidegger l'incontournable," *Actes de la recherche en sciences sociales* 5, no. 6 (November 1975): 157–61.

BIBLIOGRAPHY

Adorno, Theodor. *Jargon der Eigentlichkeit. Zur deutschen Ideologie.* Frankfurt: Suhrkamp, 1964. Translated by K. Tarnowski and F. Will under the title *The Jargon of Authenticity* (London: Routledge and Kegan Paul, 1973).

Allemann, Beda. *Hölderlin et Heidegger.* 1959. Reprint, Paris: Presses Universitaires de France, 1987.

Aristotle. *Rhétorique.* Translated by M. Dufour and A. Wartelle. Paris: Editions des Belles Lettres, 1961.

————. *La métaphysique.* Translated by J. Tricot. 2 vols. Paris: Vrin, 1981.

————. *Poétique.* Translated by J. Hardy. Paris: Editions des Belles Lettres, 1969.

Bachelard, Gaston. *La poétique de l'espace.* Paris: Presses Universitaires de France, 1981. Translated by M. Jolas under the title *The Poetics of Space* (Boston: Beacon Paperback, 1976).

Beardsley, Monroe C. *Aesthetics*. New York: Harcourt, Brace and World, 1958.

Birault, Henri. *Heidegger et l'expérience de la pensée*. Paris: Gallimard, 1978.

Black, Max. *Models and Metaphors*. Ithaca: Cornell University Press, 1962.

Blumenberg, Hans. *Paradigmi per una metaforologia*. Translated by M. V. S. Hansberg. Bologna: Il Mulino, 1969.

Bollack, Jean, and Heinz Wismann. "Heidegger l'incontournable." *Actes de la recherche en sciences sociales* 5, no. 6 (November 1975): 157-61.

Bonesio, Luisa, ed. *Nietzsche: la critica della verità*. Bologna: Zanichelli, 1977.

Borges, Jorge Luis. *Obra póetica*. Buenos Aires: Emecé Editores, 1975.

Borutti, Silvana. "Le virtù ermeneutiche dei modelli." *Materiali filosofici* 15 (September–December 1985): 62–88.

Bourdieu, Pierre. "L'ontologie politique de M. Heidegger." *Actes de la recherche en sciences sociales* 5, no. 6 (November 1975): 109–55. Translated by Peter Collier under the title *The Political Ontology of Martin Heidegger* (Cambridge: Polity, 1991).

Bouveresse, Jacques. *La parole malheureuse. De l'alchimie linguistique à la grammaire philosophique*. Paris: Editions de Minuit, 1971.

———. *Le philosophe chez les autophages*. Paris: Editions de Minuit, 1984.

Casenave, Gerald. "Heidegger and Metaphor." *Philosophy Today* (summer 1982): 140–47.

Cassirer, Ernst. *Language and Myth*. Translated by S. K. Langer. New York and London: Harper and Brothers, 1946.

Croce, Benedetto. "Noterella sulla metafora." In *Problemi di estetica*. Bari: Laterza, 1966.

Culler, Jonathan. *On Deconstruction: Theory and Criticism after Structuralism*. London, Melbourne, and Henley: Routledge & Kegan Paul, 1983.

De Man, Paul. "Theory of Metaphor in Rousseau's 'Second Discourse.' " *Studies in Romanticism* 12 (1973): 475–98.

Derrida, Jacques. "Le retrait de la métaphore." *Po&sie* 7 (1978): 104–26. Translated under the title "The *Retrait* of Metaphor." *Enclitic* 2, no. 2 (1978): 5–33.

————. *De la grammatologie.* Paris: Editions de Minuit, 1967. Translated by G. C. Spivak under the title *Of Grammatology* (Baltimore: Johns Hopkins University Press, 1976).

————. *Eperons. Les styles de Nietzsche.* Paris: Flammarion, 1978.

————. *Glas.* Paris: Galilée, 1974. Translated by John P. Leavey Jr. and Richard Rand under the title *Glas* (Lincoln and London: University of Nebraska Press, 1986).

————. *L'écriture et la différence.* Paris: Editions du Seuil, 1967. Translated by Alan Bass under the title *Writing and Difference* (Chicago: University of Chicago Press, 1978).

————. *La carte postale.* Paris: Aubier-Flammarion, 1980. Translated by Alan Bass under the title *The Post Card: From Socrates to Freud and Beyond* (Chicago: University of Chicago Press, 1987).

————. *La dissémination.* Paris: Editions du Seuil, 1972. Translated by Barbara Johnson under the title *Dissemination* (London: Athlone Press, 1993; Chicago: University of Chicago Press, 1981).

————. *Marges. De la philosophie.* Paris: Editions de Minuit, 1972. Translated by Alan Bass under the title *Margins of Philosophy* (Chicago: University of Chicago Press, 1982).

Finas, L., S. Kofman, R. Laporte, and J.-M. Rey. *Ecarts. Quatre essais à propos de Jacques Derrida.* Paris: Fayard (Digraphe), 1973.

Fontanier, Pierre. *Les figures du discours.* Paris: Flammarion, 1977.

Gadamer, Hans-Georg. *Truth and Method.* Translated by William Glen-Doepel; edited by John Cumming and Garrett Barden. London: Sheed and Ward, 1979.

Genette, Gerard. *Figures III.* Paris: Editions du Seuil, 1972.

Greisch, Jean. "Les mots et les roses. La métaphore chez Martin Heidegger." *Revue des sciences philosophiques et théologiques* 57 (1973): 433–55.

————. *La parole heureuse. Martin Heidegger entre la parole et les mots.* Paris: Beauchesne, 1987.

Hegel, Georg Wilhelm Friedrich. *Aesthetics: Lectures on Fine Art.* Translated by T. M. Knox. Oxford: Clarendon Press, 1974–75.

————. *Phenomenology of Spirit.* Translated by A. V. Miller. Oxford: Oxford University Press, 1979.

Heidegger, Martin. *Basic Writings.* Revised and expanded edition. Edited by D. F. Krell. London: Routledge, 1993.

————. *Der Satz vom Grund.* Pfullingen: Neske, 1957. Translated by R. Lilly under the title *The Principle of Reason* (Bloomington: Indiana University Press, 1991).

————. *Lettre sur l'humanisme.* Translated by R. Munier. 1964. Reprint, Paris: Aubier, 1983. Translated under the title *Letter on Humanism.* In *Basic Writings* (London: Routledge, 1993).

————. *Nietzsche.* Vol. 2. Translated by David Farrell Krell. San Francisco: Harper & Row, 1984.

————. *Poetry, Language, Thought.* Translated by Albert Hofstadter. 1971. Reprint, New York: Harper & Row, 1975.

————. *Sein und Zeit.* Tübingen: Niemeyer, 1972.

————. *Unterwegs zur Sprache.* Pfullingen: Neske, 1959. Translated by Peter Hertz and Joan Stambaugh under the title *On the Way to Language* (New York: Harper & Row, 1971).

Hesse, Mary B. "The Explanatory Function of Metaphor." In *Logic, Methodology and Philosophy of Science.* Edited by Y. Bar-Hillel. Amsterdam: North-Holland, 1965.

Janicaud, Dominique, and Jean-François Mattéi. *La métaphysique à la limite. Cinq études sur Heidegger.* Paris: P.U.F, 1983. Translated by M. Gendre under the title *Heidegger from Metaphysics to Thought* (Albany: SUNY, 1995).

Kelkel, Arion L. *La légende de l'être. Langage et poésie chez Heidegger.* Paris: Vrin, 1980.

Kofman, Sarah. *Nietzsche et la métaphore.* Paris: Payot, 1972.

Lacan, Jacques. "Séminaire sur *La lettre volée.*" In *Ecrits.* Paris: Editions du Seuil, 1966.

Le Doeuff, Michèle. *L'imaginaire philosophique.* Paris: Payot, 1980. Translated by Colin Gordon under the title *The Philosophical Imaginary* (London: Athlone Press, 1989).

Martin, Janet. "Metaphor amongst Tropes." *Religious Studies* 1 (1981).

Molino, Jean. "Métaphores, analogies et modèles dans les sciences." *Langages* 54 (1979): 83–102.

Nietzsche, Friedrich. *Das Philosophenbuch/Le livre du philosophe*. Translated by A. K. Marietti. Paris: Flammarion, 1969.

Normand, Claudine. *Métaphore et concept*. Paris: Complexe, 1976.

Palmier, Jean-Michel. *Situation de Georg Trakl*. Paris: Belfond, 1972.

Pepper, Stephen C. "Philosophy and Metaphor." *Journal of Philosophy* 25 (1928): 130–32.

———. "The Root Metaphor Theory of Metaphysics." *Journal of Philosophy* 14 (1935): 365–74.

———. *World Hypotheses. A Study in Evidence*. Berkeley: University of California Press, 1942.

Perelman, Chaïm, and Lucie Olbrechts-Tyteca. *Rhétorique et philosophie. Pour une théorie de l'argumentation en philosophie*. Paris: P.U.F., 1952.

Perlini, Tito. "Ontologia come violenza." *Nuova corrente* 63 (1973): 3–67.

Pongs, Hermann. *Das Bild in der Dichtung*. Book 1: "Versuch einer Morphologie der Metaphorischen Formen." 1927. Reprint, Marburg: N. G. Elwert, 1960.

Richards, Ivor Armstrong. *The Philosophy of Rhetoric*. 1936. Reprint, Oxford: Oxford University Press, 1971.

Ricoeur, Paul. *La métaphore vive*. Paris: Editions du Seuil, 1975. Translated by R. Czerny under the title *The Rule of Metaphor* (Toronto: University of Toronto Press, 1977).

Rousseau, Jean-Jacques. *Discours sur l'origine et les fondements de l'inégalité*. In *Oeuvres Complètes*, vol. 3. Paris: Gallimard (Bibliothèque de la Pléiade), 1964.

Saint-John Perse. *Birds*. Translated by J. Roger Little. Durham: North Gate Press, 1967.

Tarbet, David W. "The Fabric of Metaphor in Kant's Critique of pure reason." *Journal of the History of Philosophy* (1968): 257–70.

Todorov, Tzvetan. *Symbolisme et interprétation*. Paris: Editions du Seuil, 1978. Translated by C. Porter under the title *Symbolism and Interpretation* (London: Routledge and Kegan Paul, 1983).

Vico, Giambattista. *Principi di scienza nuova.* In *Opere filosofiche.* Firenze: Sansoni, 1971.

Weinrich, Harald. "Münze und Wort. Untersuchungen an einem Bild-feld." In *Festschrift für Gerhard Rohlfs.* Edited by Heinrich Lausberg and Harald Weinrich. Halle: Niemeyer, 1968: 508-21.

INDEX

abandon(ment), 18, 69, 129, 133, 140, 142, 150, 152, 175, 185n, 226, 228, 229, 257n, 262, 263, 264

abyss, 95, 122n, 139, 148–49, 151, 154, 156, 168–69

accessibility, 142, 198, 201

adaequatio, 206, 211

Adorno, Theodor, 42n

aesthetics, 33, 142, 226, 227

allegory, 62, 74, 157

Alleman, Beda, 186n

ambiguity, 27, 41n, 62, 73, 90, 150, 250

analogy, 23, 24, 26, 47, 48, 53, 55, 56, 57, 61, 74, 78, 80, 81, 82, 83, 85, 100, 109, 110, 113, 119n, 131, 132, 135, 138, 140, 142, 144, 148, 149, 152, 160, 165, 166, 169, 173, 198, 203, 221, 234, 256n, 265

appeal, 27, 146, 149, 163, 167, 171, 228, 244, 262

arbitrariness, 36, 55, 114, 136, 150, 157, 183n

argumentation, 125n, 139, 156, 175, 207, 214, 220, 232

273

Aristotle, 23, 24, 26, 28, 40n, 47, 75, 79, 80, 81, 82, 89, 106, 118n, 121n, 180, 190n, 214
attribution, 47, 62, 79, 82
Aufhebung, 75, 144
avant-gardes, 61

Bachelard, Gaston, 61
baroque, 29
Beardsley, Monroe C., 22, 40n
Beckett, Samuel, 253
begining, 23, 36, 87, 104, 152, 175, 218, 226, 249, 262
being, 74, 75, 77, 80–82, 85, 88–90, 94, 97, 102, 111, 130, 131, 137, 143, 145, 152, 153, 154, 162, 164, 167, 168, 170, 171, 172, 173, 176, 185n, 191n, 194, 217, 220, 229, 233, 264
belonging, 89, 90–91, 102, 103, 104, 164, 242, 251
Benveniste, Emile, 79
Bergson, Henri, 28
Bindung, 174, 184n
Birault, Henri, 141, 145, 180, 184n, 185n, 218, 257n, 259n
Black, Max, 22, 40n, 255n, 256n
blind spot, 75, 112
Blumenberg, Hans, 31, 42n, 259n
Bollack, Jean, 266n
Bonesio, Luisa, 41n
border, 17, 39, 77, 92, 112, 191n, 197, 217, 235, 240, 241, 264, 265
Borges, Jorge Luis, 125n
Borutti, Silvana, 256n
Bourdieu, Pierre, 42n, 44
Bouveresse, Jacques, 125n, 190n
Braque, Georges, 181

Casenave, Gerald, 186n
Cassirer, Ernst, 256n
catachresis, 61–62, 96, 106, 109, 110, 148
catastrophe, 32, 42n, 67, 91, 95–98, 110–14, 117, 148, 265
chiasmus, 123n
closedness, 198, 201–202, 239–40
clôture, 92, 93, 109, 116, 122n
code of pertinence, 50
coitus interruptus, 144, 263
communication, 45, 47, 82, 88, 164, 172, 202
comparison, 25, 61, 199
compatibility, 206–207
concept, 20, 21, 22, 23, 26, 28, 45, 46, 61, 62–64, 67, 69, 72–75, 81, 82, 86–88, 92–95, 98, 101, 103, 105–107, 111–13, 120n, 121n, 122n, 124n, 125n, 126n, 132–33, 142, 148, 150, 152, 157, 171, 185n, 204, 220, 229, 230, 233, 240, 263,
context, 21, 25, 39, 49, 50, 51, 52–55, 57–63, 99, 110, 124n, 128, 131, 134–35, 136–38, 140,

153, 165, 183n, 202, 203, 226, 229, 232

contradiction, 129, 140, 198

control, 18, 44, 45, 46, 63, 64, 69, 70, 73, 75, 100, 107, 113, 114, 116, 133, 143, 144, 145–47, 153, 158, 176, 185n, 199, 207, 228–29, 230, 233–34, 239–40, 242, 244, 247–48, 249, 252–53, 263–64

copula, 80

Croce, Benedetto, 26, 41n

cryptogram, 54

Culler, Jonathan, 260n

culture, 56

death, 77, 86, 116, 235, 236, 244–46, 248, 249, 250, 253–54

deconstruction, 44, 64, 68, 72–73, 76, 85, 86, 92, 93, 100, 103, 104, 106, 107–109, 112–13, 115–16, 196, 215–16, 230, 235–45, 247, 249–52, 254, 259n, 265

definition, 18, 21, 22, 45, 59, 60, 64, 69, 101, 106, 108, 114, 116, 125n, 149, 153, 168, 194, 198, 201, 204, 205, 230, 240

de Man, Paul, 41n

denomination, 47, 79, 85, 91

Derrida, Jacques, 15, 16, 22, 23, 27, 29, 32, 37, 38, 39, 40n, 42n, 44, 64, 65n, 67–78, 83, 85–86, 89, 91–95, 97, 99–106, 108–17,

119n, 120n, 121n, 123n, 125n, 126n, 127, 130, 143, 148, 169, 183n, 184n, 185n, 190n, 215, 216, 217, 220, 230, 234, 242–45, 248, 250, 254, 255n, 257n, 258n, 259n, 261, 262, 265n, 266n

destination, 38, 95, 96, 140, 143, 150, 159, 161, 179

destiny, 24, 116, 117, 150, 173, 231, 242, 243, 257n

deviance, 79

diachrony, 180, 191n

dialectic, 25, 80, 86, 89, 104, 218

diaphor, 180, 181

différance, 108, 109, 110, 113, 126n, 260n

difference, 32, 38, 56, 57, 59, 65n, 68, 70, 73, 74, 75, 76, 78, 80, 81, 83, 87, 89, 98, 99, 102, 103, 104, 107, 108, 110, 115, 116, 119n, 141, 148, 154, 156, 159, 163, 164, 165–69, 171, 180, 185n, 189n, 190n, 194, 195, 208, 209, 212, 230, 236, 237, 239, 241, 242, 245, 246, 247, 249, 250, 251, 253

dimension, 45, 60, 130, 154, 160, 162, 167, 173, 177, 178, 194, 195, 196, 208, 221, 225, 230, 250, 252

discourse, 19, 21, 22, 27, 34, 36, 44, 48, 50, 51, 53, 62, 63, 64, 69, 71,

77–83, 87, 88, 89, 91, 94, 95, 99, 100, 102, 103, 110, 112, 113, 116, 119n, 125n, 126n, 127, 132, 134, 135, 138, 139, 140, 141, 142, 147, 148, 149, 150, 151, 155, 157, 158, 162, 168, 173, 175, 176, 177, 181, 184n, 195, 196, 197, 198, 199, 200, 201, 202, 203, 205, 206, 209, 210, 211, 214, 215, 216, 221, 223, 225, 226, 230, 240, 241, 242, 247, 262

philosophical, 19, 20, 22, 31, 32, 33, 37, 38, 39, 45, 46, 61, 63, 64, 72, 74, 78, 80, 81, 84–89, 104, 106, 107, 111, 115, 137, 144, 178, 194, 207, 208, 212, 213, 217, 218, 222, 224, 227, 229, 231, 232–35, 263, 264

poetic, 39, 51, 78, 80, 81, 82, 83, 89, 91, 100, 104, 135, 158,

discovery, 102, 106, 204, 205, 241

discursive regime, 52, 53

displacement, 22, 28, 79, 110, 113, 114, 116, 140, 204, 216, 229, 233, 246, 247, 248

disposition, 56, 105, 111, 141, 151, 152, 241

dissemination, 74, 76, 81, 132, 265n

distantiation, 70, 88, 91, 102, 104

drift, 69, 98, 104, 117, 118n, 221, 229

eidos, 73

elocution, 40

empiricism, 106

encyclopedia, 16, 24, 93, 261

Enteignis, 152

enunciation, 49, 87, 136, 138

epiphor, *epiphora*, 23, 180, 190n

épochè, 94, 122n

equivocalness, 80, 82

Ereignis, 90, 98, 101, 102, 139, 151, 164, 174, 264

Erörterung, 90, 190n

ethicality, 198, 199, 205

ethics, 33, 114, 185n, 200, 205, 206, 207, 210, 213, 214, 215, 218, 226, 227, 228, 236, 252

etymologism, 105, 161, 188n, 229, 259n

etymology, 55, 110, 132, 138, 139, 151, 171, 175, 184n, 229, 230, 258n

exactness, 154, 171

experience, 91, 104, 146, 147, 155, 171, 172, 180, 181, 186n, 194, 207

explanation, 28, 73, 177, 205, 230, 239

exploitation, 69, 130, 131, 144, 145, 147, 197, 224

feeling, 89, 125n, 146, 170, 180

fiction, 11, 199, 208, 222, 223, 227

figurative, 25, 27, 31, 84, 86, 91, 98,

101, 255n

figure, 31, 59, 65n, 74, 94, 112, 122n

finality, 198, 202

Finas, Lucette, 125n

Fontanier, Pierre, 62

force, 28, 36, 119n, 130, 138, 142, 151, 206, 217, 243–46, 248, 249, 251, 258n, 259n, 260n

form, 24, 25, 29, 55, 56, 61, 63, 71, 72, 79, 82, 99, 103, 107, 116, 150, 154, 194, 195, 196, 199, 205, 207, 213, 226, 227, 235, 241, 243–46, 250, 259n

formalization, 198, 199, 204, 205, 206, 221

foundation, 9, 21, 31, 45, 47, 61, 75, 102, 103, 110, 111, 112, 113, 115, 141, 158, 176, 209, 215, 225, 228, 241, 265

framing, 134, 226

France, Anatole, 106

freedom, 16, 33, 58, 76, 81, 82, 95, 101, 107, 111, 114, 142, 149, 179, 193, 198, 203, 204, 205, 214, 219, 220, 224

Freud, Sigmund, 184n, 266n

futurism, 61

Gadamer, Hans-Georg, 183n, 233

generalization, 75, 76, 95, 96, 97, 101, 104, 107, 110, 111, 112, 113, 148, 163, 196, 243, 259n

Genette, Gérard, 24, 40n

George, Stefan, 173

gift, 139, 169, 170, 172, 174

gnoseology, 206

Greisch, Jean, 27, 40n, 41n, 45, 129, 139, 141, 171, 178–82, 183n, 184n, 190n, 191n, 194, 230, 256n, 257n, 258n, 262

Hegel, G. W. F., 25, 41n, 55, 75, 77, 114, 118n, 230, 258n

Heidegger, Martin, 15, 16, 20, 21, 23, 26, 28, 29, 32, 37, 38, 39, 40n, 41n, 42n, 46, 55, 69, 75, 83–86, 89–98, 101, 102, 105, 111, 119n, 120n, 122n, 123n, 124n, 125n, 126n, 127–82, 183n, 184n, 185n, 186n, 187n, 188n, 189n, 190n, 206, 210, 215–34, 255n, 256n, 257n, 258n, 259n, 262, 263, 265n, 266n

Henle, Paul, 191n

Heraclitus, 141

hermeneutics, 79, 85, 95, 100, 183n

hermeticisms, 91, 102

Hesse, Mary 205

history, 18, 19, 25, 37, 42n, 53, 57, 109, 111, 117,136, 152, 175, 196, 211, 213, 224, 257n

Hölderlin, Friedrich, 130, 186n

human sciences, 44, 100, 194, 196, 197, 198, 199, 200, 201, 202, 203, 212, 221, 223

Hume, David, 25
Husserl, Edmund, 88

icon, 96, 179, 180, 191n
idea, 24, 27, 47, 38, 48, 62, 63, 74,
   78, 80, 87, 102, 110, 113, 131,
   146, 153, 154, 155, 156, 159,
   164, 175, 187n, 209, 219, 220,
   221, 228, 237
ideology, 85, 99, 114
illness, 24, 144
image, 28, 29, 30, 49, 61, 71, 88, 96,
   130, 132, 135, 149, 151, 157,
   160, 162, 168, 189n, 219, 220,
   221, 236, 249, 255
imaginatio, 88
imagination, 29, 142, 206
imitation, 197
impertinence, 22, 48, 49, 50, 79, 85,
   86
impropriety, 22, 23, 34, 47, 62, 74,
   75, 86, 110, 113, 254
incorrectness, 54
indecidable, 9, 69, 108, 109, 110,
   112, 113, 125n, 126n, 264
inexpressible, 131
institutionality, 198, 200
intellectio, 88
intention, 19, 88, 90, 92, 114, 116,
   117, 126n, 127, 131, 165, 169,
   185n, 189n, 199, 220, 225, 242,
   244, 250, 251, 252, 256n, 260n,
   265

interaction, 19, 51, 197, 198, 203,
   215
interference, 57, 58, 137, 197
interpretability, 52, 59, 60, 135, 137
isotopy, 135

Janicaud, Dominique, 123n
justification, 28, 84, 142, 145, 150,
   174, 177, 204, 212, 213, 220

Kant, Immanuel, 42n
Kelkel, Arion L., 230, 255n, 258n
knowledge, 24, 26, 35, 64, 72, 82,
   87, 88, 104, 117, 153, 172,
   184n, 187n, 194, 197, 201, 204,
   205, 206, 209, 238, 239, 254
Kofman, Sarah, 28, 41n

labels, 29, 47, 48, 62, 171
labor of the negative, 77, 118n
Lacan, Jacques, 44, 143
language, 21, 25, 29, 34, 36, 39, 44,
   45, 47–50, 55, 56, 62, 68, 69, 70,
   74, 75, 79, 87, 88, 91, 95–98,
   100, 101, 102, 104, 105, 107,
   112, 113, 114, 117, 131, 133,
   134, 135, 136, 137, 138, 142,
   146, 149, 152, 154, 155, 157,
   160, 162, 163, 164, 165, 166,
   167, 168, 169, 170, 171, 172,
   173, 176, 177, 178, 179, 180,
   182n, 183n, 184n, 186n, 194,
   195, 197, 201, 202, 204, 205,

206, 207, 209, 220, 221, 223, 224, 227, 229, 230, 231, 232, 233, 247, 250, 251, 252, 255n, 256n, 257n, 258n, 265n

essence of, 147, 155, 163, 167, 168, 171, 176

metaphoricity of, 50

natural, 21, 39, 44, 46, 106, 137, 198, 257n

ordinary, 21, 137, 138, 198–203, 221, 230

philosophical, 19, 28, 43, 44, 70, 106, 138, 221

philosophy of, 171

Le Doeuff, Michèle, 41n

lexis, 199

limit, 22, 92, 98, 106, 159, 160, 161, 175, 178, 181, 184n, 204, 217, 225, 228, 234, 244, 255, 262, 264

linguistic, linguistics, 21, 22, 25, 29, 33, 34, 35, 38, 45, 47, 48, 54, 60, 74, 79, 88, 108, 135, 142, 147, 176, 194, 195, 205, 206, 215, 230, 255n

linguistic game, 47, 48, 54, 60, 108

literary criticism, 33, 38, 235, 237, 238, 240, 241, 243

literary theory, 29, 235, 236

literature, 21, 22, 24, 28, 29, 30, 31, 33, 34, 38, 70, 71, 72, 100, 112, 194, 196, 197, 198–203, 208, 229, 233, 235, 236, 237, 238,

240, 241, 242, 243, 244, 245, 251

Locke, John, 25

logic, 24, 25, 37, 54, 61, 69, 88, 90, 91, 93, 109, 129, 131, 140, 142, 144, 147, 149, 153, 160, 165, 172, 177, 198, 204, 205, 209, 210, 213, 224, 225, 226, 228

logical positivism, 25

logocentrism, 72

logos, 73, 133, 154, 250

loss, 76, 96, 106, 146, 147, 160, 190n, 204, 234, 243

management, 63, 130, 160, 161, 173, 216, 265

margin, marginal, 17, 29, 34, 35, 77, 98, 187n, 264

mark, *marque* , 98, 104, 109, 110, 114, 117,126n

Marxism, 40, 85, 237

Mattéi, Jean-François, 123n

meaning, 20, 21, 22, 25, 26, 31, 33, 36, 39, 46, 47, 51, 52, 54, 55, 56, 57, 58, 59, 60, 61, 63, 64, 69, 70, 74, 76, 77, 79, 81, 85, 86, 89, 93, 94, 95, 96, 97, 108, 110, 111, 112, 113, 131, 139, 140, 152, 155, 159, 160, 161, 171, 194, 195, 203, 211, 213, 216, 220, 224, 226, 229, 231, 233, 234, 235, 236, 245, 246, 247, 248, 249, 250, 253, 254, 258n, 259n,

262, 264

meaning-effect, 51, 52, 53, 54, 109, 158

metaphor

absolute, 31

and ethics, 27, 28, 41n, 118n, 206, 210, 213, 214, 217, 219, 249, 264

and knowledge, 24

as ornament, 24, 25, 29, 30, 31, 34, 71

as supplement, 24, 29

barred, 152, 156, 179

broken, 150, 153, 161, 165, 171, 177

concept (definition, description, meaning, model, notion, perception, theory) of, 19, 20, 21, 22, 23, 25, 27, 30, 33, 35, 37, 38, 39, 41n, 43, 44, 46, 47, 48, 49, 50, 51, 62, 69, 74, 75, 79, 86, 94, 101, 103, 104, 113, 131, 134, 141, 179, 184n, 205, 209, 210, 246, 247, 249

dead, 30, 49, 50, 73, 84, 85, 86, 101, 106, 107, 125n, 141, 143, 179, 183n, 236

exaltation of, 22, 29

forgotten, 27, 106, 112

history of, 23, 39

lexicalized, 49, 50, 55, 101

linked, chained, 17, 24, 62, 87, 89, 142, 151, 211, 214

living, 26, 36, 50, 78, 84, 85, 106, 107, 109, 112, 133, 141, 179, 235, 236, 244, 246, 252, 253, 259n

new, 50, 54

open, 149

philosophical, 101, 102, 112

strong and weak, 139

usage of, 19, 21, 25, 26, 28, 29, 31, 105

used, worn, 50, 85, 86, 92

metaphoric field, 42n, 30, 259n

metaphoric register, 49, 50, 51, 61, 63

metaphoricity, 33, 50, 60, 74, 85, 92, 95, 97, 183n, 204

metaphorology, 42n, 75, 259n

metaphysics, 27, 28, 31, 39, 41n, 42n, 44, 45, 46, 65n, 73, 75, 76, 80, 83, 84, 85, 86, 90, 91, 92, 93, 94, 95, 97, 99, 101, 102, 103, 106, 107, 109, 112, 113, 116, 121n, 122n, 123n, 124n, 126n, 130, 131, 132, 133, 141, 145, 152, 162, 171, 178, 185n, 186n, 212, 215, 216, 220, 221, 223, 228, 229, 232, 234, 242, 249, 254, 259n

method, 16, 18, 38, 71, 146, 249, 250, 258n, 260n

metonymy, 62, 93, 94, 115, 165

mode of discourse, 51, 63, 64, 80, 87, 88, 100, 103, 126n,

194–208, 209, 210, 212, 224, 227, 232, 255n

model, 19, 39, 46, 47, 116, 202, 204, 205, 237, 243, 246, 247, 249, 253, 256n

Molino, Jean, 256n

mourning, 116, 145

mysticism, 140, 172, 175, 177, 262

myth, 74, 265

name, 23, 34, 45, 46, 64, 103, 111, 125n, 130, 143, 145, 148, 162, 164, 165, 166, 167, 170, 171, 173, 174, 215, 216, 241, 248, 251, 264

naturalism, 208

Nazism, 42n

neographism, 110

neologism, 106, 155

network, 50, 56, 59, 60, 63, 64, 165, 169, 229, 250

Nietzsche, Friedrich, 26, 27, 29, 41n, 42n, 46, 73, 85, 106, 126n, 141, 142, 185n

nomination, 132, 161, 165, 168, 171, 173, 183n

Normand, Claudine, 40n

noun, 21, 22, 23, 79, 91

Olbrechts-Tyteca, Lucie, 207, 256n, 257n

onoma, 24

ontic, 164

ontology, 24, 79, 81, 82, 87, 89, 164, 178, 181, 186n

onto-theology, 82–83,

openess, 198, 202

origin, 25, 28, 34, 36, 56, 60, 63, 69, 73, 74, 75, 76, 85, 98, 106, 107, 112, 113, 114, 132, 152, 162, 169, 173, 174, 215, 220, 221, 229, 233, 236, 258n, 265

overcoming, 77, 86, 101, 102, 103, 130, 131, 186n, 232, 234, 242

paleonymy, 250

Palmier, Jean-Michel, 186n, 188n

paradigm, 68, 205

paradox, 21, 117

paralysis, 88, 151

participation, 80, 82, 83, 108

pathos, 27, 138, 151, 264

Peirce, Charles S. 21, 191n

Pepper, Stephen C., 31, 42n

perception, 30, 33, 36, 46, 47, 56, 57, 58, 125n, 132, 152, 173, 178, 195, 197, 210, 239, 242, 255n

Perelman, Chaïm, 125n, 207, 214, 256n, 257n

Perlini, Tito, 125n

persuasion, 214

pertinence, 49, 50, 58, 61, 76, 85, 207, 214, 225

philosophy, 15, 16, 17, 19–21, 22, 23, 24, 25, 26, 28, 29, 31, 32,

33–36, 37–39, 40, 42n, 44–46, 51, 59, 62, 63, 64, 67, 68, 70–78, 81, 82, 83, 84, 85, 87, 88, 90, 93, 99–104, 105–108, 110, 111, 112, 113, 114, 115, 116, 117, 125n, 126n, 136, 137, 139, 143, 145, 146, 148, 150, 152, 153, 161, 173, 175, 176, 178, 180, 181, 193–221, 223, 224, 225, 227, 228, 229, 231, 232–35, 240, 241, 242, 247, 248, 262, 265

Plato, 24, 28, 80, 86

plurivocality, 18, 150

poetic, 39, 51, 75, 78, 79, 80, 81, 82, 83, 87, 89, 90, 91, 100, 111, 130, 135, 138, 151, 155, 157, 158, 160, 161, 162, 168, 170, 173, 175, 181, 183n, 186n, 191n, 199, 204, 205, 221, 223, 226, 227, 230, 233, 235

poetics, 24, 33, 38

poetry, 10, 26, 31, 39, 51, 78, 80, 81, 82, 83, 84, 87, 89, 90, 91, 97, 100, 101, 104, 106, 111, 125n, 130, 132, 135, 138, 140, 142, 150, 153, 154, 155, 156, 157, 158, 159, 161, 162, 164, 167, 168, 169, 170, 171, 173, 174, 176, 180, 181, 182, 186n, 188n, 194, 196, 197, 198, 199, 200, 201, 202, 203, 207, 212, 223, 225, 230, 234, 235, 237, 262, 265

politics, 42n, 100, 176, 177, 215, 260n

polysemy, 76, 80, 81, 85, 94, 142

Pongs, Herman, 61

positivism, 89, 106

poststructuralism, 29, 237, 242

predicate, predication, 79, 80, 83, 85, 111

producer, 175, 198, 199, 200, 201, 203, 204, 208, 210, 215

propaganda, 202

proper, 22, 23, 27, 34, 45, 47, 55, 57, 58, 60, 62, 71, 73, 74, 75, 76, 77, 84, 85, 86, 91, 94, 95, 96, 98, 100, 101, 102, 110, 113, 137, 139, 148, 172, 216, 221, 242, 257n, 260n

proximity, 39, 73, 75, 83, 97, 98, 101, 112, 135, 138, 149, 156, 157, 164, 169, 230

psychoanalysis, 29, 34, 38, 40, 237

psychology, 138, 153, 196

public, 49, 195, 198, 201

quasi metaphor, 97, 101, 217

quotation marks, 12, 229, 230, 231

radicality, 18, 68, 111, 117, 247

rationalism, 28, 214

rationality, 16, 24, 26, 31, 35, 63, 73, 74, 108, 158, 198, 204, 205, 212, 214, 220, 224, 233, 236, 252

reader, 53, 54, 56–59, 61, 65n, 69,
71, 79, 129, 134, 136, 137, 142,
143, 151, 156, 158, 177, 197,
199, 201, 208, 225–28, 237, 241
realism, 208
reality, 28, 68, 74, 79, 80, 88, 89, 96,
115, 131, 153, 172, 180, 191n,
197, 198, 203, 211, 212, 220,
222, 234
reason, 28, 107, 140, 144, 146, 147,
154, 158, 185n, 213, 220, 225,
232, 234, 253, 262
reference, 22, 33, 37, 39, 49, 51, 52,
54, 61, 79, 87, 89, 96, 103, 115,
134, 136, 139, 146, 184n, 210,
215, 221, 229, 240, 265
referent, 49, 50, 60, 97, 111
referral, 21, 130
religion, 82, 207, 215, 226, 227
Renan, Ernest, 106
representation, 27, 56, 57, 73, 84, 89,
93, 96, 131, 132, 133, 141, 144,
145, 146, 147, 149, 150, 151,
152, 154, 157, 158, 160, 161,
162, 163, 164, 165, 167, 168,
170, 171, 175, 178, 179, 181,
204, 218, 219, 220, 221, 223,
228, 229, 232, 233, 255, 263
reproduction, 58, 76, 168
resemblance, 24, 81, 90, 108, 169
responsibility, 214
restraint, 105, 142
retreat, *retrait*, 68, 91, 94, 95, 98, 99,

122n, 123n, 124n, 148, 164
reverse metaphorization, 73
rhetoric, 21, 24, 25, 26, 28, 32, 33,
36, 38, 40, 59, 71, 74, 79, 93, 94,
136, 142, 143, 151, 153, 154,
155, 207, 213, 214, 215, 229,
231, 232, 247, 257n
rhetorical figure, 21, 26, 28, 79, 247
rhetorical question, 231
Richards, Ivor A., 22, 40n
Ricoeur, Paul, 9, 24, 26, 32, 40n, 63,
67–70, 78–91, 92, 93, 99–103,
109, 117, 118n, 126n, 127, 131,
133, 179, 183n, 190n, 191n,
204, 207, 256n, 258n, 266n
rigor, 18, 25, 69, 142, 150, 152, 262
romanticism, 25, 29
root-metaphors, 31
Rousseau, Jean-Jacques, 25, 41n
Rousset, Jean, 244
Ruf, 149, 186n

sacred, 145, 151, 153, 158, 168, 175,
176, 213, 226
Saint-John Perse, 181, 191n
Saussure, Ferdinand de, 57
sayable, 44, 63, 265
Schlegel, Friedrich, 208
Schritt zurück, 147, 174
science, 21, 31, 50, 63, 82, 99, 100,
106, 114, 119n, 146, 150, 153,
155, 160, 161, 173, 176, 181,
182n, 187n, 190n, 195,

196–207, 209, 210, 212, 220, 221, 222, 223, 224, 225, 230, 233, 240, 244, 256n, 260n

semantic, 24, 48, 62, 64, 76, 79, 83, 85, 86, 87, 88, 90, 104, 139, 151, 155, 171, 184n, 198

semiotic, 38, 79, 85, 91

sign, 51, 61, 62, 72, 77, 126n, 220

signification, 21, 25, 83, 87, 88, 109, 113, 119n, 139, 160, 171, 174, 196, 243

signifier, 29, 49, 50, 56, 108, 216

silence, 29, 115, 162, 163, 164, 167, 168, 170, 231

similarity, 59, 82, 108

sociology, 42n, 177, 237

song, 160

speakable, 165, 195

speculation, speculative, 70, 78, 80, 81, 82, 83, 87, 88, 89, 90, 101, 102, 103, 104, 117, 119n, 125n, 126n, 263

speech (ordinary), 90, 194, 196–204

Sprache, 123n, 131, 137, 140, 149, 154, 155, 157, 163, 164, 168, 176, 185n, 186n, 187n

step back, 147, 148, 168, 215, 244

strategy, 23, 33, 111, 242, 244, 245, 250, 251, 254

stricture, 112, 204

structuralism, 29, 65n, 237, 238, 239, 240, 241, 242, 243, 249, 259n, 260n

structure, 21, 32, 33, 42n, 56, 57, 69, 71, 72, 76, 80, 81, 86, 89, 92, 112, 121n, 123n, 132, 139, 146, 148, 151, 153, 165, 168, 200, 204, 213, 218, 225, 235, 236, 243, 244, 246

style, 27, 28, 29, 35, 68, 69, 70, 71, 105, 141, 145, 247

subject, 40, 54, 61, 72, 76, 89, 96, 111, 112, 118n, 128, 136, 138, 183n, 214, 231, 240, 241, 252, 255n, 259n

substance, 63, 73, 99

substitution, 24, 34, 79, 85, 86

suffering, 36, 141, 142, 143, 145, 146, 151, 154, 155, 156, 159, 160, 167, 179, 181, 201, 263

supplement, 24, 29, 49, 52, 61, 94, 110, 134, 135, 136, 137, 183n, 205, 208

surrealism, 29, 61, 135

symbol, symbolic, 49, 62, 109, 151, 198, 220

symbolism, 29

synecdoche, 62

syntax, 44, 76, 91, 136, 199, 218, 224

system, 16, 18, 20, 25, 27, 30, 35, 37, 49, 57, 60, 71, 74, 76, 88, 106, 112, 146, 166, 167, 169, 170, 184n, 189n, 208, 211, 221, 225, 236, 239, 240, 246, 250, 261, 263

Tarbet, David W., 42n

tautology, 139, 140, 155, 168, 171, 190n, 262, 266n

techné, 133

technology, 144

tenor, 97, 111

tension, tensional, 22, 49, 50, 61, 62, 69, 80, 86, 87, 88, 184n

text, 19, 20, 22, 30, 32, 33, 34, 35, 40, 51–55, 57–61, 65n, 69, 70, 71, 72, 73, 74, 75, 77, 93, 95, 108, 128, 129, 130, 133–35, 136, 137, 140–46, 149, 150, 151, 153, 154, 155, 156, 157, 158, 162, 169, 175, 176, 177, 178, 179, 181, 182n, 186n, 189n, 196, 199–203, 205, 206, 207, 208, 213, 216, 217, 222, 225–29, 233, 235–38, 240, 241, 243, 244–47, 249, 250, 251, 252, 263

texte général, 77

theology, 82, 119n

negative, 108, 265

theory, 16, 18, 19, 20, 21, 23–25, 27, 33, 37–40, 43–48, 50, 51, 63, 64, 67, 68, 71, 73, 74, 79, 81, 82, 86, 87, 92, 100, 103, 104, 113, 138, 141, 205, 211, 221, 235–55, 256n, 260n, 264

thinking, thought, 16, 18, 22, 27, 29, 30, 36, 39, 45, 68, 70, 73–75, 77, 83, 84, 86, 88–95, 97, 99, 102, 103, 104, 105, 107, 109, 111, 113, 114, 115, 117, 129, 132, 139, 141, 144–47, 150, 151, 152, 153, 157, 160, 161, 162, 163, 164, 168, 170–74, 176, 178, 180, 182, 189n, 210, 215–25, 226, 227, 231, 232, 233, 250, 251, 253, 254, 257n, 258n, 262, 263

nonrepresentational, 132, 133, 152, 153, 161, 218–19, 227

Thomas Aquinas, Saint, 82, 83

threshold, 10, 19, 70, 71, 145, 151, 156, 159, 160, 161, 193, 228, 263

Todorov, Tzvetan, 256n

totalization, totalizing, 45, 113, 250

trait, 55–57, 84, 94, 98, 99, 124n, 135, 138, 144, 148, 165, 166, 169, 181, 206, 234, 264

Trakl, Georg, 130, 154, 155, 156, 157, 159, 186n, 188n

transfer, 21, 28, 79, 84–85, 91, 130, 131

transport, 23, 24, 190n

trope, 28, 40, 59, 92, 94, 106, 113, 121n, 122n

truth, 20, 24, 26–28, 33, 46, 69, 74, 76, 77, 80, 82, 89, 99, 102, 103, 110, 112, 114, 115, 128, 129, 131, 143, 146, 153, 157, 158, 168, 169, 171–73, 175, 176, 185n, 187n, 191n, 198, 199,

200, 206–208, 210–15, 217, 218, 221, 224, 225, 228–34, 244, 247, 250, 251, 252, 254, 255, 256n, 264

Überwindung, 130
unconscious, 30, 40, 226
Ungesprochene, 131
Unheimlichkeit, 171
univocity, 69, 93, 110, 132, 150, 199
unspeakable, 90, 131, 140, 148, 160, 163, 165, 174, 175, 176
unthinkable, 56, 75, 76, 101, 109, 114, 152, 160, 175, 216, 250

vagueness, 69, 140, 171, 204, 221, 227, 238
Valéry, Paul, 193, 255n
vehicle, 95, 96, 97, 111
Verborgenheit, 94
Verhüllung, 94

verifiability, 63, 199, 200, 206, 211, 217, 224
verification, 176, 198, 199, 203, 207, 210, 211, 214, 224, 228
verificationism, 89
Verweisung, 21
Vico, Giambattista, 25, 40n
vitalism, 28

wear, *usure*, 27, 41n, 86, 92, 121n
Weinrich, Herald, 42n
Wheelwright, Philip, 190n
Wisman, Heinz, 266n
Wittgenstein, Ludwig, 87, 190n
world, 44, 56–58, 77, 82, 84, 89, 133, 144–47, 154, 159, 162, 164–74, 194–96, 199, 200, 203, 206, 208, 209, 210, 212, 213, 234, 237, 245, 246, 249, 256n
world-effect, 208